SCRIPTURAL TRACES: CRITICAL PERSPECTIVES ON
THE RECEPTION AND INFLUENCE OF THE BIBLE

26

Editors
Claudia V. Camp, Texas Christian University
Matthew A. Collins, University of Chester
Andrew Mein, Durham University

Editorial Board
Michael J. Gilmour, David Gunn, James Harding, Jorunn Økland

Published under

LIBRARY OF HEBREW BIBLE/
OLD TESTAMENT STUDIES

699

Formerly Journal for the Study of the Old Testament Supplement Series

Editors
Claudia V. Camp, Texas Christian University
Andrew Mein, Durham University

Founding Editors
David J. A. Clines, Philip R. Davies and David M. Gunn

Editorial Board
Alan Cooper, Susan Gillingham, John Goldingay,
Norman K. Gottwald, James E. Harding, John Jarick, Carol Meyers,
Daniel L. Smith-Christopher, Francesca Stavrakopoulou, James W. Watts

BERTOLT BRECHT AND THE *DAVID* FRAGMENTS (1919–1921)

An Interdisciplinary Study

David J. Shepherd and Nicholas E. Johnson

LONDON • NEW YORK • OXFORD • NEW DELHI • SYDNEY

T&T CLARK
Bloomsbury Publishing Plc
50 Bedford Square, London, WC1B 3DP, UK
1385 Broadway, New York, NY 10018, USA
29 Earlsfort Terrace, Dublin 2, Ireland

BLOOMSBURY, T&T CLARK and the T&T Clark logo
are trademarks of Bloomsbury Publishing Plc

First published in Great Britain 2020
This paperback edition published in 2021

Copyright © David J. Shepherd and Nicholas E. Johnson, 2020

David J. Shepherd and Nicholas E. Johnson have asserted their right under the Copyright, Designs and Patents Act, 1988, to be identified as Authors of this work.

For legal purposes the Acknowledgements on p. xiii constitute an extension of this copyright page.

Cover design: Charlotte James

Cover image: David before Saul (I Samuel 17:57-58), 1923, Lovis Corinth
© Harvard Art Museums/Fogg Museum, George R. Nutter Fund

All rights reserved. No part of this publication may be reproduced or transmitted in any form or by any means, electronic or mechanical, including photocopying, recording, or any information storage or retrieval system, without prior permission in writing from the publishers.

Bloomsbury Publishing Plc does not have any control over, or responsibility for, any third-party websites referred to or in this book. All internet addresses given in this book were correct at the time of going to press. The author and publisher regret any inconvenience caused if addresses have changed or sites have ceased to exist, but can accept no responsibility for any such changes.

A catalogue record for this book is available from the British Library.
Library of Congress Control Number: 2019956618

ISBN:	HB:	978-0-5676-8564-3
	PB:	978-0-5677-0483-2
	ePDF:	978-0-5676-8565-0
	ePUB:	978-0-5676-8567-4

Series: Library of Hebrew Bible/Old Testament Studies, ISSN 2513-8758, volume 699
Scriptural Traces, volume 26

Typeset by: Forthcoming Publications Ltd

To find out more about our authors and books visit www.bloomsbury.com and sign up for our newsletters.

Hat man sein 'warum?' des Lebens,
so verträgt man sich fast mit jedem 'wie?'

—Friedrich Nietzsche

For our families

CONTENTS

List of Tables	ix
List of Figures	xi
Acknowledgements	xiii
A Note on the Text	xv
List of Abbreviations	xvii

INTRODUCTION: BRECHT'S *DAVID* FRAGMENTS 1
   Brecht and the Bible 1
   Brecht's *David* in Fragments 4
   Left for Dead: Forgetting Brecht's *David* Fragments 6
   The Bible and Its Survival/Afterlife 9
   The Survival of Samuel and the After/Laterlife of Brecht's *David* ... 13
   Bringing Brecht's *David* to Life:
       Translation, Performance and Survival 18

Chapter 1
THE *DAVID* FRAGMENTS IN TRANSLATION 22
   Preface to the Translation 22
   The *David* Fragments: A1–A8 25
   The *David* Fragments: B1–B11 32
   Previously Uncollected *David* Fragments 68

Chapter 2
BRECHT'S *DAVID* AND THE BIBLICAL DAVID:
URIAH, BATHSHEBA, ABSALOM AND JESSE 72
   Brecht and David: A Question of Character 72
   Uriah (and Bathsheba) 77
   Absalom 80
   Jesse 87

Chapter 3
BRECHT'S *DAVID* AND THE BIBLICAL DAVID:
JONATHAN, SAUL AND DAVID 97
   Jonathan 97
   Saul 104
   David 113

Chapter 4
BRECHT'S *DAVID* AND OTHER ADAPTATIONS:
FEUCHTWANGER, ZAREK AND GIDE 125
   David and Saul on Stage 125
   Lion Feuchtwanger's *König Saul* 127
   Otto Zarek's *David* 139
   André Gide's *Saül* 151

Chapter 5
THE *DAVID* FRAGMENTS IN PRACTICE AND PERFORMANCE 164
   Clearing the Stage: *David* in Germany (1995) 164
   Setting the Stage: *David* and Practice-as-Research in Ireland 168
   Preparing the Stage: *The David Fragments* Workshops (2015–2017) 177
   On Stage: *The David Fragments* (2017) 188
   Beyond the Stage: Impacts and Absences 195

CONCLUDING REFLECTIONS: AFTER *DAVID* 198
   Entangled Lives: The *David* Fragments,
      the Biblical David and the Young Brecht 198
   Entangled Methods:
      Theatre/Brecht Studies and Biblical Reception Studies 202
   Entangled Afterlives: *Goliath* and the Survival of Brecht's *David* 208

BIBLIOGRAPHY 217
   Bertolt Brecht's works 217
   Other Works Cited 218

Index of References 227
Index of Authors 230
Index of Subjects 233

List of Tables

Table 1	Structure of the *Arbeitsfassung* text of *David* (1995) with sources	166
Table 2	Stages of *The David Fragments* practice-as-research project, 2015–2018	178
Table 3	Structure of the final performance text of *The David Fragments* (2017) with sources	188
Table 4	'Casting' grid from *The David Fragments* production notebooks, June 2017	190

LIST OF FIGURES

Figure 1   Young Brecht (James Ireland)
           with ensemble and title at the end of the Prologue   191
Figure 2   The ensemble during 'Brechts Anonymous'   192
Figure 3   The ensemble during 'Saul and David',
           with Young Brecht in the foreground   193

All production photos are © Kasia Kaminska (used with permission)

ACKNOWLEDGEMENTS

The journey from this project's inception to its completion was possible only due to the hospitality and generosity of many institutions, collaborators, colleagues and friends. We wish to thank all at Bloomsbury, especially Dominic Mattos, Sarah Glynn, and the series editors of Scriptural Traces first and foremost, for their consistent support of the project from its inception and their careful stewardship of this publication. Both authors have benefited from extensive collegial input from within the Biblical studies and Brecht studies communities, without which this project would not have been possible: Tom Kuhn, Antony Tatlow, and Phoebe von Held in particular gave freely of their time and expertise. Erdmut Wisizla and the staff of the Bertolt-Brecht-Archiv kindly facilitated our research in Berlin, while the representatives of both Suhrkamp Verlag and the Brecht Estate were encouraging regarding our permissions at every stage. We appreciate also the seminal contribution of David Jobling – the first biblical scholar to take up Brecht's *David*.

The theatre production of *The David Fragments* on which this research is based was supported by grants from the Society for Old Testament Study (SOTS) and two sources from Trinity College Dublin: the Provost's Fund for the Visual and Performing Arts and the Trinity Association and Trust. The research could not have progressed without the collaboration of the Trinity Long Room Hub, Trinity Centre for Biblical Studies, Loyola Institute, the Samuel Beckett Theatre, and Trinity Centre for Literary and Cultural Translation: we thank our colleagues and support staff at these institutions. For first approving our work and then for their robust academic engagement, we thank the conference committees for '(Un)performable & (Un)translatable' at Trinity College Dublin (May 2017) and SOTS Summer Meeting at Kings College London (July 2017).

In addition to the artists and sources identified in the bibliography and notes, the practice and research for this paper arose from a collective process with the *David* ensemble, and the authors wish to acknowledge the full ensemble's contributions. Artists involved in the 2017 productions in Dublin and London were Marc Atkinson, Jen Aust, Leonard

Buckley, Ferdia Cahill, Honi Cooke, Will Dunleavy, Richard Durning, Benedict Esdale, Colm Gleeson, Martha Grant, James Ireland, Hugo Lau, Colm McNally, Aoife Meagher, Grace Morgan, Laoise Murray, Mary Sheehan, Michael Stone, and Colm Summers. The German-language David ensemble that worked to perform 'B10' in German at Probe 2016 included: Conor Brennan, Neimhin Gunning, Seamas Hyland, Shannon Huggard, Eh-Jae Kim, Sarah Lucey, Hannah Moody, and Órla Wittke. Collaborators who engaged in our research process in 2015 and 2016, as well as correspondence and forms of research support since then, include, in addition to those named above, Mark Ball, Enda Bates, Dominic Glynn, Nathan Gordon, James Hadley, Leo Hanna, Michael Hofer, DeVon Jackson, Kerill Kelly, Lorna Kettle, and Carl Vogel. Special thanks is due to Kasia Kaminska for her excellent photography and associated permissions to reprint here.

The translator wishes in particular to acknowledge the key figures involved in his orientation to the slippery (but highly structured) archipelago that is the German language: mentors Géza von Molnár, John Paluch, and Ingrid Zeller, further supported in this specific project by translation assistants Jenni Schnarr and Peter Krauch, as well as by the hospitality of Katrin Wächter, Martin Urmann, and Mark Barden in Berlin. The 2018 Brecht-Tage at the Literaturforum im Brecht-Haus, facilitated by Matthias Rothe and Astrid Oesmann, provided a valuable learning experience. Markus Wessendorf, editor of the *Brecht Yearbook / Brecht-Jahrbuch* 44, gave useful editorial feedback and support to our article '*The David Fragments* in Performance', some elements of which reappear here within Chapter 5.

Lastly, we express our gratitude to our families, who have been a wellspring of support and meaning through the thick and thin phases of this project, and to whom this work is dedicated.

A Note on the Text

Authorship and Contributions. This book is a work of dual and co-equal authorship arising from shared research and conceptual collaboration between the authors. David Shepherd worked as corresponding author for the proposal stage and permissions; Nicholas Johnson worked as corresponding author and final editor for the submission and proofing. Shepherd led on the fabrication of Chapters 2, 3, and 4; Johnson led on chapters 1 and 5. The authors created the introduction and conclusion together, and all editing work was essentially collaborative. Future citation of any part of the academic text should be attributed to both authors. The sole exception is the new translation of the *David* fragments and the excerpt from Zarek's *David*, which can both be attributed to Johnson as translator, though numerous annotations and selections among the alternatives supplied were made by Shepherd. See the Preface to the Translation in Chapter 1 for a full account of how the translation process unfolded.

Permissions. Brecht's *David* fragments and relevant diary entries appear courtesy of the Estate of Bertolt Brecht and Suhrkamp Verlag. We acknowledge Gallimard and the Gide Estate for their guidance regarding quotation of André Gide. We thank Camden House/Boydell and Brewer for permission to include elements of our essay 'The David Fragments in Performance', appearing in *Brecht Yearbook / Brecht Jahrbuch* 44 (2019), within Chapter 5.

Cover Image. Lovis Corinth's 1923 'David before Saul (I Samuel 17:57–58)' appears courtesy of the Harvard Art Museums/Fogg Museum, George R. Nutter Fund. Photo © President and Fellows of Harvard College.

Italicisation Conventions. The following conventions have been followed in the use or non-use of italics:
    CASE 1: The *BFA* section called *David* is what we refer to as Brecht's *David* fragments. It is these that have been translated newly. Their

collection under the title *David* as a "work" of sorts justifies this italic and creates this distinction.

CASE 2: We talk about the biblical king David and the David story, always without italics.

CASE 3: We talk about our 2017 production as *The David Fragments*.

List of Abbreviations

BBA	Bertolt-Brecht-Archiv, Akademie der Künste, Berlin
BFA	*Große kommentierte Berliner und Frankfurter Ausgabe* of Brecht's complete works
CBQ	*Catholic Biblical Quarterly*
DDR	Deutsche Demokratische Republik
EE	Electronic Edition (Suhrkamp Brecht Notebooks Project)
EEF	Electronic Edition Forum (Suhrkamp Brecht Notebooks Project)
JSOT	*Journal for the Study of the Old Testament*
NB	*Notizbücher* or Notebooks
NRSV	New Revised Standard Version
NT	New Testament
PaR	Practice-as-Research
PDF	Portable Document Format
STEM	Science, Technology, Engineering, and Mathematics
TCD	Trinity College Dublin
VT	*Vetus Testamentum*
WTJ	*Westminster Theological Journal*
WWI	World War I

INTRODUCTION:
BRECHT'S *DAVID* FRAGMENTS

Brecht and the Bible

In a 1928 interview with the Berlin magazine, *Die Dame*, when Bertolt Brecht was asked which work of world literature had exerted the greatest influence on him, he famously answered: 'You will laugh: The Bible'.[1] That Brecht expected the interviewer to find such an answer laughable says much about Brecht's own awareness that the Bible's influence on the plays for which he had already become well known was by this point neither conspicuous nor uncomplicated. In *The Threepenny Opera*, for instance, which had premiered in Berlin barely a month earlier, while the Bible is referred to and quoted not infrequently, the tone is obviously satirical – hardly what his mother Sophie would have hoped for when she sat down in their flat in Augsburg to read Bible stories to the young Eugen, as her own mother had to her.[2] Indeed, once Grandma Brezing had moved to Augsburg, she took over Eugen's biblical education herself, not only regaling him and his brother Walter with tales from Scripture, but also fielding their questions and invariably underlining the moral of the story.

Moreover, wherever the young Brecht went, it seems, the Bible was there waiting: at the Lutheran 'Barefoot' Church of course, where the family worshipped, but also at the Barefoot's Primary School, where Scripture featured prominently in the carefully curated religious curriculum.[3] Here, in Buchrucker's *Die Biblische Geschichte* (*Biblical History*),

---

1. *BFA* 21, 248.
2. See Stephen Parker, *Bertolt Brecht: A Literary Life* (London: Bloomsbury Methuen, 2014), 10, 12 for these and other details of Brecht's early childhood.
3. For an exhaustive account of the young Brecht's religious education and its impact on his early work, see Eberhard Rohse, *Der frühe Brecht und die Bibel: Studien zum Augsburger Religionsunterricht und zu den literarischen Versuchen des Gymnasiasten* (Göttingen: Vandenhoeck & Ruprecht, 1983), from which details offered here have been drawn.

the young Brecht and his fellow pupils were introduced to the full sweep of sacred history from the origins of humanity in Genesis through to the end of the Acts of the Apostles in the New Testament.[4] Buchrucker's *Biblical History* followed Brecht and his fellow pupils from the Barefoot *Volkschule* to the *Realgymnasium*, where it was used for a further four years of grammar school before giving way to Luther's Bible itself. It is thus hardly surprising that the young Brecht's first play, written in the summer of 1913 and published the following January in *Die Ernte* (*The Harvest*), was entitled simply *The Bible*.[5]

Set in the Netherlands during the Thirty Years War, this one-act play is – perhaps predictably – saturated in biblical quotations, gently problematising a young girl's Christ-like desire to sacrifice herself for her town, but robustly rejecting the religious legalism of the grandfather who succeeds in thwarting her. As others have noted, in *The Bible* Brecht seeks to subvert dogma that passes for religious truth, for the sake of revealing a truth more essential and elemental to the Christian faith. While *The Bible* anticipates his later plays by eschewing the biblical context for a more 'modern' one, the young Brecht's first play is nevertheless transparently dependent on the story of Judith of Bethulia, introduced to him not by Buchrucker, whose apocryphal interests extended little further than the Maccabees, but rather by the German poet and playwright Friedrich Hebbel (1813–1863), whose play *Judith* (1840) left a lasting impression on the young Brecht.[6]

Interestingly, a passing reference in his diary already in the spring of 1913 suggests that Brecht's very first dramatic ambitions drew biblical inspiration not from the apocryphal Judith, but rather from Samson, a character more firmly lodged in the Protestant canon of the Old Testament and thus well-introduced to him by his early biblical education.[7] Brecht's confession two days later – 'I am not progressing with the drama. It falters'[8] – probably explains why nothing has been preserved of the play by which we may judge his efforts, but the boy's conviction at the time

---

4. Ibid., 405–9.

5. *BFA* 1, 7–15.

6. For the controversy arising from Brecht's review of Hebbel's *Judith* see below, p. 118. For discussion of Hebbel's influence on Brecht's *Die Bibel*, see Rohse, *Der frühe Brecht und die Bibel*, 122–8 and Saeko Ishikawa-Beyerstedt, *Friedrich Hebbels Einfluss auf die Moderne: Seine Rezeption in dramatischen* (Marburg: Tectum, 2014), 59–62.

7. *BFA* 26, 19 (29 April 1913).

8. *BFA* 26, 19 (31 April 1913): *Im Drama komme ich gar nicht vorwärts! Das stockt.*

that the play would have been 'very funny' may suggest a *Samson* rather nearer in spirit to the satirical works of Rudolf Presber – which he reports the following day to have found entertaining – than the sober-minded Samson to which he was introduced by Buchrucker.[9] Had Brecht already felt at this stage the admiration for Frank Wedekind that he did a few years later, one wonders how he would have reacted to the knowledge that Wedekind was, at the same time, in the middle of writing a *Samson* of his own.[10] While Wedekind's *Samson; or Shame and Jealousy* was published by one of Brecht's own eventual publishers, Georg Müller, in Munich in 1914,[11] it was banned from the city's stages in June of that year, only receiving its premiere there in a closed performance some four years later on 6 May 1918.[12] By that time, of course, Brecht himself had come to Munich, but Wedekind was dead, and Brecht had long since been captivated by a biblical hero less famous for his strength than his sling.

That the stories of David and his predecessor Saul eventually attracted Brecht's dramatic attentions may reflect in part the larger share of the religious curriculum they commanded: Samson, occupying a mere four chapters of Judges, was passed over quickly, while David and Saul, monopolising more than half of the first book of Samuel and all of the second, received a rather fuller treatment. Nevertheless, while we will see below that Brecht's treatment of David and Saul is very much fragmentary, so too in its own way was Brecht's school curriculum, which notes some but not all of Saul's faults, and passes over, perhaps predictably, the graphic familial dysfunction which besets David's house in the aftermath of his adultery with Bathsheba.[13] Perhaps most striking of all is the fate of

---

9. While the curriculum afforded much less space to Samson than David (see Rohse, *Der frühe Brecht und die Bibel*, 405), it is quite possible that the former would have featured among the Bible stories told at home.

10. According to Artur Kutscher, *Frank Wedekind: sein Leben und seine Werke*, Vol. 3 (Munich: Georg Müller, 1922–1931), 136–41, while Wedekind began his first draft of *Samson* toward the end of January 1913 and finished it in Rome in the first week of July, the second act was apparently reworked at the end of that month.

11. Frank Wedekind, *Simson oder Scham und Eifersucht, dramatisches Gedicht in drei Akten* (Munich: Georg Müller, 1914).

12. The play was banned by the police, despite most members of the Censorship Advisory Board approving it. For discussion of the banning of this play and other works of Wedekind in the context of theatrical censorship in Germany and especially in Munich, see Gary D. Stark, *Banned in Berlin: Literary Censorship in Imperial Germany, 1871–1918* (New York: Berghahn Books, 2009), 55–83.

13. For the initial inclusion of David but the exclusion of Saul, see the curriculum sampled by Rohse, *Der frühe Brecht und die Bibel*, 391–8; for the inclusion of Saul and a fuller treatment of David, see ibid., 405–6.

David's battle with Goliath: while the curriculum both describes and illustrates this episode, we will see below that David's famous monomachy with the Philistine is conspicuous (indeed remarkably so) by its absence in Brecht's *David*, or at least that part of it found in the fragments preserved for us, to whose description and composition we now turn.

Brecht's David *in Fragments*

In the tenth volume of the *Große kommentierte Berliner und Frankfurter Ausgabe* of Brecht's works (*BFA*), the editors attribute nineteen fragments, predominantly from Brecht's notebooks of 1919–1921, under the title *David*. Eight of these fragments (A1–A8) are essentially notes toward possible structures of an envisioned *David* play about the life of the biblical king, while eleven (B1–B11) are mostly fragments of dialogue.[14] The range of styles contained among the B-fragments is broad: some are as short as a paragraph (such as the B5 'Absalom' fragment, which reads more like a snippet of poetry), while the longest fragment, B10, includes dozens of characters and runs to more than three thousand words in the German. Arguably the most 'complete' scene is B9, a dialogue between David and Saul, probably written (as discussed in Chapter 4) in direct response to the David and Saul scene composed by Otto Zarek in 1920.[15] These published fragments were our initial source material for the translation (Chapter 1) and subsequent research, writing and theatrical process. However, as the editorial notes for the *BFA* already suggest, and as our archival work in Berlin at the Bertolt-Brecht-Archiv of the Akademie der Künste (*BBA*) confirms, the texts are significantly more diverse in origin than their collection under the single title *David* suggests.

---

14. The editors of the *BFA* Vol. 10.1 and 10.2, Brecht's *Stückfragmente und Stückprojekte* ('play fragments and play projects'), use 'A' to designate notes, outlines and synopses, and 'B' to indicate scenes or dialogues. 'C', a further designation used in other parts of the volume to apply to commentary by Brecht on a given project, does not apply to the *David* fragments, although Brecht did comment on the project in his diaries (captured in other volumes of the *BFA*). The arrangement of fragments is notionally chronological (from early to late), but given the notorious state of Brecht's notebooks and loose-leaf annotations that are often undated, chronology is not always possible to establish accurately. There is also evidence of some outright editorial error, as in the case of *David*'s A5 (see Chapter 1 n. 19, p. 28).

15. See diary entry of 27 July 1920, *BFA* 26, 130. For English, see Bertolt Brecht, *Diaries 1920–1922*, ed. Herta Ramthun, trans. John Willett (London: Eyre Methuen, 1979), 12–13.

March 1919 seems to mark the first phase of Brecht's work on staging the David story. His design collaborator and friend Caspar Neher writes in his notebook on 4 March 1919: 'Brecht wants to write a new Drama: David and Bathsheba: Absalom'.[16] Hans Otto Münsterer's diary from the same week, in an entry on 10 March 1919, confirms that Brecht is writing this 'massive' new drama, but refers to it under the title *Absalon oder der Beauftragte Gottes* ('Absalom or God's Chosen One').[17] Three days after that, Neher begins drawings for the play under the title *Der König David*.[18] That these three different titles occur within a nine-day period suggests a project very much in flux, but also implies that it had a good amount of Brecht's attention at the time. The lack of direct traces in Brecht's surviving notebooks of this early phase of work is conspicuous, however, and by the time Brecht writes a title (A2) in his own hand – likely sometime between January and March 1920[19] – it has changed again to *Der Sieger und der Befreite* ('The Victor and the Liberated'). By the summer of 1920, Brecht refers to three new titles: 'Saul and David' (30 July), 'David Amid the Eagles' (20 August) and finally 'David' (6 September, and thereafter, into 1921). While the *BFA* annotations suggest it is 'justified to speak of two different play projects', the full range of titles, ideas and emphases that actually emerge from close examination of Brecht's notebooks and those of his artistic associates suggest a rather more complex picture.

Brecht's diaries from this period, collected in Volume 26 of the *BFA*, form a parallel but previously uncollected record of fragments associated with *David*, including comments, plans and even dialogue. We have restored the most significant of these to their place within the *David* fragments, and include new translations of the passages at the close of Chapter 1. Without associating David as a character too strongly with Brecht, there is no doubt that the personal experiences of the young playwright inform how David is written, and the diaries are one area where the

---

16. The Neher diaries from 1917–1920 are included as a supplement to Bertolt Brecht, *Notizbücher 1 bis 3 (1918–1920)*, Vol. 1, ed. Martin Kölbel and Peter Villwock (Berlin: Suhrkamp, 2012), 428. In our English translation we have converted the name Neher writes as 'Bath-Seba' to 'Bathsheba'.

17. Ibid., 457. Münsterer writes 'Absalon' for 'Absalom'. *Beauftragte* carries more of a sense of 'agent' or 'representative' than 'Chosen One' (which would be closer to *Auserwählte*), but we follow the translators of Münsterer here, as well as selecting the option with the most biblical resonance.

18. Ibid., 370.

19. This dating is based on Caspar Neher's notes of 8 January 1920 and 23 March 1920, where this title is referenced in both entries. Ibid., 444 and 450.

overlap is apparent. Often a single diary entry will compress the activities of theatre practice, romance, friendship, and multiple writing projects, all seen through the lens of Brecht's personal emotional landscape. The dynamic of autobiography as a feature of Brecht's process, especially in the 1920s, has been regularly discussed within Brecht studies. Klaus Völker articulates the situation as follows:

> Brecht never wrote anything deliberately autobiographical, even though many of his plays, prose works and especially poems contain personal experiences and record the attitudes and standpoints of friends and acquaintances. He did not regard his diary entries and biographical notes primarily as literary forms; their main purpose was to provide him with material.[20]

What is notable when reading Brecht's diaries of the *David* period is how vibrant and comprehensive the interaction between the personal, the collaborative and the literary seems to be in this period, with many entries moving seamlessly between his personal life and his multiple projects. Following a formulation that H. Porter Abbott applied to the fiction of Samuel Beckett, perhaps what is happening in this phase is not autobiography, but rather *autography*: writing the self.[21] John Willett, introducing his translation of the early Diaries, articulates it also as a personal *mythos*, a construction of a dwelling: 'the world which he was thus forming for himself was a strange pot-pourri of classical, biblical and wildly exotic elements, to be seen at its most impressive perhaps in his vivid yet basic, down-to-earth version of the David story'.[22]

Left for Dead: Forgetting Brecht's David *Fragments*

When Hans Otto Münsterer, Brecht's childhood friend, sat down to commit to paper his recollections of the 'Young Brecht' and his *David*, he had the benefit of his own notes, clippings and diaries from the time.[23] Of course, in doing so, what he cannot have had – whether at the time or

---

20. Klaus Völker, *Brecht: A Biography*, trans. John Nowell (London: Marion Boyars, 1979), 13.

21. For an elaboration of 'autography' and literature, see H. Porter Abbott, *Beckett Writing Beckett: The Author in the Autograph* (Ithaca: Cornell University Press, 1996).

22. John Willett, 'Introduction: Brecht on the Threshold', in Ramthun, ed., *Bertolt Brecht Diaries 1920–1922*, xviii–xix.

23. For some reflections on Münsterer's process, see the editors' comments in Hans Otto Münsterer, *The Young Brecht*, trans. Tom Kuhn and Karen J. Leeder (London: Libris, 1992), xviii.

even much later when he compiled his account – was anything like the range of sources for Brecht's *David* on offer to the reader of this volume. And yet, even allowing for the probability that Münsterer may have had some material which we do not, what turns out to be most noteworthy is that his own impression of the work was so favourable. Thus, in recalling one scene relating to Absalom, Münsterer insists that it was 'an exposition Brecht might have been proud of in his maturity'.[24] Indeed, despite his frank acknowledgement of the complexity of Brecht's *David(s)* and the problems they posed for Brecht, Münsterer goes on to extol the virtues of the work and its potential: 'What I do know is that even years later, I was convinced that this play, had it been completed, would have numbered amongst the greatest works of all German drama'.[25] Even allowing for Münsterer's caveat regarding its completion and his tendency to eulogise Brecht and his work at points, his numbering of a completed *David* amongst the greatest works of Brecht (let alone of all German drama) is remarkable, given that by the early sixties, the 'greatness' of many of Brecht's works was already widely recognised. But most significant of all is the fact that Brecht's *David* – which Münsterer remained convinced might have been so long remembered – was soon left for dead.

Of course for those with a knowledge of German and access to the standard edition of Brecht's works, *David*'s fragmented corp(u)s(e) as described above has been readily available for examination.[26] Indeed, the *BFA*'s editorial notes represent an invaluable resource, pointing suggestively as they do to signs of life in Brecht's *David*; but, working within the understandable constraints of the *BFA*, they can only begin to do so. Likewise, the recent and very welcome publication of the facsimiles of the notebooks containing many of the fragments themselves offer valuable insights into the genesis of the *David* fragments (amongst others).[27]

Yet, if all this suggests that scholarship knows where the Brechtian *David*'s body lies, it is curious that it has been left so undisturbed, even by that small tranche of scholars interested in Brecht and the Bible.[28]

---

24. Ibid., 80.
25. Ibid.
26. *BFA* 10.1, 120–42.
27. For a list of the volumes already produced and those in preparation, see: http://www.brecht-notizbuecher.de/editionsplan/. Our project has made extensive use of the first three volumes (see full citations in bibliography) and ancillary PDFs, as well as the electronic editions (EE) and 'EE Forum' spaces online.
28. See, for instance, the following studies which explore interesting and even important aspects of the relationship between Brecht's work and the Bible, but offer no substantial engagement with Brecht's *David*: G. Ronald Murphy, *Brecht and the*

Rohse's voluminous study of Brecht's biblical formation, the value of which has already been seen above, does begin to, in effect, poke at the body of Brecht's *David*, again pointing to potential themes or motifs seen elsewhere in Brecht's early writings and to the potential value of connecting the *David* fragments not only with David's own reflections on them in his diaries, but also with other literature with which they might usefully be compared. Nevertheless, in the nearly four decades since Rohse devoted those four suggestive pages to Brecht's *David* fragments, it is clear that the latter have been left to 'rest in peace' even by those who are specifically interested in the representation of Saul and David in the German theatre of the late nineteenth and early twentieth centuries.[29]

Of course, the fact that Brecht's David has been left in the sort of 'peace' which passes for benign neglect certainly has something to do with the 'pieces' in which Brecht left his life of *David*, some of which are very fragmentary, and only two of which appear even remotely 'finished' in the loosest sense of that word. Indeed, it is surely a measure of how little life Brecht scholars assume there to be in his *David* that there has been so little interest thus far in searching for signs of life in it, even in an era in which interest in other Brecht fragments has blossomed.[30]

Accordingly, it is not entirely surprising that one of the most substantial investigations of Brecht's *David* fragments in recent times is the work of someone whose primary expertise is in Biblical rather than Brecht

---

Bible: A Study of Religious Nihilism and Human Weakness in Brecht's Drama of Mortality and the City (Durham: University of North Carolina Press, 1983); Thomas O. Brandt, 'Brecht und die Bibel', in *Die Vieldeutigkeit Bertolt Brechts* (Heidelberg: Stiehm, 1968), 13–27; Ilja Fradkin, 'Brecht, die Bibel, die Aufklärung und Shakespeare', *Kunst und Literatur, Sowjetwissenschaft* 13 (1965): 156–75; Siegfried Melchinger, 'Brecht und die Bibel', in *Sie werden lachen – die Bibel: Überraschungen mit dem Buch*, ed. Hans Jürgen Schultz (Stuttgart: Kreuz Verlag, 1975), 227–38.

29. While the study of Inger Nebel, *Harfe, Speer und Krone: Saul und David in deutschsprachigen Dramen 1880–1920* (Gothenburg: Acta Universitatis Gothoburgensis, 2001) has proven very useful for the present study (not least in Chapter 4 below), the methodological approach it adopts and the sheer number of productions it considers explains in part why it has so little to offer in relation to Brecht's *David* beyond what is obvious on a first reading of the *BFA* and its notes.

30. See for instance the 2018 Brecht-Tage in the Literaturforum im Brecht-Haus (Berlin), which took 'fragments' as a theme, as well as the special topic section within *Brecht Yearbook / Brecht Jahrbuch* 44, and most especially the volume *Brecht and the Writer's Workshop: Fatzer and Other Dramatic Projects* (London: Bloomsbury, 2019) edited by Charlotte Ryland and Tom Kuhn, the latter of whom has offered crucial and sage advice at many stages throughout this project.

studies.³¹ Written for other biblical scholars first and foremost, David Jobling's study of the *David* fragments is naturally more concerned with how the Brechtian reflexes of David and other characters relate to their biblical incarnations than is Rohse's work, but like the latter – and arguably to an even greater extent – Jobling also recognises and begins to explore the significance of rival efforts like that of Otto Zarek, as well as the relevance of the Brecht's diaries and his other writings. While Jobling tries (perhaps mistakenly) and fails (probably inevitably) to assemble the Brecht's fragments into a coherent picture or 'life' of David, several of his intuitions regarding the value of reading Brecht's David in light of the young Brecht will find confirmation in the present study.

Why the most recent and substantial treatment of Brecht's *David* has been produced by a biblical scholar is partly explained by Jobling's existing interest in Brecht. However, his acknowledgement of a methodological turn toward the reception of biblical texts invites consideration of how this turn, and the notion of 'survival/afterlife', offers a frame for our investigation of Brecht's interpretation of David and the biblical stories associated with him.³²

The Bible and Its Survival/Afterlife

Of all the possible starting points for reflecting on the potential fruitfulness of the notions of 'survival' and 'afterlife' for the present study, perhaps the most obvious is Yvonne Sherwood's *A Biblical Text and its Afterlives: The Survival of Jonah in Western Culture* – a book which has perhaps more than any other helped to popularise the concept of 'afterlife' in biblical reception studies.³³ While Sherwood's simple equating of the 'afterlife' of the Bible with its 'reception history' in her introduction continues in various quarters,³⁴ a more interesting point of departure for our purposes

---

31. David Jobling, '"David on the Brain": Bertolt Brecht's projected play "David"', in *The Fate of King David: The Past and Present of a Biblical Icon*, ed. Tod Linafelt, Claudia V. Camp and Timothy Beal (London: T. & T. Clark, 2010), 229–40.

32. Ibid., 240.

33. Yvonne Sherwood, *A Biblical Text and its Afterlives: The Survival of Jonah in Western Culture* (Cambridge: Cambridge University Press, 2000).

34. See, for instance, the work of Anthony Swindell, *Reworking the Bible: The Literary Reception-History of Fourteen Biblical Stories* (Sheffield: Sheffield Phoenix Press, 2010), who refers to 'after-life history' in his preface (ix) and reverts thereafter to 'literary reception-history' and the terminology of Genette (especially 'hypertext' and 'reworking'). A subsequent book by the same author, *Reforging the Bible: More Biblical Stories and their Literary Reception* (Sheffield: Sheffield Phoenix Press,

is the way the 'Afterlife' of her title is and is not invoked elsewhere in her work. As has been noted by others, Sherwood's treatment of Jonah is not easily corralled into the stables of Hans-Robert Jauss or Hans-Georg Gadamer, so familiar to students of biblical reception.[35] However, while the opening pages of Sherwood's *Jonah* offer little by way of sustained reflection on method, she does eventually come nearest to parsing her title in a discussion under the heading: Of Survival, Memes and Life-After-Death: On Jonah's Infinite Regurgitation and Endless Survival. As this title and the discussion that follows it suggest, Sherwood turns out to be much less interested in the 'life after death' of Jonah than what we might call its 'life-after-life', which she explores by means of Hugh Pyper's notion of the biblical text as '" meme"…a cultural unit that ensures its own survival by grafting itself onto, and incubating itself in, human culture and the human mind'.[36] The evolutionary 'DNA' of this metaphor – which Sherwood borrows from Richard Dawkins via Pyper – is also made clear from her emphasis on Jonah as a biblical text whose remarkable fitness ensures its apparently endless survival in popular culture, as it is infinitely regurgitated (like Jonah himself) in countless variations. While the considerable purchase of both Sherwood's evolutionary and alimentary metaphors is clear, so too is the absence of any meaningful reflection on the eschatological potential of the 'afterlife' metaphor which she invokes both in the title of her discussion at this point and in her book as a whole.

2014), continues in the same vein. See too Christine E. Joynes and Christopher C. Rowland, *Women of the New Testament and their Afterlives* (Sheffield: Sheffield Phoenix Press, 2009), whose opening paragraph illustrates the simple equation of 'reception history' with 'the study of biblical women's "afterlives"' (1), and Diane Apostolos-Cappadona, 'Introduction', in *Biblical Women in the Arts: Biblical Reception* 5 (London: T & T Clark, 2018), who sees the 'diversity of methodological approaches' reflected in the collected essays as exploring the 'afterlife of a biblical figure or narrative' (1), but does not theorise the term in any way. Likewise, Kelley Harness, 'Theatrical Reliquaries: Afterlives of St Mary Magdalene in Early Seventeenth-Century Florence', *Biblical Women in the Arts: Biblical Reception* 5 (2018): 159–84.

35. As noted by Holly Morse, 'What's in a Name? Analysing the Appellation "Reception History" in Biblical Studies', *Biblical Reception* 3 (2014): 243–62, who uses Sherwood's work (and the wide variety of labels which have been applied to it) as props to illustrate the terminological and methodological morass within biblical reception studies.

36. H. S. Pyper, 'The Selfish Text: The Bible and Memetics', in *Biblical Studies/Cultural Studies: The Third Sheffield Colloquium*, ed. J. C. Exum and S. D. Moore (Sheffield: Sheffield Academic Press, 1998), 70–90.

A clue to Sherwood's insistence on construing 'afterlife' in evolutionary terms rather than eschatological ones may be found in Todd Linafelt's deployment of the very same two notions of 'survival' and 'afterlife' in his very stimulating *Surviving Lamentations: Catastrophe, Lament and Protest in the Afterlife of a Biblical Book*.[37] In a helpful introduction, Linafelt makes clear that he is interested not only in Lamentations as 'survival literature' – the work of those who have survived significant trauma – but also in the 'survival' of Lamentations in its subsequent interpretive 'afterlife'. What is also clear from his discussion is that Linafelt's understanding of the notions of 'afterlife' and 'survival' depends on his reading of Walter Benjamin's famous essay known in English as 'The Task of the Translator', from which he quotes:

> Just as the manifestations of life are intimately connected with life itself without signifying anything for it, a translation issues from the original – not so much from its life as from its 'afterlife' [*'Überleben'*]. For a translation comes after [*später*] the original [*das Original*] and for the important works, which never find their chosen translator at the time of their birth, is a stage of continued life [*Fortleben*].[38]

From this quotation (without the German), Linafelt draws the following conclusion: 'A translation then participates in the survival of a text (its afterlife) and ensures its survival (or continued life) in succeeding generations'.[39] While Linafelt goes on to amply and interestingly illustrate Lamentations' interpretive 'survival' and 'continued life', a reading of the rest of his book reveals him to be as little interested in the metaphor of 'afterlife' as Sherwood, despite its prominence in both their titles. This is all the more curious in the case of Linafelt, since unlike Sherwood, he actually goes to the effort of mining Benjamin's essay for 'afterlife', in outlining his own theoretical approach.

But what is perhaps most interesting about the absence of any meaningful deployment of the metaphor of 'afterlife' in the studies of Sherwood and Linafelt is that it turns out to be equally absent from Benjamin's essay itself, despite their and others' efforts to extract it along with the notion of 'survival'. Certainly the 'survival' of Benjamin's notion of 'survival' has

---

37. Todd Linafelt, *Surviving Lamentations: Catastrophe, Lament and Protest in the Afterlife of a Biblical Book* (Chicago: University of Chicago Press, 2000).

38. Ibid., 27–8; German in parentheses from Walter Benjamin, 'Die Aufgabe des Übersetzers', in *Gesammelte Schriften*, Vol. IV/1 (Frankfurt am Main: Suhrkamp, 1972), 9–21 (10).

39. Linafelt, *Surviving Lamentations*, 28.

been aided by Jacques Derrida's well-known translation of '*Überleben*' with '*survie*' and his insistence that it represents a continuation of life rather than 'life-after-death'.⁴⁰ It is also worth noting that Benjamin's reference in the quotation above to 'later' (*später*) in the same breath as *Überleben* and *Fortleben* ('progressing life') clearly implies that the latter admits of a kind of temporality – reflected in 'earlier' and 'later' stages of life.⁴¹

But it is equally clear that in the original German text of Benjamin's essay, 'Die Aufgabe des Übersetzers', neither *Überleben* nor *Fortleben* (to which Benjamin reverts in the essay) have much at all to do with *Nachleben*, the eschatological/spectral connotations of which in German are nicely captured by 'afterlife' in English. Indeed, the fact that *Nachleben*/Afterlife (with its religious connotations) doesn't appear even once in Benjamin's essay seems unlikely to have been accidental, given its widespread currency in scholarly discourse in German in the late nineteenth and early twentieth century.⁴² It is thus an unfortunate irony that an English mistranslation in Benjamin's famous essay *on translation* has led to so many erroneously associating him with the notion of 'afterlife' – a metaphor which his essay may well have intentionally avoided and in which it certainly shows no interest.⁴³

40. Jacques Derrida, 'Des Tours de Babel', trans. Joseph F. Graham, and 'Appendix: Des Tours de Babel', in *Difference in Translation*, ed. Joseph F. Graham (Ithaca: Cornell University Press, 1985), 165–248 (222).

41. See the translation above and the original German text in Benjamin, 'Die Aufgabe des Übersetzers'.

42. The use of the term by Otto Immisch and others is well illustrated by Daniel Weidner, 'Life after Life: A Figure of Thought in Walter Benjamin', paper presented at the conference *Afterlife: Writing and Image in Walter Benjamin and Aby Warburg*, Universidad Federal de Minais Gerais, Belo Horizonte, Brazil, October 2012. See http://www.zfl-berlin.org/tl_files/zfl/downloads/personen/weidner/life_after_life.pdf. Weidner notes that Benjamin's 'Die Aufgabe' does not mention 'death' (p. 9) but mistakenly sees Benjamin's references to Holy Writ later in the essay as a belated marker of a religious component in Benjamin's understanding of 'afterlife' – a misstep which follows from his failure to note the absence of *Nachleben per se* in the essay. Further context is supplied by the very learned discussion of Aby Warburg's use and understanding of *Nachleben* in Ulrich Raulff, '"Nachleben": A Warburgian Concept and its Origins', a lecture delivered on the occasion of the 150ᵗʰ anniversary of the birth of Warburg in 2016 (https://www.youtube.com/watch?v=u6Hgw8ooams).

43. As argued very persuasively by Caroline Disler, 'Benjamin's "Afterlife": A Productive(?) Mistranslation in Memoriam Daniel Simeoni', *TTR: traduction, terminologie, redaction* 24, no. 1 (2011): 183–221. Brennan Breed, *Nomadic Text: A Theory of Biblical Reception History* (Bloomington: Indiana University Press, 2014),

Of course, the further but rather more fortunate irony is that because Sherwood's and Linafelt's titles are haunted by an 'afterlife' which turns out not to exist after all in Benjamin's work, they end up following him 'faithfully' in neglecting it in favour of 'survival', which turns out to be the operative term in both their titles.[44] While a correction of the misreading of Benjamin noted above rightly allows his (and Sherwood's and Linafelt's) understanding of textual and cultural translation to be properly 'disenchanted', the shared term 'vie/leben/life' – at the heart of both the notions of 'afterlife' and 'survival/continuing life' – suggests the possibility that the two need not be mutually exclusive in reception studies generally or indeed in our exploration of Brecht's life of *David*. Indeed, how notions of 'afterlife' might be compatible after all with that of 'survival' in our study of Brecht's fragments may be illustrated by a remarkable episode found in 1 Samuel, the very book on which Brecht's *David* depends.[45]

The Survival of Samuel and the After/Laterlife of Brecht's David

While Brecht himself shows no interest in the figure of Samuel – the prophet who anoints first Saul and then David as king – close attention to the unique account of Samuel's spectral survival in 1 Samuel 28 suggests a stimulating analogy for exploring not only the relationship between the biblical and Brechtian lives of David, but any biblical life and its afterlife/survival in culture.

In 1 Samuel 28, King Saul – beset by fear of the Philistine army and bereft of divine guidance – journeys in disguise to Endor to seek out one of the very mediums he had previously banished from his kingdom (1 Sam. 28). Once Saul has allayed the woman's fear of doing so, she agrees to Saul's request to 'bring up' Samuel, the prophet who first anointed Saul as king before eventually opposing him and anointing

---

4, 169, seems also to mistakenly associate Benjamin and Derrida (and Sherwood) with the use of *Nachleben*, but rightly notes that their interest is in fact in 'survival'.

44. For Jonathan Z. Smith, 'Religion and Bible', *JBL* 128, no. 1 (2009): 5–27 (23 n. 27), it is the 'spectral tone' of 'afterlife' which leads him to prefer 'paraphrastic' translations of *Nachleben*, such as 'continuing life' and 'survival'. In following Smith, Christine Joynes, 'Revisioning Women in Mark's Gospel Through Art', *Biblical Reception* 5 (2018): 83–98 (95 n. 6) adds that she does not wish to 'to imply that somehow the real life of the text ceased prior to its reception' – which she evidently feels the use of 'afterlife' might imply.

45. For discussion of the reception of this episode in the German theatre see Chapter 4, pp. 125–7 below.

David in his place. What makes the request extraordinary is that three chapters earlier the reader is told that Samuel has died and been buried at his home in Ramah (1 Sam. 25.1). That Samuel must be 'brought up' (1 Sam. 28.8, 11, 13, 14, 15) almost certainly points to the widely held belief in the Hebrew Bible that while Samuel has been buried in his family tomb, he has also gone 'down' to *She'ol*, the final destination for all living beings at the end of their earthly lives.[46]

While 1 Samuel 28 is more (indeed exclusively) interested in Samuel's survival rather than his death, the latter is clearly assumed as we will see and may not be subtracted from the equation. Samuel is evidently one of the '*living* dead' (and therefore not '*dead* dead'), but if not summoned up by Saul and the medium, he is effectively 'left for dead', by virtue of being cut off from the land of those not yet dead.[47] Put another way, while our and Saul's *awareness* of Samuel's survival may depend on his 'summoning up', his survival *per se* does not, indicating that Samuel's afterlife – both before and after his coming up to the 'land of the living' narrated in 1 Samuel 28 – might be considered as merely one more 'stage [*Stadium*] of continued life [*Fortlebens*]'.[48]

At the same time, the need for Samuel to be 'brought up' makes clear that this later 'stage' of Samuel's 'continuing/progressing life' does nevertheless belong to a different place, indeed to a different world, not only populated by a different cast of characters but also displaying its own character in various ways.[49] While precious little is offered by 1 Samuel 28 to allow for the reconstruction of this world, in theory at least, it seems

---

46. For a general discussion, Brian B. Schmidt, *Israel's Beneficent Dead: Ancestor Cult and Necromancy in Ancient Israelite Religion and Tradition* (Winona Lake: Eisenbrauns, 1996) and Philip S. Johnston, *Shades of Sheol: Death and Afterlife in the Old Testament* (Leicester: Apollos, 2002) whose argument founders, however, when suggesting that *She'ol* is a less likely destination for the righteous than the wicked.

47. The notion of the dead 'rising' seen here is clearly related to notions of 'resurrection' of which the Hebrew Bible offers tantalising glimpses (Isa. 26; Dan. 12; Ezek. 37) and on which subsequent Jewish literature and the New Testament linger at considerable length. However, as Francesca Murphy, *1 Samuel* (Grand Rapids: Brazos/Baker, 2010), 258 notes, what 1 Sam. 28 imagines is not so much a resumption of the life *before* death (however different in various respects) suggested by resurrection, so much as a temporary recall from a life *after* death to which Samuel will seemingly happily return.

48. Benjamin, 'Die Aufgabe', 10.

49. For discussion of *She'ol* see n. 46 above. Indeed, it is interesting that despite no record in the Hebrew Bible of anyone in normal circumstances seriously wishing to go to *She'ol*, Samuel seems unhappy at being summoned from there. As A. Graeme Auld, *I & II Samuel: A Commentary* (Louisville, KY: Westminster John Knox Press,

obvious that to understand Samuel's 'afterlife/survival', one should seek to understand something of that perhaps quite different world from which he comes.

For all that the 'later' Samuel inhabits a different world, it should be noted that the woman's successful summoning of him also points to continuities with 'earlier Samuel':

> The woman said to Saul, 'I see a divine being coming up out of the ground'. He said to her, 'What is his appearance?' She said, 'An old man is coming up; he is wrapped in a robe'. So Saul knew that it was Samuel, and he bowed with his face to the ground, and did obeisance. (1 Sam. 28.13-14)

That it is Samuel rather than some other figure who appears is in fact confirmed by his appearance and the observable similarity of 'later-Samuel' to 'earlier-Samuel' not least with respect to his robe.[50] Indeed, it seems essential to the exercise of recognising 'before' and 'after', that something remains of what was 'earlier' in that which comes 'later'.

It is, however, not just what may be 'seen' which marks the continuity between the Samuel who survives death and the Samuel who is survived; this continuity is also marked by what is heard.[51] Thus, in responding to Saul's complaint that God has given him the 'silent treatment', Samuel is at pains to point out that what he says to Saul now in his continuing life is what he had already said at an earlier stage (namely, before death):

> The LORD has done to you just as he spoke by me; for the LORD has torn the kingdom out of your hand, and given it to your neighbor, David. Because you did not obey the voice of the LORD, and did not carry out his fierce wrath against Amalek, therefore the LORD has done this thing to you today. (1 Sam. 28.17-18)

2011), 328 notes, *hirgaztání* suggests Samuel is not merely 'disturbed' but rather 'violently shaken'. For an interesting suggestion of the promise of thinking about reception history in terms of 'movement', see Breed, *Nomadic Text*.

50. As Robert Polzin, *Samuel and the Deuteronomist: A Literary Study of the Deuteronomic History; Part Two: 1 Samuel* (Bloomington: Indiana University Press, 1989), 218 notes, the identification of Samuel by means of his robe is hardly surprising given his long association with it in 1 Samuel, beginning with his mother's annual gifting of a robe to him after he is devoted to the temple (1 Sam. 2.19).

51. That what is heard underlines this continuity of identity is recognised by Murphy, *1 Samuel*, 255, who notes in this connection that 'the voice is the voice of Samuel'.

'later Samuel' may be identified with 'original/earlier Samuel' by Saul and the reader, because Samuel says here what he had said to Saul some thirteen chapters earlier in 1 Samuel 15 regarding the price of his disobedience in choosing to spare Agag, king of the Amalekites, and some of their animals. Indeed, 1 Sam. 28.17 largely echoes 1 Sam. 15.18 to prove the point.

Although what is seen and heard of Samuel confirms that it really is Samuel after all despite his death, the text also signals that the Samuel who survives has changed.[52] For instance, despite the resemblance of what Samuel says 'after' (1 Sam. 28) to what he said 'before' (1 Sam. 15), his interpretation of God's original orders to entirely annihilate Amalek as God's 'fierce wrath' (ḥărôn-'appô; v. 18) is new to both Saul and the reader. Whence has this new information come? The observation that the Hebrew phrase does not appear elsewhere in the books of Samuel, but does in 2 Chron. 28.11; 29.10; 30.8 might suggest that the information comes from the later world of the Chronicler's History. But whatever the source of this change, Benjamin's insistence that in a text's 'progressing/ continuing life...even words with fixed meaning can undergo a maturing process' might be readily applied here to the 'later' evolution of 'earlier' Samuel's message.

Indeed, the further transformation of that message is reflected in the new information which 'later' Samuel goes on to supply: namely, that Saul's worst fears will be realised imminently in the defeat of his kingdom by the Philistines, the death of him and his sons, and the beginning of their own 'afterlives' with Samuel in *She'ol* (v. 19). While 'later' Samuel's prediction of future events confirms that he is the 'same old prophet', here he goes beyond simply saying old things in new ways by bringing genuinely new information from the world beyond the grave – information which prompts a dramatic response from Saul, who falls flat on his face in fear (v. 20). What should also be noted, though it is less conspicuous, is that the transformation of 'earlier' Samuel's message also involves omissions – indeed much of the dialogue of 1 Samuel 15 has been 'lost' in later-Samuel's retelling of it.

How then might this remarkable vignette of Saul's summoning up of Samuel point toward ways of exploring the 'afterlife' of Brecht's *David* fragments? The fact that comparison of 'later' Samuel with the 'earlier' Samuel above points to both similarities and differences between two

---

52. Exemplifying Benjamin's observation ('Die Aufgabe', 12) that 'in its progressing life [*Fortleben*] – which it could not be called if it were not a transformation and a renewal of something living – the original is changed [*ändert sich*]'. The reflexive on the last verb suggests a slightly different translation: 'changes itself'.

discrete stages of his 'continuing/progressing life' encourages a similar comparison of the 'original' (biblical) David with the David who lives on in Brecht's fragments. Accordingly, in the present study, we unashamedly ask how does the 'later-life' of Brecht's *David* relate to the 'earlier-life' of David disclosed by the ancient biblical books of Samuel? More specifically, we interrogate the ways in which Brecht's *David* follows the biblical tradition (especially with respect to character development), and in what ways (if at all), Brecht's *David* reflects a reaction to or even subversion of the earlier (biblical) lives of David found in 1 Samuel.

No less than Samuel in 1 Samuel 28, it is clear that Brecht's *David* comes from a very different world than the 'original' David – the world of post-war Munich ca. 1920, a world populated by Brecht and those within his orbit. Thanks to the diaries of Brecht (and others) and a wide range of historical sources of which we may avail, this world out of which Brecht's *David* emerges is far more accessible than the shadowy underworld of *She'ol* from which Samuel is summoned: thus, we consider what light this world might shed on the afterlife of David in Brecht. So, for instance, while very much wishing to avoid falling prey to the 'biographical fallacy', we ask how Brecht's life/lives of *David* and their various characters and interests relate to the characters and interests reflected in the life/lives of the young Brecht himself, especially as disclosed by his own diaries.

Mindful that Brecht was writing much else in addition to *David* and these diaries at this time, we further consider to what extent the interests and characters of *David* resonate with those found in his other theatrical and poetic writings of the period. Indeed, recognising that Brecht was far from the first writer to be attracted to David and that the 'later' life of David consists of an astonishing number of 'afterlives', including many theatrical incarnations, we also ask how the characters and interests of Brecht's *David* relate to those of other theatrical interpretations of the David stories produced prior to and at the time of his own work.

That the 'summoning up' of the later Samuel for interrogation in 1 Samuel 28 requires a 'stirring' or 'shaking' suggests that it is no mean feat, and perhaps explains in part Saul's insistence on collaboration with a medium, whose specialist skills were clearly required. Interestingly, while other afterlives of David have been explored with the traditional tools of biblical studies, the fragmentary quality, dramatic character and opacity of Brecht's *David* soon suggested that its interrogation, like Saul's interrogation of Samuel, would require specialist expertise and interdisciplinary collaboration.

Bringing Brecht's David *to Life:*
Translation, Performance and Survival

In the case of authors or works that have been 'left for dead', the figure of Samuel's *medium*, a living figure who traffics in intercessions with the dead, invokes the parallel concept of 'mediation'. Both translation and performance are theorised as a form of mediation, implying that they are actions that take place between the moment of textual production (by an author) and textual reception (by an audience). The definition of 'mediation' that is associated not only with different 'media' but also with negotiation between two parties is useful here, because in moving between languages or between bodies and spaces, there are always gains and losses to be balanced. The translator, or any of the numerous people involved in a stage performance, all have roles to play in building a bridge between the audience of *now* and the vision originally perceived, internalised and then articulated by an author in the past. Theatrical mediums and mediators – translators and dramaturgs, directors and actors, designers and stage managers – are all working in tandem to ensure survival of our cultural past, but they bring with them a set of contemporary values and interests. Finding the right balance between tradition and innovation such that a resurrected figure or reinvigorated work can be recognised, and that its underlying thought may 'go on' (*Fortleben*): this is the main challenge in such work.

Thus, one of the initial gestures in the collaboration around *The David Fragments* in production – the outreach from the biblical side to the theatre side to offer Brecht's texts for mutual investigation – could be considered our 'Saul to Endor' moment. Such a request implies two important concepts underlying our interdisciplinary approach: first (in terms of methodology), that there is a special form of insight arising from theatrical practice that would be of benefit to the other discipline in pursuing the research; and second (in terms of research questions), that there are specific challenges involved in understanding Brecht's *David* fragments which might require performance to overcome. Crucial to such interactions, based on our experience and understanding, is that the methods and research questions cannot be held entirely apart, or else one discipline ends up working purely in service of the other, never 'entangling' productively in order to generate new forms of knowledge.[53] In a research environment

---

53. Recent critiques of an older model of 'reciprocity' in interdisciplinary encounters, accounts which often ignored power imbalances between research partners coming from different training, backgrounds or institutions, have led to a new discourse around the 'entanglement' of research questions, which allows interdisciplinary

increasingly focused on 'impact', given the power of theatre and performance to vivify narratives, there is always a risk of instrumentalisation. Rather than focusing on the creative arts only for the sake of communication or entertainment, this encounter took theatre practice seriously as a means of research. The affirmative response to the call to 'raise up' Brecht and *David* also connected to broader trends at our institution and in the Irish higher education sector. The discourse of 'practice-as-research' (PaR) has migrated from drama departments in the United Kingdom, where it has been extensively discussed since the turn of the current century, to a distinctive local model of PaR involving inter-departmental collaborations around challenging, unperformed, or theoretically 'unperformable' texts. The *David* project, extending in its active phase for approximately 26 months (April 2015–June 2017) and dedicating a further 24 months to research and dissemination (July 2017–July 2019), was the third such project at Trinity College Dublin since 2013.

Certain peculiarities of the *David* material – namely its fragmentary nature, its unclear relation to later (but better-known) Brechtian theatrical aesthetics, and the fact that it was not yet fully available in English – all suggested that a translation followed by a theatrical 'workshop' process would unlock some of the texts' mysteries. Actors seeking to perform dramatic material must explore all possible avenues of meaning, aided in their investigation by a director and/or dramaturg; their intuitive and kinaesthetic modes of exploration uncover features of the text – often, its literary motifs and character motivations – that might have eluded even a close reader. Designers interpreting Brecht's rough notes, especially in relation to broader knowledge of the scenographic traditions of his period, might illuminate new readings as well. At the same time, the possibility of generating fresh academic methods or new knowledge is not generally why producers agree to produce live theatre (an extravagantly expensive activity for something so ephemeral). In short, this was not a project that drama would have come to without the prompt of interest from the biblical studies side, and the research, had it been conducted solo by either side, would have been significantly less rich: the expertise brought to bear around the specificities of David as a biblical figure, and one represented extensively in the nineteenth- and twentieth-century canon that influenced Brecht, opened new avenues theatrically as well. The inclusion of a biblical researcher as a named role within the theatre process – with David Shepherd ultimately serving as dramaturg, co-author

---

work to have a less binary structure. See Felicity Callard and Des Fitzgerald, *Rethinking Interdisciplinarity across the Social Sciences and Neurosciences* (Houndmills: Palgrave Macmillan, 2015).

and co-adaptor, on a co-equal basis with Nicholas Johnson's work as translator and director – was an essential ingredient. The fusion of creative and academic intelligences, buttressed by the combination of professionals and students within the ensemble, were all required to ensure the particular form of 'survival' for Brecht's *David* that we present here.

This book begins with the essential first step of the whole process: a translation of Brecht's *David* fragments, offering their first complete version in English, further enhanced by several 'uncollected' fragments that are not part of the *BFA* and by an extensive apparatus of annotations.[54] The next two chapters explore comparisons and (more often) contrasts between Brecht's *David* and the biblical David, mining these as 'translations' of a different sort that shed light on biblical reception as well as Brecht's early evolution as a writer. The fourth chapter examines some of Brecht's influences and sources among his contemporaries, exposing the many 'mediators' of his era who kept David alive for him. The fifth and final chapter considers the *David* fragments in performance in both 1995 and 2017, offering extensive documentation and reflection on our own process of staging *The David Fragments* with an early-career ensemble. Though the separation of these stages is designed to guide the reader to their own area of greatest interest, it is important to note that the biblical and theatrical research is fully interlocking and wholly intertwined: there are numerous annotations and insights that derived from our practice within the first four chapters, just as the originating biblical research undergirds our final chapter's exploration of the texts' afterlife (*Nachleben*) in the studio and the theatre.

We have sought to construct, from the fragments offered by Brecht and our own diverse processes of investigation, research and writing, a vessel that will bear Brecht's thought a small bit further. Walter Benjamin wrote of just such a goal in his essay on translation:

> Fragments of a vessel that are to be glued together must match one another in the smallest details, although they need not be like one another. In the same way a translation, instead of imitating the sense of the original, must lovingly and in detail incorporate the original's way of meaning, thus making both the original and the translation recognizable as fragments of a greater language, just as fragments are part of a vessel.[55]

---

54. A short preface to the translation will discuss the editorial and translational approach in greater detail.

55. Walter Benjamin, 'The Task of the Translator', in *Selected Writings, Vol. 1: 1913–1926*, ed. Marcus Bullock and Michael W. Jennings (Cambridge: Harvard University Press, 2002), 260.

The burden to be 'recognisable' or to serve a 'greater language' is the zone of greatest friction for the aspiring 'medium'. How would Samuel's story be different, for example, if he had not been recognised on his return? Fear attends the process of confronting a Brecht who has returned from *She'ol*: what if the authorities who watch over Brecht's afterlife – guardians of rights or the scholarly record – are displeased? Is it a requirement that the Brecht arising in the *David* fragments, in a new translation or a new performance, be 'Brechtian' in some particular way? This idea of a certain self-similarity being required exists in productive friction with Benjamin's emphasis on evolutionary process and change over time, a notion that echoes Sherwood's invocation of the 'gene' and the 'meme'. In the biological world, mutation, adaptation and evolution are key to the survival of the phylum. The fruits of our collaboration reveal that the theatrical and biblical ecologies are not so different from the world at large: that survival of an author might be linked to the recovery of forgotten texts, which we hope have been productively mutated, adapted and evolved here.

Chapter 1

THE *DAVID* FRAGMENTS IN TRANSLATION

Preface to the Translation

This translation of the *David* fragments of Bertolt Brecht, their first appearance in English, is an exercise in multiplicity: different layers of meaning fight for supremacy within these texts, while manifold individual word choices compete for selection by the translator. All translators have found themselves in this same hall of mirrors: it could usually go either this way or that, and there is a special joy in moments that are constrained to just one option (a rare event in Brecht's texts generally). The spirit of these fragments is manifested in the attempt to serve multiple audiences: first, the translation and accompanying notes seek to facilitate further scholarly research (whether in Brecht studies, Biblical studies, German studies, or drama/performance studies); second, they seek to capture and disseminate some results of practice-as-research into these texts (explored in detail in Chapter 5); finally, they are offered as a potential performance source text or a prompt for choreography, for those interested in staging, reading or adapting Brecht's early fragments.

It may be useful to expose the process by which this translation of dramatic material has progressed from an initial 'literary' or 'faithful' translation through rehearsal and performance and then ultimately into print. The process of translation that contributed various strata to the following text included six sequential stages, which are enumerated below:

- **Transcription** of the German as edited in the *BFA*, for which the translator is the audience. The process of transcription forces close reading of the original language and creates a document with the formatting required for a rehearsal script.

- Translation into the **'faithful'** English, which has collaborators (actors, designers, dramaturg) as an audience. This draft is focused on discovering and communicating Brecht's intended meaning in the original language, and in the case of non-dramatic material in translation, is generally the final stage.

- A **'rehearsal adaptation'** which has collaborators (actors, designers, dramaturg) as an audience. This draft is usually produced by the creative team collaboratively, especially the dramaturg and director working in tandem. It focuses on the exigencies of performance in terms of actor and audience needs, especially as relates to clarity. Such a draft might reflect more significant changes such as cuts to sections that do not make sense to anyone or do not fit within the allotted time of performance; the focus is on 'playability' of a line's action, rather than accuracy to Brecht's original language, in cases where these seem to be in opposition.

- A **'run draft'** produced at the last stage of rehearsals, which has stage management and technical crew as an audience (so that they can accurately identify what is really going to happen on stage during the production and find their own cues). This draft reflects what is actually being said and done by actors on stage, recording what is transpiring as opposed to the aspirational script that began the rehearsal process.

- An **'archival comparison'** produced after the project is concluded, with scholarly reflection and preparation for publication as an aim. By comparing both the German transcription and the multiple translation versions to the manuscript originals held in the Brecht archive, decisions on indistinct areas become easier, and possible variations in choices become more available.

- The final text presented here: a **'playable translation'** that integrates all of the above, originating in the authorial 'faithful' translation but reflecting alterations shown to be functional by field testing with actors in front of audiences, as well as later information gained from archival explorations and dramaturgical research.

Some of the fragments do not conform to the layout of a traditional dramatic script, but appear as lists or narrative prose. Reflecting the editorial strategy of the *BFA*, the authoritative German published source for the *David* fragments, this arrangement has retained the designations A1–A8 and B1–B11 as titles. Later chapters of this book will refer to sections by those names, which were used throughout the rehearsal process to designate particular scenes. Dialogue has been formatted as theatrical script according to house style, so the lineation does not reflect either the *BFA* or the archive. Footnotes indicate where substantial changes have been made from Brecht's original word choice, where variant alternatives that may have a bearing on meaning were explored, where capitalisation or punctuation are idiosyncratic in a way that affects meaning, where biblical citations offer insight into Brecht's source material or where archival work revealed uncertainty.

After the final *BFA* fragment (B11), in this chapter we include new translations of several previously uncollected *David* fragments drawn from the first three volumes of Brecht notebooks from 1918–1921 (published by Suhrkamp) and the *Journale* from this period (published in the *BFA*, and previously translated by John Willett in *Diaries 1920–1922*). The entries are partial, excerpting only the elements that are clearly related to the *David* project in its various iterations; subsequent chapters will tease out more oblique connections and biographical elements related to the narrative of *David*'s development.

Initial translation work based on the *BFA* was undertaken by Nicholas Johnson in Berlin, London, Dublin and New York between late August 2015 and December 2015. Revisions to the 'faithful' translation through workshops, rehearsals and performance with actors occurred between May 2016 and July 2017 in Dublin and London. Amendments and some footnotes arose from visits to the Bertolt Brecht Archive and Akademie der Künste archives in Berlin in 2018. Annotations to this translation are co-authored by David Shepherd, co-adaptor/co-author and dramaturg for the production of *The David Fragments*.

The translator acknowledges the kind permission of Suhrkamp Verlag, the Wylie Agency and the Estate of Bertolt Brecht to produce this translation. Translation assistance was provided by Jenni Schnarr and Peter Krauch, and all members of the *David* ensemble, including all readers and actors involved from 2016 to 2018, were integral to the development of the text that results here.

Nicholas Johnson, Dublin 2019

The David Fragments: A1–A8

A1

First Scene[1]

Wooden structure[2] with pallid sky. David and Absalom. Bathsheba. Behind they cry for Uriah. David demands Absalom.

Second Scene

Absalom by the river in the tavern. Fishermen. Soldiers. Whores. They tell the story of David and Bathsheba and that she is pregnant.[3]

Third Scene

Wooden structure with mottled night sky. Bathsheba and Uriah. Bathsheba to the bath.[4] Uriah remains there. David and Absalom. Meal. Letter.[5] Absalom and Uriah embrace off.[6] With Absalom many soldiers.[7] David stays back with Bathsheba, who is pregnant.

---

1. This sequence of scenes introduces Absalom as a character (2 Sam. 13–18) into the narrative of David, Bathsheba and Uriah (2 Sam. 11–12). It appears in BBA 459/73, part of the archival '*Lose Blaetter – 1*' collection of loose-leaf related papers, preceded by a fragment from *Im Dickicht der Städte* (BBA 459/72) and followed by B1 (BBA 459/75–76). It dates to Summer 1920 and is available as part of the Electronic Edition of the Brecht *Notizbücher*.

2. Brecht uses *Der Holzbau*, which carries the sense of a 'building' of wood. 'Structure' was used to give the impression of something unfinished, transparent or partial, because this would be more evocative for a stage designer than 'building'. The word recurs across the *David* texts, as does the material of wood.

3. The account of David and Bathsheba and the pregnancy is found in 2 Sam. 11–12.

4. Brecht uses *ins* rather than *im*, suggesting a progression of going rather than being in already. David and Bathsheba's relationship begins when he sees her bathing on a rooftop (2 Sam. 11.2)

5. David's orchestration of Uriah's death is facilitated by sending a letter with him back to the battle front with instructions to his general (Joab) to have Uriah placed in the heat of the battle (2 Sam. 11.14-15).

6. Brecht's *umschlungen ab* is ambiguous; it could refer to an offstage embrace or an embrace during the exit from the stage. The translation sought to retain the odd locution and open possibility here.

7. Absalom's insurrection against David (2 Sam. 15–18) employs soldiers.

Fourth Scene

Yellow tent. Uriah and Absalom. Uriah alone, in his shirt. (Absalom newly[8] back with the treasonous soldiers!) Bathsheba and Uriah. Absalom. Insurrection.[9] Uriah doesn't believe in goodness, he goes to David, to beg for his life.[10] Bathsheba sends him in advance. Uriah, the seed of death, sits among the zealots.[11]

Fifth Scene

David's wooden hut. Bathsheba is brought. Uriah comes. He is to be sent away after the letter. In the meantime, the child of Bathsheba is strangled.[12] But Uriah comes, and David flees with him. Bathsheba remains, alone, back with the child.

Sixth Scene

Absalom's tent. Unmasking of Uriah.[13]

Seventh Scene

Vineyard. Death of Absalom.[14]

---

8. 'Newly' could also refer to 'recently' or similar temporal conditions; English does not have a comfortable translation for the inserted adverb *erst* in this context.

9. 2 Sam. 15–18.

10. For discussion of how much the biblical Uriah knows about what David has done, see below, pp. 77–80.

11. *Uria, der Todeskeim, sitzt unter den Begeisterten.* This translation reads the commas as apposition (i.e. *Todeskeim* is describing Uriah himself, not a second element in a series); 'seed of death' is a fairly direct translation of this evocative coinage, though *Keim* in isolation also carries the sense of 'embryo' or 'germ'. 'Zealots' is a somewhat idiosyncratic translation for what could be just 'enthusiasts', but here the word with greatest biblical resonance was selected.

12. The first child of David and Bathsheba (the fruit of their adultery) dies shortly after birth and its death is seen as a fulfilment of the prophecy of judgement (2 Sam. 12). For Brecht's early conviction that David was directly responsible for this child's death, see pp. 72–3 below.

13. Though a fairly direct translation pair with 'unmasking', *Entlarvung* in the German carries a more powerful sense of emergence related to leaving behind the larval stage of animal development, of maturation and metamorphosis.

14. For discussion of the death of Absalom in the fragments and in Brecht's writing beyond them see pp. 80–7 below.

A2

The Victor and the Liberated

3. Act

The sun is pulled across the sky by a cord. The act lasts the length of the full day, during which Bargan sits on the wall. But behind the scenes is stamping and drumming, as well as a barbaric song to be heard, coming ever nearer. This is Absalom.

5. Act

End: the stars begin to run into one another.[15] It grows dark ahead. The curving star-paths!

A3

The red tree,[16] brown, in which Absalom is hanging in the end, brown sky, pastures, glistening eyes. Wind.

A4

Three notes, a broken a-minor VII[17]
The degenerate who left his wife – 20 years and then comes back. He finds the wife besieged by dandies, a whore. And he says: although I have neither right nor claim, I nonetheless lament, that mercy has not befallen me.[18]

---

15. Brecht uses the more literary and spiritual term *Gestirne*, which the translation 'stars' doesn't quite cover; the term also implies heaven, celestial bodies or luminosity in the night sky.

16. *Rotbaum* is literally translated here as 'red tree' in contrast to the brown colour that marks the rest of the line, as it is unclear what species or type of tree Brecht might be referring to; one appropriately biblical and regional option is cedar, although since *Zeder* also exists in German, it is not certain that this was intended.

17. 'a-minor broken' is an alternative possibility. BBA 10462/68, where this fragment appears, shows that Brecht originally misspelled *a-mol* without the second *l*, and the Roman numeral *VII* appears after *gebrochen*, which has been restored here after having been left out of the *BFA* (even though its meaning is unclear). As a-minor is the key of the famous *allegretto* (second movement) of Beethoven's seventh symphony, this is one possibility.

18. The referents remain unclear for the pronouns in this line, in terms of any relation to biblical narrative.

A5

Uriah, standing on his rights as a general (certificates of honour), while David fucks his wife.[19]

A6

David-End[20]

He stands up, with a complicated face, somewhat laboriously, sluggishly, on the rocks, and walks back slowly like a rhinoceros, inward between the trees.[21]

A7

1[22]

2

Jonathan tells Saul of David, who is returning from his victory over

---

19. This text is aligned with BBA 503/047–048 and appears on the back of printed stationery from the Gotham Hotel, New York City, which was popular with German expatriates. As Brecht did not visit New York until much later, it seems likely that this fragment dates from after the other *David* fragments, which means it should be aligned either with the 1942 film project *Uriasbrief* or the *Goliath* project, both unfinished.

20. The original appears in NB 11, 26v.1–7, BBA 10450, and dates from 1921, after the encounter between Brecht and Zarek about Zarek's *David*. The entry shares a page with one of the fragments of the project *Mormonenpapst*, a film project based on the life of Joseph Smith (founder of the Church of Jesus Christ of Latter-Day Saints) with particular focus on the report of him having had forty wives.

21. *Er steht auf, mit kompliziertem Gesicht, etwas mühselig, schwerfällig, in die Brüche gegangen, und geht langsam wie ein Nashorn hinter, zwischen die Stämme hinein.* A difficult passage for several reasons, but three elements are notable: the idiomatic expression *in die Brüche gegangen* correlating with the idiomatic use of 'on the rocks' (not literally on rocks); the spatial directions *hinter* and *hinein* that seem to imagine a possible staging or actor direction; and the word *Stämme*, which could refer to 'tribes' (also relevant to the David story, of course), 'trunks' of trees or 'logs' of cut trees. The resonance with *Holzbau* from earlier fragments is preserved by the choice of 'trees' in the translation here, as is the link to 'family trees' (maintaining the 'tribes' possibility). The only mention of David's incapacity in old age is found in 1 Kgs 1.1 where he cannot stay warm. See also 1 Kings 2 where he is on his deathbed.

22. BBA 10459/73–74. The handwriting of A7 (1-9) is neater than in other fragments, possibly suggesting an earlier date.

Goliath.²³ Covenant between him and Jonathan.²⁴ Saul grows fond of David.²⁵ ('When I stretch a few guts over a piece of wood, it gives a strong sound and I can sing to it. Perhaps you'll fall asleep, when I sing to the guts?'²⁶

3

Saul's spear-throw²⁷

4

David's farewell from Jonathan.²⁸

5

David appals his city. Saul wants to catch him. The priest feeds him.²⁹ Saul comes. They receive him with cries, as a victor. ('The Philistines yield like ears of corn in the wind, when I become visible: I only see the corpses of them.³⁰ But David I hate, because he is my enemy. Show him to me, so I can drill through him!')

---

23. In 1 Samuel, Jonathan does not (first) tell Saul of David after he kills Goliath, because Saul meets David before his combat with Goliath. However, see 1 Sam. 17.31-39.

24. 1 Sam. 18.1-3 contains Jonathan's initial covenant with David; for discussion see pp. 98–102 below. There is a multivalence in the German *Bund* that 'covenant' does not quite capture; alternatives could be 'bond' or 'alliance'. The alliance implied can be military or friendly, or both.

25. The expression *Saul gewinnt David lieb* is vitally important here to our reading of the relationship, as it is often used to express romantic or erotic attraction, as well as platonic affection (somewhat more rarely). For discussion see p. 113 below.

26. Brecht does not close the parentheses. These traces of the writer's process, including gaps and elisions, have been maintained here (for example in the blank 'scene 1' in this fragment) and throughout our translation.

27. The biblical Saul repeatedly tries to kill David with a spear (1 Sam. 18.10; 19.11; 20.33). For Brecht's fuller development of this, see B9 below.

28. David and Jonathan part memorably twice: in 1 Sam. 23.18 and 2 Sam. 20.42. In both cases Jonathan leaves David.

29. 1 Sam. 21 finds David fleeing from Saul into the city of Nob, where a priest feeds him.

30. Literal rendering of a somewhat awkward original: *Ich sehe nur ihre Leichen von ihnen.* Altered from the text used for performance, which was the more playable 'I see only their corpses'.

6

The cave. Saul forgives David.[31]

7

David among the Philistines.[32] The son of the priest.

8

Jonathan goes into battle.[33]

9

David becomes king.[34]

A8

1[35]

David and Jonathan

2

Saul suffering. Jonathan.[36] David

3

The victor David. Michal. The foreskins.[37]

---

31. In 1 Sam. 24, David encounters Saul in a cave, declines to kill him but feels guilty for even cutting off a corner of his robe. Saul acknowledges that David is more righteous than him and that he will be king, but never explicitly pardons him.
32. David seeks refuge from Saul with the Philistines (the Israelites' enemies) on two occasions (1 Sam. 21 and again in 1 Sam. 27 and 28).
33. Jonathan goes into battle on numerous occasions: 1 Sam. 13 (vs. Philistines); 1 Sam. 14 (vs. Philistines heroically); 1 Sam. 31 (where Saul and Jonathan die).
34. David is anointed king by Samuel in 1 Sam. 16 but is only made king over Judah in 2 Sam. 2.4 and over Israel in 2 Sam. 5.3.
35. BBA 10364/13v. Dates (indirectly) to June 1920, and appears in NB 8 (*Notizbücher* Bd. 2, 434–5) in both facsimile and transcription.
36. Brecht in fact uses 'ditto' marks – " – in place of Jonathan's name in the MS, directly under where 'Jonathan' is written on the first line. We follow the *BFA* in including the full name here.
37. The bride price Saul asks for his daughter Michal and receives from David consists of Philistine foreskins (1 Sam. 18.25, 27). Brecht inserted the name of Michal above the line at some point after it was written.

4
Saul and David.[38]

5
David flees. The 10000[39]

6
Saul and David, rest[40]

7
David

8
Saul to Endor[41]

9
Saul dying and David

---

38. Perhaps more fully developed as B9, below; for discussion, see pp. 112–13 below.

39. David regularly flees for his life from Saul (1 Sam. 18–21); Brecht references David's flight and Saul's mention of David's killing of 'ten thousands' (1 Sam. 18.7-8) in B9 below.

40. Brecht's term *Schonung* contains a variety of meanings, including the notion of care and protection; in adjective form, *schonungslos* means 'pitiless' or 'unsparing', as well as sometimes 'blunt'. In this case, a term has been selected that includes the dramaturgical sense of refuge and stillness after battle, because of its position in the scene list.

41. In 1 Sam. 28, Saul goes to Endor to ask a medium to summon up the ghost of Samuel (the prophet who initially anointed Saul as King and then anointed David in his place) to seek his guidance as the kingdom slips away from him. For this episode in other adaptations of the Saul material, see pp. 130, 134, 153, 155, and 162 below.

The David *Fragments: B1–B11*

B1

Wooden Structure with Pallid Sky[42]

***David** sits in white robes. A fat man.*[43]

David

I love all my children. But above all I love my child Absalom.[44] He always reminds me of his mother. He has her hair, and he's vain about it.[45]

The Man

Every man in Israel is vain about Absalom's hair.[46]

David

Because I love him, that's why I forgave him for killing his brother.[47]

The Man

He only did that because he loved his sister Tamar, whom his brother defiled.

---

42. This manuscript appears in BBA 459/75–76, part of the archival '*Lose Blaetter – 1*' collection of loose-leaf related papers, preceded by A7 (BBA 459/73–74) and followed by B10 (BBA 459/77–91). It dates to Summer 1920 and is available as part of the Electronic Edition of the Brecht *Notizbücher*.

43. It is unclear in the text whether this refers to David's interlocutor or to David himself.

44. There are various references to David's yearning or affection for Absalom (2 Sam. 13.39; 14.33; 2 Sam. 18.33; 19.4), and David's grief following Absalom's failed coup and death is seen by his general Joab as evidence of David's unwarranted and unreciprocated 'love' for his son.

45. Brecht crossed out *Ihr Haar hat er* before settling on *Er hat ihr Haar*. See BBA 459/75.

46. There is no explicit reference to Absalom's vanity in the books of Samuel, but the narrator's note of Absalom's great beauty and its public acknowledgement in 2 Sam. 14.25, as well as the fact that he weighed his hair after it was cut in the following verse, finds a resonance in Brecht's characterisation of Absalom here.

47. For discussion of Absalom's killing of Amnon for raping Tamar, seemingly referenced here, see p. 80 below.

David

He loved her too. But you came on business?

The Man

You want many men to settle themselves on the plains and make the fields fertile. But the soldiers you sent me for that, they don't love the plough.[48] They want to go back to the army.

David

Tell them: they should go out to the fields, and whoever has the best field after a year shall go back to the army.[49]

The Man

Then you'll lose the best farmers within a year, my lord.

David

You have the brain of a crane. They have the same brain, my friend: their fields will give them pleasure, and I have to get them whipped when they get back to the army.[50]

The Man

That's what I think too. But I have in mind the story[51] of a man, where I'm at a loss about what to do. He had squeezed a field out of someone else with false papers and now, after seven years, it came to light. He had made much of the field, but now he has to give it back again. I don't want to lose him.

---

48. The text of BBA 459/75 is not clear at this point. Brecht crossed out *wollen* and wrote a word that looks like *lieben*, but Suhrkamp went with *heben*, in reference to 'lifting' the plow. 'Love' was selected here because it seems more likely as a correction for the crossed-out *wollen*.

49. *BFA* has the line *sollen wieder zum Heere dürfen*, but BBA 459/75 does not have the added 'e' on *Heere*. The added 'e' can be a dative masculine ending in more antiquated German.

50. In BBA 459/75, the line is *Ihre Äcker werden ihnen selber Freude machen und sie ich muß sie peitschen lassen, wenn sie wieder zum Heer sollen.* Suhrkamp is missing the underlined 'sie' that appears in the manuscript.

51. It is unclear whether the manuscript reads *Gesichte* (face) or *Geschichte* (story/history). We follow *BFA* in reading *Geschichte*.

David

The theft of a field can't be allowed.[52] Tell him, he should decide whether he wants to keep the field and get beaten by the man he stole it from, or neither of the two.[53] If he wants the beating, he should have it, but the field too,[54] because he loves it and I need good fields. The other guy, I'll give him a new field.

The Man

But what if he doesn't want the beating?

David

Then he should get it even more so, because then he stole for love of stealing, not for the field. Do you have anything else interesting?

The Man

I brought a Syrian sheep with me, my Lord.

David

That I've got to see. But now, look at the sky and the rooftops over there! I love these moods, that only consist of the pale air.[55] Don't you?

The Man

Yes, I love them too.

---

52. 1 Kings 21 recounts the story of Ahab, a king of Israel long after David, whose theft of a vineyard and prophetic indictment for it bears a certain resemblance to the story of David's 'stealing' of Uriah's wife Bathsheba and his own prophetic indictment by means of a story of a stolen 'lamb' – a story which prompts David's righteous indignation before he realises his own guilt (2 Sam. 11–12).

53. Brecht wavers in the manuscript between *behalten* and *bekommen wolle* in reference to the field. The translation seeks to capture both senses here, of retaining and receiving.

54. *BFA* prints the word 'Akker' in this line, following the rule of German orthography that an end-of-line hyphenation changes 'c' to 'k' – it is not a misspelling of *Acker*. Review of the manuscript (*BFA* 459/76) confirms that Brecht wrote *Acker*, so this apparent spelling variation arises only from the textual layout of *BFA*.

55. *Ich liebe diese Stimmungen, die nur aus bleicher Luft bestehen.* 'Stimmung' can refer to ambience, mood or temper, and is etymologically related to *Stimme*, the word for 'voice'. 'Mood' was selected for its multiple resonances here, since the word can refer to atmosphere, music or the self.

David (*stands up*)

Anyway, drag me to your sheep. It's unforgivable.

Exit with arm on his shoulder.

Soldiers with **Absalom** within:

B2

Bargan[56]

Sometimes I feel the longing to do something bad. But then I can't find anything. I say to you, there's so little! It seldom works. Without chance, never.

——[57]

Lots of people get cramped up longing for white lilies, people without bread or schnapps. Some almost die yearning for a rope that strangles them all by itself, as if it could haul them up to heaven.[58] Some want a wide bed and have a woman who loves like a saw — before they annoyed me and I wouldn't do what they wanted. Now I annoy them and I fulfill their wishes.

---

56. Bargan is a figure appearing in Brecht's prose of the same period, and he features in a series of short stories in which the irrationality, laziness and charisma of a masculine leader is held up as evidence of the arbitrariness of God. For discussion of the homoeroticism of one of them, 'Bargan gives up', in relation to the *David* fragments, see below, pp. 110–11. In BBA 11087/16v, NB 3 (Bd. 1 170–171), Brecht writes: '*Bargan für David / Koloman für Absalom / Hete für Bathseba / Ur für Uria*' (see 'Previously Uncollected David Fragments' below, p. 68) which seems to warrant the otherwise surprising inclusion of B2 in the *BFA*'s *David* fragments.

57. Brecht does not supply a name here, but it seems clear that the dash indicates another character's speech.

58. *Einige sterben fast vor Sehnsucht nach einem Strick, der sie von selbst erwürgt, als ob er sie in die Himmel zöge*. In performance, this was rendered: 'Some nearly die just yearning for a bit of rope to strangle themselves with, as if it could haul them up to heaven'. Though easier to perform, this missed the emphasis in the German that the rope is doing the action on its own.

B3

David

What's going on with this immoderate Absalom? That one has to kill him like a rabid dog?[59] Why better than any measure: why does Absalom want to die? My son Absalom had such soft hands that doves would not fly away.[60] Why does he want to strangle necks, so that his neck must be strangled?[61] Why does Absalom want to go into the dark ground? Why is he dying in the midday hour, when it's so hot and no one can get him water? Before a woman can get a single breath, he will smile about it!

Absalom

I want to throw away what my hand can grasp. It's too small. I don't want what I can have: because it's too little. I want there to be more than there is. I want to throw my hand away! I want to punish Heaven: I throw my beaten body before it! To the radiant heaven, the shameless![62]

B4

5

—We come from Koloman![63]
—Did you see Koloman?
—Yes. He had sad eyes in a brave face!
—How's that?
—His face knew that he could have had it all, if he stretched out his hand. Only the eyes knew that 'all' was too little.

---

59. For discussion of B3 and Brecht's other 'Absalom' fragments and writings and their relationship to the biblical tradition of Absalom's failed coup and violent death (2 Sam. 15–18), see pp. 80–7 below.

60. The association between Absalom and hands is a persistent image throughout the *David* texts, the prominence of which was highlighted especially in the exploratory, physical improvisation work by the ensemble following their initial reading of the texts.

61. The biblical Absalom famously dies after being unseated from his mount when his head is caught in the branches of a tree. See further, pp. 80–7 below.

62. Cf. B5, the poem 'Of Absalom', and the treatment of hands as an image. The stage direction 'They look at their hands' also occurs in B10, in relation to the Beggars and David.

63. Koloman seems to be a name invented by Brecht, as it does not appear in the biblical tradition. Its association with the *David* texts is with Absalom, as noted above in B2 (n. 56).

B5

OF ABSALOM[64]

Stretched out
He lies now. Nothing held him
Lying there, in his whole length.
No more orders
Does he give. Never rises up
On call. Stretched out
He lies slain, who towered
And fulfilled is the revolt
From oppression he towered[65]
Mute and scornful toward the stars.
Never cursing, never helping: he
Folds the hands! They lay in the lap.
He never grasps, he never resists
Instead, he lays down the hands.
Pointless this bygone pressing[66]
He left with a shrug
The dying / in the wood a
Beautiful corpse, stretched out —

B6

Koloman *last word of the fourth act:* I have in my mouth a bitter taste.

---

64. The first line of this text, which is lineated as a poem, is *von Absalom* in the German; this could mean 'by', 'of' or 'about' Absalom. As the death of Absalom (2 Sam. 18.5-15) appears to be the subject of the poem, 'of' was chosen. For discussion of this poem and Brecht's other 'Absalom' fragments and writings and their relationship to the biblical tradition of Absalom's failed coup and violent death (2 Sam. 15–18), see pp. 80–7 below.

65. *Aus der Bedrängnis erhob er sich. Bedrängnis*, the word used by Brecht translated here as 'oppression', has a sense both of being 'bound' and under pressure, as well as a sense of distress.

66. *Sinnlos bedrängt abseits gegangen*: a challenging line, somewhat unclear in the German. Literally, a version might be 'senselessly oppressed gone apart'; *abseits gegangen* is also the term used for 'off-side' in football.

B7

—⁶⁷

But right at the end
He still found the word
See, he still saw, because it was dark already
The path in the last light
And that God already forgot, turning away his face
Listen: he screamed and the voice resounded.
All the heavens cheered, as he crossed over
As he l a i d the weapons from his lame hand⁶⁸
And surrendered and went away
As one liberated!

Chorus
Someone said something, before he went
What did he say?
He said:

One of us, who had fallen
said

B8

David

I must have your body, because the drunkard goes away, the breeze, the red hair!⁶⁹ Besides I need more brandy! *Grabs during the following the iron cup and drinks.* They've left something inside. They're not so bad.

---

67. The dash is again interpreted here as denoting dialogue, a speaker not yet identified by Brecht in his assembly of the draft materials.

68. We follow Brecht's and the *BFA*'s unusual spacing of the verb *legt*, indicating emphasis.

69. *Ich muß deinen Leib haben, weil der Säufer weggeht, der Wehende, das rote Haar!* The line is challenging in German; *der Wehende* can also mean 'wave', but 'breeze' was selected here for the strong links to 'wind' in all its forms throughout the *David* texts. If the reference to 'hair' here is related to B1's references to the hair of Absalom and his mother Maacah, the daughter of Talmai, King of Geshur (2 Sam. 3.3), then Brecht's David may here be expressing his carnal desire for her, though she is not referenced explicitly anywhere in the *David* fragments.

David

Come up here, my son Absalom, here you can see the sky of midday and how it turns green.

B9

SAUL AND DAVID[70]

Saul and David enter. Saul has his arm on David's shoulder,[71] and David has a lyre in his hands.

Saul

Come in with me, my child![72] The rabble scream in the alleys, they're drunk again like always. The animal is always drunk. It smells the blood of the slain and cries, when it sees you, and stares at your hands, because you're the victor, and you can see its rotten teeth. But I'm glad that you haven't become arrogant, because many believe that a man becomes more, when he does something. That's a heresy, don't you agree? Why should a beast be more than a tree? Don't you agree, my child? A beast is not more than a tree, sit down, there, so I can see your face, it's gotten leaner, was it so much trouble to win? You see, in your face there's almost nothing there, it's like a green field in spring, with lots of wind. That's why you also have no heart, no heart yet, my child.[73]

---

70. Covering BBA 10459/14r–21r, this fragment is dated 28.7.20 and appears to have been completed in a single sitting. For discussion of the probable circumstances, see pp. 147–9 below. Pagination of the archival document was confused historically and in some extant references, because the final page was listed in the archive as 459/27 (the German 1 looks like a 7 without a crossbar, but 21 is indeed the correctly numbered final page). The manuscript, published as an Electronic Edition *Anhang* to the Bertolt Brecht *Notizbücher* was used in rehearsal in the manner described in Chapter 5 (see p. 193), with the actors performing edits and amendments during the course of the piece, according to Brecht's drafting process.

71. For the potentially homoerotic qualities of this scene, see pp. 113–15 below.

72. The biblical Saul refers to David as *Běnî* 'my son' in 1 Sam. 24.16 (Heb. v. 17) and 1 Sam. 26 (vv. 17, 21, 25), but nowhere uses the Hebrew word for 'child', which is nearer to '*Kind*', used by Brecht's Saul repeatedly here in his first speech and elsewhere in B9.

73. While Saul alleges here and below that David has no heart, 1 Samuel notes that after Saul's anointing, God gave him a different heart (10.9) and that after his disobedience, God anointed David because he was a man after 'God's own heart' (13.14).

David *is silent and adjusts the lyre.*

Saul

And about the victory: I don't care. They say I killed a thousand. You have ten thousand, they say, a thousand are nothing anymore, times move on.[74] But I think: it's better to kill a thousand and have peace, than if you have to kill ten thousand to win. That'll give you a lean face and bad sleep, too. They all have nails and hides and a heart and guts and a mother, and one doesn't kill them like flies. Naturally you have no heart, my child, but I forgive you for it.

Looks at him.

David

Should I sing a song?[75]

Saul

Yes. Sing! I listen to you, because I know you then. When someone sings, one sees his teeth, and beneath that, whether he has something in his stomach. But I want to know why y o u sing.[76] Tell me!

David

Your face changes and your hands get calmer.

Saul

What business of yours are my hands? A lot occurs to me when I hear singing. I never listen to the words. Then I see my enemies clearly, and I know how I punish them. That makes me calm.[77] It's as if the strength

---

74. Saul's speech here seems to reflect the reference in 1 Sam. 18.7-8 to David's greater military prowess – the celebration of which greatly angers the biblical Saul.

75. While the biblical David is associated with singing thanks to the Psalms and his lament for Saul and Jonathan in 2 Sam. 1, no singing is mentioned when David plays music for Saul (1 Sam. 16.16, 23; 18.10). For discussion of Brecht's David as singer and the song which he sings here, see pp. 121–2 below.

76. Again, the idiosyncratic spacing of 'you' follows the *BFA* practice of indicating emphasis in this way.

77. *Dabei beruhige ich mich.* The fluid 'oral' translation, 'That makes me calm', doesn't quite capture the German sense of *Dabei*, which could mean 'thereby' or 'therefore' in the sense of logical progression.

gathers into me, like water in a well. But the song doesn't matter at all to me, my child.

David *sings sitting, forward on the table, where the lyre sits bent; he sings to* ***Saul*** *in his face, and* ***Saul*** *leans back:*

David

Strong is the bull, who can't see the sky!
He strolls in the sun and stomps down the grass!
    Ha! Laugh in Judah and clap,
    For the bull is strong.
Strong is the bull, but the grass is stronger!
He stomps it down, but it sees the sky,
    And picks itself up again.
    Ha! Laugh in Judah and clap,
    For the stronger grass.

David *tunes the lyre.*

Saul (*clapping*)
That's a good song. Does it go on?

David (*singing*)
He who looks at clouds, is like the stone
Stuck there, not going forth, and not drinking![78]
    Ha! Laugh in Judah and clap,
    For the stone is stuck.
Stuck is the stone, but he who is blind
Cannot see the clouds. Isn't it good,
    To have a big mouth?[79]

---

78. *Der die Wolken ansiehet, ist wie der Stein / Der festsitzt. Aber der Stein muß nicht / Fort und geht nicht zur Tränke.* The compression of the line in English follows the melodic requirements of the music created to accompany Brecht's lyrics for the *David Fragments* performance (composed by Leonard Buckley). The sense of the stone being free because it is not forced to proceed (*muß nicht / Fort*) relates to Brecht's interest in various types of inaction, in relation to David. For more on this, see pp. 113–15 below.

79. *Maul* is normally used for the jaws of animals. While *Duden* identifies the most common usage of the phrase 'ein voll Maul haben' as relating to having enough to eat or drink, there is an idiomatic usage (regionally related to the Pfalz, not far from Augsburg) that is closer to *Angeber* or *Großmaul*, akin to the idiom 'he has a

Ha! Laugh in Judah and clap,
Because you're not blind!

David *tunes the lyre.*

Saul

Hold on, I don't understand the song. It makes no sense, my child.[80]

David

And the water swells up by the full moon[81]
And is water no more. But the lion
Dies of hunger, when he just lies there.
Strong are those, who just do what they must
And stronger those, who make nothing of it[82]
For the hailstones don't hit them, and those
That do hit them, they don't destroy them.
   Ha! Ha! Laugh in Judah, laugh and clap,
   Clap in Judah, that you can still laugh!

Saul (*clapping*)

That is a good song. But in the middle it's weak. It's the same with your face, it's sometimes good, but it has red hair,[83] when the sun shines on it. But I love you anyway,[84] not because you killed ten thousand for me, and not because your face is sometimes good. But now I'm much calmer,

---

big mouth' in English; as David is later described (in B10) as having *ein gewaltiges Maul*, this meaning was chosen. See *Deutsches Wörterbuch von Jacob und Wilhelm Grimm*, s.v. 'Maul', online at http://tiny.cc/4mnviz.

80. The theme of the (in)comprehension of David is a recurring one in B9 and B10; see pp. 107–8, 122.

81. *BFA* transcribed this as *Und das Wasser schwillt bei Vollmond und / es wird nicht mehr Wasser.* However, on consultation with BBA 10459/17r, 'im Mund' appears to have been a first draft; 'bei Voll' is written in afterwards, with the 'im' crossed out. Again, the translation follows the song as performed.

82. *Und stärker sind, denen es nichts ausmacht.* Though the line seems to translate the German fairly directly, a nearer idiomatic meaning would be *And stronger are those who don't care.* The line is translated here as performed/sung.

83. See B8 above.

84. For Saul's love for David here and elsewhere in B9 and its relationship to the biblical Saul's profession of love for him (1 Sam. 16.21) and other theatrical interpretations of Saul's feelings for David, see pp. 108–13 and 142–62 below.

I'm nearly full. And it seems to me that you are a bit emptier than before, you've shouted too much; when I speak, I get stronger. That's why I talk, and you think that I'm just chatting, but I'm consuming you. Did you never wonder why I chat so much to you, even though you're a kid?[85]

David

I think: it lightens your burden.

Saul

Why do you want to lighten my burden? What has nothing inside it is already light![86]

David

When one lies in water that flows, one is light too.

Saul

I didn't know that. One must swim under one's own strength.

David

Maybe one doesn't have to swim.

Saul

You don't often contradict me, although I love it. But what you're saying is nonsense. You have no capacity for logic. You make your way from hundreds to thousands. That you can see in your face.

David

I can't think as much as you.[87] It makes me miserable.

---

85. The verb repeatedly translated here as 'chat' is *schwatzen*, which carries a stronger sense of 'gossip' than is perhaps apparent here.
86. *Warum willst du mich erleichtern? Leicht ist, was keinen Inhalt hat!* Brecht does not include the word 'burden' a second time, but the translation here follows what emerged through performance, where the repetition helped to escalate the drama between David and Saul.
87. Brecht originally wrote *Ich denke* before crossing out *denke* and continuing the line with *kann nicht soviel denken*; this internal edit of David's thought process was retained in the performance script.

Saul

Does it now? Does it make you miserable? I think that myself. But I recover myself and it cools me down, when I see your face. It's only a plain full of wind.[88]

David

Do you never get weak, when you say 'why' and it's worse than catching flies?[89]

Saul

No. Only if nothing occurs to me. I pay it no mind, child. When I think about it, then it comes first. But it's a cold air around me, which I have to warm up. That's why I'm lonely, because nothing touches me, and nothing changes me.[90] I tell you, often I'm freezing at night, and I beat the women and sleep anyway on the cold stones, so I feel the bones that I have, and then it's a little better. Sometimes it doesn't work, though, it lasts many weeks and nothing says anything and I can't let the walls speak and the grass never grows and everything is naked and it disgusts me. Now that I say this, it's easier for me, but you don't understand it and I see in the field with the wind,[91] I said it and I'm never alone.

Looks at **David***. Is silent, waiting.*

But sometimes it's like if God has forgotten me alone, like it's a tree that stands in black, stony depths and is so far grown from its roots, it scares itself. Can't you feel that?

---

88. *Es ist nur eine Fläche voll Wind. Fläche* is interesting and poetic here, as it can mean 'face' in the sense of 'surface', but it is also the technical term for plains or flat areas of land.

89. *Wirst du nie schwach, wenn du warum sagst und es ist schlimmer als Fliegen fangen?* A fairly literal translation, the line nonetheless poses challenges; the quotes around 'why' were added to assist performers in decoding meaning. The repeated image of flies (and catching them) marks all of B9 and elements of B10.

90. *Darum bin ich einsam, weil um mich nichts vorgeht, und nichts ändert mich.* '*um mich nichts vorgeht*' is closer to the locution 'around me nothing happens' – this translation follows the flow of the performer, after numerous edits and alternatives attempted in rehearsal.

91. Brecht crossed out *dein Gesicht* – 'your face' – and replaced it with *das Feld mit dem Wind.*

David

I don't know what you mean. Can't you lie in the sun or swim or kill enemies? Perhaps that helps?

Saul

You understand nothing. You're as dumb as your bull and as gutless as your grave. You slaughter ten thousand men with nails and hides like you and play on the lyre and it's enough for you, as if you were lying in the sun! You loaf around here and eat my figs and catch flies and drink my milk and have your nails washed on your feet and trim them and 70 years pass, they always grow back. And now you make a face like you don't understand me, or as if it irritates you that you're this way, but I know you, you're as evil as a poison fruit that hangs in the mouth and says nothing and thinks nothing. I have no voice, and for what does he have a mouth?[92]

David stands up.

Saul

Now you stand up too? Did you kill ten thousand to stay sitting, when you're offended? But now I've hit you, the stone flies forward, he can't hold it back anymore. Sit down again, I feel for you. I want to let you sing again, that will be fun for you, and then I'll clap, you can tell the story to the chambermaids.[93] Tell them too that I love you and can't be without you, tell them, how I am and that I can't hold my tongue before you, that I gossip, that I'm miserable.

Stands up, stretches out strongly.

---

92. This line is transcribed in the *BFA* as '*Ich habe keine Stimme und wozu hat er sein Maul!*' The 'wozu' implies a question, but the *BFA* editors ended the sentence with an exclamation mark; as it is at the border of the page, we think this is uncertain, so we have translated this as a question based on syntax. Complicating the meaning of the line further, the difference between *keine/sein/kein* is also unclear in the handwriting in this passage in BBA 10459/19v. This translation follows the choices made in the *BFA* – *keine* followed by *sein* – but alternatives are possible and would affect meaning.

93. Brecht crossed out *Knechten*, which means 'laborer' or 'bumpkin' and a word that implies a masculine listener, before writing *Mägden*.

Now everything is different between us, my dear. I always wanted to keep it secret,[94] but now I've talked too much.[95] I feel sorry for you.

Silence. **David** *makes a move to exit.*

Where do you want to go? Are you going right into the courtyard with the news?

David (*coolly*)

I don't know what you want. I don't want to upset you.

Saul

I don't understand how you can be so calm. Do you not realise that here a man has almost bared his soul to you?[96]

Silence.

But now I pity you.

Takes a deep breath.

It's better for me, my child. You haven't yet seen a man who dared so much as I. I am a man and I said this. I said it *to you*, who has no heart, not yet a heart. I humiliated myself before you, not everyone can do that. The proud ones can't do it, that I know, and those with nothing in them, they can't either, that's for sure. Who has nothing, can be nothing, I see that now. I'm grateful to you, that you were there, and I love you still a bit, I like to see your face and I love it when you sing, come and sing again to me soon, now that I'm in better mind, what do you say to that, that I love you?

Silence.

---

94. For the relationship of Saul's 'secret' in B9 to that found in Gide's play *Saül* see pp. 151–62 below.

95. *Ich habe es immer verschweigen wollen, aber jetzt habe ich dich um deinen Kopf geredet.* The translation is somewhat free with the idiomatic possibilities of the second half of this line.

96. *Merkst du nicht, daß sich hier ein Mensch beinahe entleibt hat?* The word *entleibt* here could imply nakedness, but an alternate reading could refer to suicide (*sich entleiben*).

But now it never touches me again, that you still say nothing and that I just said to you that I love you, I, King Saul. I'm grateful to you, that you were *there*, when I uncovered myself,

He takes him by the shoulder, leads him away

although you said nothing and had no feelings, it revived me.[97] It didn't put me out, and the hailstones did not hit me.

David (*under the curtain*)
I am glad that my song revived you.

Off.

Saul (*stands struck*)
What do you say? Your song? What revived me? Is it only your song? You're glad?

He runs across the stage and gets the spear.

But it continues, your song, it's not done yet, your song. Strong are those who do there, you say, what they

throws the spear

M U S T.

Cries off

You say!

Curtain.

---

97. *wiewohl du nichts sagtest und kein Gefühl hattest, erquickte es mich.* The verb choice of *erquicken* is notable in the biblical context, as the word appears in the Luther Bible (1912), Mt. 11.28: '*Kommet her zu mir alle, die ihr mühselig und beladen seid; ich will euch erquicken*'. In the NKJV, this is rendered: 'Come to me, all you who labor and are heavy laden, and I will give you rest'. David uses the same verb in his reply.

B10

White, sunny wall, on which squat the **Beggars**. Enter **Two Men** from right.[98]

First

I don't believe in them. They are... figments! Saul also doesn't believe in them. Sometimes they make noise and then they get their throat cut. Me, I don't give a damn about the Philistines!

Second

Saul doesn't either. But I'm telling you, that does him no good. Every year they've been there. They've burned cities to the ground and killed men. They disappeared again and then they came back, every spring stronger and meaner.[99] OK then, they are figments, Saul doesn't give a damn, we're getting eroded by figments.[100]

First

That you have from the arms traders, my friend! They're always drunk because they earn too much. Who dies from flies? I won't hear a word against Saul. THAT is a king![101] Saul and his son Jonathan, there are the eagles![102] I saw their eyes. They are not mortal, my friend! God has something in store for Judah! Let the flies fly.

*Behind, strolling across the square, showing his back, lazy **David** sits on the wall.*

---

98. Dating from the summer of 1920, this is the most extensive (if not the most 'complete') of the *David* fragments. It aligns with BBA 10459/77–86, 93.

99. According to 2 Sam. 11.1, spring is when kings go out to war.

100. The manuscript is unclear on the verb. *BFA* transcribes the line *wir werden von Hirngespinsten zerfressen werden*, but BBA 10459/77r is transcribed with *gefressen* instead. The difference in meaning is between 'eroded' and 'guzzled' (*fressen* is the form of eating done by animals and is generally not applied to humans). As the conflict described seems to be more akin to an irritation rather than utter destruction, 'eroded' seemed preferable here.

101. In the *BFA*, added spaces were used here to indicate emphasis, but in the manuscript the emphasised word *Das* is simply underlined.

102. In David's lament for Saul and Jonathan in 2 Sam. 1.23, he praises them as being 'swifter than eagles.' For the reference to 'David Amid the Eagles' in Brecht's diary, see p. 5 above and p. 138 below.

Second

I don't doubt Saul. — Do you know the young lad, sitting on the wall?

Thinks.

Even though some people say he's insane, I don't doubt him!

First

Who said that, that Saul is insane?[103]

Grabs his front.

Confess, out with it! Who told you Saul is insane?

Second (*shaking him off, cold*)

I don't know. Some. When you were young and still in diapers, I saw Saul, as he was and how the others were around him, then. They slept in robes made of skin, and no one went to the waste-pits without weapons,[104] and men had faces and the voices that came out of them were different than today, and they spent their lives just keeping the flies off. And they said what they thought, even when they believed, that God could be [ ].[105] Grow up first, young man, before you open your mouth. We only see your milk-teeth.

He goes.

---

103. In 1 Samuel (esp. ch. 16) an 'evil/troubling spirit' plagues Saul and prompts the recruitment of David to soothe his spirit with music (so, B9).

104. In 1 Sam. 24.3, Saul retreats into a cave (perhaps leaving his weapons behind him) to relieve himself, leaving him vulnerable to being killed by David, who is hiding deeper in the cave.

105. See BBA 10459/77v. Brecht inserted the line *Und sie sagten was sie dachten, auch wenn sie glaubten, daß Gott wäre* between the two other lines. Something is scribbled in the manuscript but it remains unclear, perhaps crossed out, so the Herta Ramthun 1974 transcription (a key source for both *BFA* and the *Notizbücher* editions) uses […] in its place. The gap left in the *BFA* was retained in performance as a silence, as though it was impossible to speak of what God could be, or as though there was a risk of blasphemy or some punishment if the actor spoke it aloud, again revealing the performative possibilities hidden within manuscripts.

First

(*looking after him, kicking with his leg, calls thinly*)

Now he runs! Look how the old one runs, look! That's good fun! The Philistines are behind you!

To the **Beggars***:*

He makes leatherware for the cavalry! I was being clever:[106] you heard that from the arms traders, I said, but he noticed right away and swallowed heavily and flew off the handle and let the oldest bag of wisecracks go![107] And all the while his daughter has a kid and his son is completely depraved!

First Beggar

He is an old man, and you are a young man, and you just grabbed him by the chest.

Second Beggar

Someone should show him. He has a chance.[108] Show it to him![109]

Third Beggar (*standing up*)

Say it one more time, that the old guy wasn't right about the waste-pits and that everyone could say what they wanted, and it was a much better time, say the opposite, kid!

---

106. *Ich habe mich ganz zweideutig ausgedrückt.* The word *zweideutig* has no ideal English equivalent and captures, in a single word, the notion of an expression having more than one meaning: 'ambiguous' or 'ambivalent' are both possibilities. The choice of 'clever' here reflects a more basic selection, to facilitate audience understanding in performance.

107. *ließ die ältesten Spruchbeuteleien los!* A coinage clearly intended as an insult, the term seems related to the nineteenth-century insult *Windbeuteleien* ('windbag'), with *Spruch* ('sayings' or 'axioms') substituted for *Wind*.

108. *Er hat eine Gelegenheit.* The translation here uses the more literal translation, but to make sense of this with the actor in performance when the referent 'he' was unclear, the line 'this is the moment!' was substituted.

109. *Zeigt's ihm!* Though literally 'show it to him' as translated here, this expression has the sense of 'Get him!' in the German.

*Walking up to him, he grabs him. The other two **Beggars** stand up slowly and walk toward them.*

The Man

It was just a bit of fun. Of course it was better in the old days. It's a misunderstanding. There's David, the son of Jesse, whom you know, he knows me. Good day, David!

***David** looks at the sky.*

The First Beggar

(*looks toward **David**, slaps **The Man** on the shoulder*)

What is this one?

David

A clean man. He washes himself every day, Jonas!

The First Beggar

Here?

Hits him on the cheek.

Second Beggar

Let him run, otherwise he howls. What do you think, David?[110]

David

He won't howl, I know him. He won't bat an eyelid.

The First Beggar

(*hits the back of his neck*)

Good boy!

*Two men, **Jonathan** and an **Officer**, arrive. Behind them, **Soldiers**.*

---

110. David's views are regularly solicited in B10; for further discussion see pp. 115–20 below.

The Officer

What are you doing there?

The First Man (*joyful*)

Is that you, Isaac? I'm glad to see you. Come here and show them!

The Officer

Why are you beating this man? Shut up, you pack of flies! What are you doing hitting someone here? You are a bag of pus![111] Shut your mouth! You can scream in the stocks. Get him!

*The **Soldiers** seize the **First Beggar**.*

Jonathan (*putting his hand on his shoulder*)

Wait a little! (*to **David***) You were watching! What happened?[112]

David looks at the sky.

Officer

What did you see? You can't open your mouth?

David (*looking at him impudently*)[113]

On the contrary! (*to **Jonathan***) A dove flew over there.[114] Have you ever studied a flying dove?

---

111. *Du bist eine Eiterbeule!* 'Bag of pus' is a literal translation of this insult; an alternative would be 'You're an abscess!' It does not read idiomatically in either German or English.

112. For the Brechtian Jonathan's tendency to ask questions in this scene, see pp. 101–3 below.

113. Brecht's characterisation of David as impudent/impertinent persists through B10; for further discussion in relation to perceptions of the young Brecht, see, pp. 115–22 below.

114. This whole section refers to *Tauben*, which can be translated in English as either 'dove' or 'pigeon'. There is a case for both; 'pigeon' would be more typical of the street and rougher in character, perhaps in keeping with the nature of David in B10, but 'dove' has the stronger biblical resonance, and was selected for our production.

Officer

This is an impudent little cub, my Lord, I'm sorry![115]

Jonathan

How do doves fly?

David (*superior,*[116] *slowly*)

They enjoy it. One should let them fly. They can't do it well.

Jonathan

You mean, one should let doves fly?

David (*looks at him, a bit more affably*)

The main thing is: one should sit there by oneself. Otherwise one sees nothing.

Jonathan

What kind of man is this beggar?

People gather.

David

He is quarrelsome, lazy, greedy and philosophical. He left a woman and gossips. He loves me, that's it.[117]

Jonathan

Why don't you help him?

---

115. *Das ist ein unverschämter Flegel, Herr, entschuldige!* The word *Flegel* is somewhat archaic in usage, and could scan as 'lout' or 'cad' in British English; 'cub' is a more zoological rendering and was preferred by the actor.

116. *überlegen* is the word describing David, but because of a lack of context, either the adjective 'superior' or the adverb 'thoughtfully' could be applied. The translation choice reflects the actor's performance of the line.

117. *Mich liebt er; sonst nichts.* An alternative translation of the line could be: 'He loves nothing else than me'. Here, as in B9 (see below), the emphasis is on David as one who is the object of devotion/love.

David

Why? So his nails grow?[118]

Jonathan

It wasn't much of an art, to hit this young man?[119]

David

My friend Joshua had a house and a vineyard, when he started to bother himself with art. When he stopped with that, as he had to, then he was a dead man. Then he had nothing more than too much water.

Jonathan

How so?

David (*smirking*)[120]

He did nothing that wasn't art. Having a house and making children and all that, he almost never bothered himself. But then he noticed that peeing also wasn't an art. That's why he died. He couldn't stand the art.

*The **People** laugh.*

Jonathan

Let the beggar go! You can go! (*to the **Officer***) Tell my father, I'm not coming till tonight! (***Officer** off and **Jonathan** to the **Beggar***) What do you think about his story?[121]

---

118. Cf. B9 and Saul's comments to David about his nails growing or his nails being cut.

119. *Es war doch keine Kunst, den jungen Menschen zu schlagen?* This line, and the subsequent story, depend on the word *Kunst* heavily, and in rehearsal we oscillated between using 'art' and using 'trick' for this translation, since *Kunst* also carries a sense of the artificial. Neither word adds/makes a great deal of sense to/ in the dialogue, as the parable appears to set up David as a kind of nonsensical (but charismatic) storyteller.

120. Brecht crossed out *lächelt* to write *grinst*, exchanging a smile for a smirk: this is an indicative emendation relevant to the development of David's character.

121. For discussion of David's brief story here and reaction to it, see pp. 103, 106 below.

The First Beggar (*snidely*)

A greyhound! It's worthless! He would have let me sit there. First he sent me to him! Pig!¹²² (*Angrily.*) He wanted it! The young lad said: Saul is the eagle in Judah, and the older one: he is insane! Then the boy grabbed him, and this one said, we should help the old one! See there, look how he is!

The Third Beggar

Don't listen to him, my lord! That's David, the son of Jesse, a good lad, he suns himself here. He doesn't want anything that others want,¹²³ he's much too lazy, isn't that so, David?¹²⁴ We watch the doves here, we two, nothing to it! He just has opinions on everything, my lord! Just opinions!¹²⁵

A Group of People

Hoho! Up, all of you! The Philistines have invaded Gad!¹²⁶ Into your houses, all of you, the Philistines have overrun the cities! 400 lie slain in Gad! And there's one there, whose name is Goliath, as strong as twenty men! Get into your houses!

Jonathan (*calm*)

Calm down! The King Saul knows this and has put out the call. Go home to your houses, all of you, and keep the women indoors, so that it's silent, Saul wants to think. We are going to think about what should happen next. I am Jonathan!

---

122. *Ein Windhund! Sie taugt nichts! Er hätte mich sitzen lassen! Zuerst hat er mich hingeschickt auf den! Schwein!* This fragmentary speech is not very clear in German or English, and was performed by the actor in a kind of spluttering stutter, indicating indignation.

123. *Er will gar nichts, die Andern wollen.* A slight elision in the English translation was necessary in performance.

124. For discussion of the Brechtian David's indolence in this scene and its resonance with Brecht's reflections elsewhere, see pp. 113–15 below.

125. In contrast to B9, Brecht's David in B10 is full of opinions. See pp. 115–20 for discussion of David's resonance with the young Brecht on this point.

126. While Gad is the name of both a tribe and a region in Israel (see Josh. 13.8 and 13.24), it is at some distance from the Philistine littoral; it is also (with Ga) Brecht's cipher for Germany (in later work such as the *Me-Ti*) and is obviously similar to 'Gath', the Philistine city famously associated with Goliath.

The People[127]

Hail, Jonathan! Hail, Jonathan, who has killed 500![128]

Slowly departing. One hears the calls of 'hail' long after.

Jonathan

What did the old one say?

The Second Beggar

He said that the Philistines will come and all the old sayings, my lord. One knew everything that he was saying.

The Third Beggar

Judah was a warlike people, he said, now they're dealers! But he himself was a dealer, in leather goods![129]

Jonathan (*to David*)

Did you think he's right?

David

He was once right.

Jonathan

Does that fade?

David

When he was young, he was right.

---

127. Brecht shifts between *Volkshaufe* (a group or clump of people) to *Das Volk* and does not standardise the mode of identifying individual speakers in these groups for the remainder of the scene.

128. Given the earlier references in B9 to Saul's 'thousand' and David's 'ten thousand' (see above), this may well be intended as a case of damning with faint praise or even sarcasm.

129. *Juda war ein Kriegsvolk, sagte er, jetzt sind es Händler! Aber er war selbst ein Händler mit Lederzügen.* 'Dealers' could be translated here as 'traders' or 'salespeople' as well; it is notable that the linkage of an entire Jewish tribe to shop-keeping plays into certain anti-Semitic tropes in the Germany of this period.

Jonathan

Then why did you help him?

David

Because he needed it. He had the wrong opinion.

The First Beggar

That's his old nonsense![130] He gives old people advice! He sits there and makes up wise sayings for old people!

Jonathan

What do you think about the warlike people?

David

It used to be that people grew up stronger. But making war they didn't have time to make good children. Power with iron and leather was all very well. Soon now you'll have to sell them.

Jonathan

And you don't serve? Never worn the armour?

David

It's too heavy. It's iron.[131]

Jonathan

You don't think much of the Philistines?

David

One has to chase them off. What a waste of time![132]

---

130. *Das ist so sein Geschwätz!* While 'nonsense' was selected for playability, the sense of *Geschwätz* normally includes gossip or scurrilous rumour.

131. While there is no mention of weight, in 1 Sam. 17.39 the biblical David famously rejects the armour offered to him by Saul because it limits his mobility and he is unaccustomed to it.

132. Brecht uses a slightly unclear phrase, possibly an unfamiliar or regional idiom: *Es ist schade um die Zeit*. This could refer either to the time spent here talking (as we played it in performance, 'pity about the time') or about the times in general ('pity that we live in such times').

The Third Beggar

The kid before said the same thing to the old guy. David said: They're flies! To hell with them!

Jonathan

That sounds strong, you love that! What do you do all the time?

David (*impudent, yawning*)

Sound strong.

Jonathan

You always sit here? What are you, then?

The First Beggar

Lazy. Lazy's what he is. He is lazy. Otherwise nothing. That's his career.

Jonathan

Should one be lazy?

David

No.

The Third Beggar

He says something different every day. It's bad with him! Yesterday he said: I must be as lazy as a quail. Then I'll know from the white clouds whether it will rain or not.[133]

A Group of People

The Philistines have invaded! Saul has called all the men to the city walls! Come, everyone!

Jonathan *disappears into the crowd.*

The Second Beggar

What's the truth about the war, David?[134]

---

133. Cf. B11, where part of this sentence recurs.
134. For the Brechtian David's distinctly unenthusiastic attitude toward (the) war in relation to the young Brecht's own attitude and experience, see pp. 118–22 below.

David

Go anywhere where you can catch flies. Here you're probably going to be disturbed. They are running around like ants, but without sense, just to any purpose, and the fattest heroes will want to spit undisturbed, namely in your face, my friends.

The Second Beggar[135]

But King Saul orders us to go into battle.

David

No one in Judah can command us anything. We are free as the birds in the wind. No one in this patch of earth can call us anything, Gibeon,[136] we are like the clouds, to hell with them! And in the whole world no one can tell us what to do, that's freedom!

The Third Beggar

That's beautiful, how you say it! But King Saul will chase us down!

David

We are sand fleas, Gibeon. King Saul won't chase sand fleas.

The Third Beggar

Will you go with us into the mountains, until Saul has finished off the Philistines?

David

Here we won't get anything else.[137] The cripples will multiply like mould after the rain. And they'll cry, they had their legs in Gad.

---

135. The next four lines were inserted later. They appear on the loose page BBA 10459/93r and are appended to an 'x' mark in the MS. Notably, they include the first appearances of the name 'Gibeon', which seems to apply to both the second and third beggar in this exchange. In performance this confusion (and the paradoxical 'no one in this patch of earth can call us anything, Gibeon') was played for laughs.

136. Gibeon is the name of a person in 1 Chron. 8.29; elsewhere it refers to a city (famous for securing a treaty which preserved it and its inhabitants in the face of Israelite invasion; see Josh. 9).

137. *Hier werden wir nichts mehr in die Zähne kriegen.* This idiom often refers to eating things, but can also apply to catching/receiving things.

The Second Beggar

That's it then, we run, before someone presses an iron shield into our hands! (*looks at his hand.*) Mine is white and has a damn fine skin, it's not for dirty work, my child. Let's see yours!

They show each other their hands. From a distance cries and whistles of many men.

A Pack of People (*coming slowly onto the stage*)

Hoho, there's David, the son of Jesse, who threw Joseph in the ring. He has a big mouth.[138] He'll have something to say about the war!

One

Tell us, doesn't it rain now and then into your mouth, David? I mean: when you speak to the birds of the sky?

David

No. If it's raining the birds don't fly. But I've been meaning to talk with you for a long time, Ismael. You have to sell your corn before the rainy season, since you were just talking of the rain. Then it will spoil and get cheaper.

Ismael

He's always joking. But thank you, you do understand the corn.

Submerged in the crowd.

The Third Beggar

David, my friend, tell us something of the war with the Philistines. WHAT's your opinion?[139]

The Group of People

What do you think, David? What do you think?

---

138. *Er hat ein gewaltiges Maul.* Cf. 'voll Maul' references in B9 (nn. 79 and 92); *gewaltiges* carries the possible senses of both enormity and violence, which 'big' doesn't fully capture.

139. Emphasis reflects underlining in the MS and transcription of BBA 10459/85v; the *BFA* used extra spacing.

David

You will defeat the Philistines.

The Group of People

Bravo! That's what we'll do! He could be right! Go on, tell us more!

David

I see their corpses lying in the valleys of Gad and the birds that peck out their eyes.

The Group of People

Then there will be lots of corpses, do you mean that too?

David

Yes. Many of you, who will eat dinner later tonight, will lie in four days stiff in the good air.

A Woman

You all have to take care!

Laughter.

David

Your corn will rot in the fields, but you will die gloriously. And what are all the fields in the world against a hero's death! Your women will stay chaste, even when you are away for four years, since the wives of heroes are themselves heroines. You will run out of air, you'll hold your throat and the air goes out and you see blood, your own, and it runs away, and you will lean pale against trees and fade away, but your children will speak of you and of Saul, who defeated the Philistines.[140]

A Man

(*in a choking voice, gripping onto his own throat*)

That is a good speech, right there!

---

140. The biblical Saul (thanks sometimes to his son) enjoys numerous military successes against the Philistines, including the one following David's triumph over Goliath, which this scene seems to anticipate.

Second Man

He paints it so clearly that you sweat. But what he says about our children, that may be true.

Third Man

Really, the audacity![141] He's a green boy teaching old men. He spits in the mouths of grown men! He needs a spanking.

The First Beggar

He's laughing at all of you!

The Crowd

Green, that's what he is! Spank him! Why doesn't he go among the warriors! That's it with this wall-perching![142]

The First Beggar

He perches lazily here and gossips like an owl and in the evening he stands up lazily and heads to the river with the birds![143] This laziness has annoyed me, to the limit! Such a young lad!

One

Somebody should wake him up! A few kicks in the arse and he'll be glad to hold his tongue.

The Third Beggar (*worried, stands up*)

What are you thinking, David? You've blabbed again! We're going to the palace, it's time. Leave the people!

---

141. *Eigentlich ist es eine Unverschämtheit* translates more precisely as 'Actually, it's an impudence', but this translation reflects the more free version used in performance.

142. *Es ist aus mit dem Andiemauerhocken! BFA* transcribed this with hyphens: *An-die-Mauer-Hocken!*

143. *am Abend steht er faul auf und geht fort an den Fluß zum Vögeln!* A sexual double entendre is clear in the German's use of the noun *Vögeln* in this context, since the verb *vögeln* is equivalent to the verb 'to fuck' in English; the Hiberno-English use of 'birds' in our translation (an Irish slang term for 'women') carries the same double entendre with less vulgarity.

The One

Not a chance! Stick around! Now we want to see!

The Crowd

Stay there!

David (*calm, seated*)

I'm coming later, Gibeon! I'll head down to the river with them and we'll sort this thing out. You and you and you, you three should be enough to beat a young lad half to death. We four will be heading off soon, out there, where there are no soldiers, but you all would like me to tell one more little story, wouldn't you?

The Crowd

Give him a smack in the face! Aren't you ashamed of yourselves? Him tell another? Get close around him, so he can't head off, and then let him tell. So.

The One Man organises the people in front of David. One can't see him anymore.

David

In the mud there lay a tortoise. There was a war between a pine tree and a briar, when she was three hundred years old. So the briar bush spoke: should I flee, old tortoise? The tortoise said: No, stay there. Wrap around the pine and stay there. So the thorns wrapped around the pine, and the pine was pricked and began to shrink away. Two hundred years passed that way, my dears, and then the briar asked: should I uproot this pine tree, good tortoise? My roots are reaching against his. The tortoise said: no, leave them be. Then came the wind one night and the briar held against the pine and was not overturned. But after another hundred years the briar said: Should I reach my roots back to the stream, great wise tortoise? So the tortoise, who was six hundred years old, crawled to the stream to check it out and help the briar and not disappoint him, and she fell in the stream and drowned.

A Man

What happened then?

The Third Beggar

Don't you see that it's over? Idiot!

Second Man

It's a good fable, only hard! But the meaning is very clear!

Woman

David is nobody's fool! But what does the fable mean?

One (*laughing*)

There stands the hen and doesn't understand! Yes, fables, those are manly things! It's perfectly clear and the hen doesn't understand. Hahahaha!

One (*hitting **David** on the shoulder*)

You did well there. It's a deep fable![144]

A whistle.

David

Shut up a second!

An Older Man *enters from left. He whistles.*

David

Let me go! (*somewhat urgently.*) Arrange yourselves around me! I want to quickly take a leak in those bushes there!

Tries to leave.

One

Who's whistling there – it's Jesse! David, your father is here![145]

---

144. For discussion of the Brechtian David's 'fable' and response to it within the scene, see pp. 91 and 116 below.

145. The biblical account of Jesse does little to prepare the reader/audience for his appearance here in B10 or the characterisation of his relationship with the Brechtian David. For further discussion of B10's David and Jesse in relation to their biblical incarnations and the young Brecht's own relationship to his father, see pp. 87–96 below.

The People *draw back.*

David (*sitting again*)

I was just coming home, Father.

A few laughs.

Jesse

Will I see you soon, eh, you pig? Were you just coming home? You had a few things to take care of, eh? Arrange yourselves around me, eh? You bloody bag of lies.[146]

One (*laughing*)

Now he's holding his water for him. He must have run away from home! Give it to him, Jesse! He's teaching the old ones! He's mocking the greybeards! Give it to him, Jesse!

Jesse (*friendly, as from a distance*)

Sitting well, my son? Are you not sitting on a pebble, David? Isn't there a date pit, where you are sitting? Raise yourself up a little, listen up. Your father is a bit worried on your behalf!

David (*cheekily*)

I don't have any dates to eat, father. And I don't eat pebbles any more.

Jesse

So, you've eaten them all up? You even want to eat my roof and the stove too? Should I slaughter the lamb for you, that you let fall into the gorge? Eh? Should your old, sick father muck out the stables with his old hands, with your dirt under his nails,[147] my dear son? Should your father walk through the fields in the slush, until there's blood in his shoes? Eh?

David

No.

---

146. *O du verfluchter Lügenbeutel!* The term 'bloody' served here for an English-accented performer, but *verfluchter* is closer to 'damned' or 'cursed'.

147. *mit den Nägeln deinen Schmutz* would be translated literally as 'with the nails your dirt', so this slightly free translation seeks to make sense of the flow of the line more logically.

Jesse

What kind of answer is that, again?

*Throws a stone at **David**, that doesn't hit him.*

David

Take care with those stones, father! One day you might hit me!

Jesse

If only I had already! May God curse my good heart! Didn't you hear something spoken of, that something is not completely clean somewhere, my dear son? Has no one made you aware that there is a war going on in your homeland? Do you want to stay here? So tell me!

David

Yes.

Some (*laughing*)

They're a couple of odd ducks, these two! – They understand each other. – He has said exceptionally clever things about the war, Jesse, old honoured skin![148]

David

My father is no old honoured skin.

Stands up.

Jesse

You're standing up, youngster? You want to take a look at the clouds, see if it's not raining, my son? In rain you don't go to war, eh? Not in the rain, is that it? Express yourself, you exceptionally clever gobshite![149]

---

148. *ehrliche Haut* is an honorific nickname, generically used as a familiar term for an older person, that does not sound as unusual in the German as it does in English. No substitute was attempted in rehearsal, but the sense was still clear.

149. *ungemein kluger Schwätzer* suggests an unusually clever 'babbler' or 'gossip', but in the Hiberno-English context, 'gobshite' played very well for the audience and carried the sense.

David

My father has herded swine with no one here.[150]

Jesse

Don't suck up to them, young man! Don't start any funny business here, I'm not letting you out of my sight, don't even try it! You can't resist, your mother is waiting for you with your iron armour, boy.

He turns right around and goes to the rear. **David** *follows him lazily and reluctantly from some distance. He mumbles.*

David

I'm not putting on any armour. But I'll take my slingshot with me![151]

They disappear. **The Crowd** *laughs.*

B11

SAUL. ISMAEL.[152]

Ismael (*of David*)

He sits on a wall and looks at the sun. He's as lazy as a quail. He eats figs that people give to him for singing songs, but only when he wants to. In the autumn he works. He has opinions about everything. He says, for example, that one must be as lazy as a quail. Then one could be brought so far as to know just from the clouds when it's going to rain.

---

150. *Mein Vater hat hier mit keinem die Säue gehütet.* Brecht deploys an idiom dating from the sixteenth century that loses much of its sense in translation; essentially, he is saying that his father is not familiar to anyone there, seeking to play the card of his own social status.

151. An obvious foreshadowing of the biblical David's preference for his slingshot to Saul's armour in preparing for his monomachy with Goliath (1 Sam. 16–17).

152. Aligns with BBA 10364/14r, in NB 8 (Bd. 2, 436–37). Seems to have been incorporated within the B10 scene, rather than being part of a separate attempt at a different scene; many of the lines and images recur.

Previously Uncollected David *Fragments*

Notebook 3, January–February 1920[153]

Bargan for David
Koloman for Absalom
Hete for Bathsheba
Ur for Uriah

Monday 13 September 1920

The third part of the *David* play, where the old man shuffles alone through the chambers and speaks with the elders, Saul, Jonathan, Absalom, fat bodies in pallid air, all four in an aquarium.[154] David is forced into defense, against the wall, he speaks. Listen! He speaks of an aqueduct.[155] It was built with difficulty. There were stones to be drilled through. Israel has no blacksmiths.[156] It was a slippery, subtle, strong work, one had to stay strong. David speaks of this, when he sees that someone laughs. Saul laughs.[157] 'Are you laughing, Saul? It wasn't easy.' Jonathan asks: 'Where is it? Is it working well? Do many scoop water from it?' He says, pensively: 'It is mouldering.[158] No one needs it anymore. But that doesn't matter. That wouldn't matter.' He alarms himself, because he didn't do what was right. Did he not know that it was right to be lazy,[159] not to want

---

153. Located in BBA 11087/16v; published in *Notizbücher* Bd. 1, 170–1.

154. While in A1 Brecht brings together characters (Uriah/Bathsheba/Absalom) whose paths never cross in the biblical tradition, nowhere in the *BFA* fragments does David appear with Saul, Jonathan (both of whom disappear from the narrative in 1 Sam. 31) and Absalom (who is mentioned for the first time in 2 Sam. 3.3 but only enters the narrative proper much later, in 2 Sam. 13).

155. *Wasserleitung* could be any kind of water conduit, including an underground culvert or sewer pipe. While 1 Kings 20.20 associates a (water) conduit with Hezekiah (a later king of the Davidic dynasty), this conduit and the actual water tunnel found in Jerusalem (often associated with Hezekiah) have no association with David himself.

156. In the biblical tradition, Jonathan's daring raid against the Philistine garrison at Michmash is prefaced with an editorial note: 'Now there was no smith to be found throughout all the land of Israel for the Philistines said, "The Hebrews must not make swords or spears for themselves (1 Sam 13:19)"', meant to explain the absence of weaponry amongst the Israelites (apart from Saul and Jonathan).

157. Laughter is referenced infrequently in the Hebrew Bible (see Gen. 18), but never in stories associated with David.

158. The verb *zerfallen* is used for various states of destruction and disrepair; 'moulder' was used here because of the connection to water pipes.

159. For the laziness of Brecht's David see B10 above and pp. 113–15 below.

to change anything, to be human? Why hadn't he done it?[160] Of course, Saul was to be protected. Made great gestures against David and the others, they were wonderful, David bowed to them, but they must also be paid by David.[161] Saul, a great man, but David must protect him.[162] That was not easy. Never did David want to leave things how they were, go where they went. Didn't Saul go under in spite of everything, if they had only seen! Absalom, of Saul's tribe,[163] also wanted to go under, that was the same man, large, imperturbable, imperious, walking through walls, he had to be protected. One scarcely had time to take his insurrection seriously, it was such an insane thing, it almost overwhelmed one, by accident, so it had to be dealt with quickly, without dignity or beauty, ignobly. And Absalom was not to have been saved.[164] But they both had followed their own heads, wanted to go through the wall, the wall was stronger, the heads shattered like eggshells.[165] He, only he, had made the wall, dealt against himself, played politics, believed that one could do something 'provisionally'.[166] He was unworthy, he proves his worthiness at last only thus: that he gets broken, thus, that he remains conscious and nonetheless says 'yes'. Solomon remains, whom he loathes, his son and

160. *Wußte er nicht, daß faul sein das Richtige war, nichts verändern wollen, menschlich sein? Warum tat er es nicht?* Willett abbreviates this line substantially, to 'Did he not realise that the right thing was to be idle?' The additional questions that follow are all included here.

161. *Machte große Gesten gegen David und die andern, sie waren wundervoll, David verbeugt sich gegen sie, aber sie mußten von David bezahlt werden.* The payment that David has to make could refer either to the gathered people or to the gestures. Willett suggested the latter reading by changing the verb to 'paid for'; this translation leaves it uncertain.

162. While the David of B9 is certainly solicitous of Saul's feelings, the biblical David actually spares Saul's life in 1 Sam. 24 and again in 1 Sam. 26, despite being hunted by Saul.

163. Because in the biblical tradition Saul is a Benjamite and Absalom a Judahite son of David by a Geshurite wife, the two are not from the same tribe. Brecht seems to be suggesting that they are instead kindred spirits.

164. For more on Absalom's insurrection in the *BFA* fragments, see A1, B3 and B5 above, and for their relationship to the biblical tradition see pp. 80–6 below.

165. *Aber diese beiden hatten nach ihrem Kopf gehandelt, er wollte durch die Wand, die Wand war stärker, die Köpfe zerbrachen wie Eierschalen.* To 'follow one's head' is less of an idiom in English; this expression in German would be more normal for a horse than a person, i.e. to go of one's own accord, rather than being led.

166. *vorläufig* was translated by Willett as 'just for the time being'; the term is often applied to 'interim' or 'temporary' measures.

heir, 'this guy'!¹⁶⁷ Glossy and empty, the dealer, the sage, the windbag, the diplomat, the priest.¹⁶⁸ Solomon, who protects no one, who kills no one,¹⁶⁹ who 'uses' everyone, who twists everything, finds everything easy, who gets it in his sleep. Solomon, who cannot be broken, the trumpet-trader, the heir, the stand-up guy.¹⁷⁰ Solomon, beloved of a hundred women, God's boy-toy,¹⁷¹ Israel's throne-weight.¹⁷² The whole: the downfall of the strong man.

10 March 1921

DAVID

While he waits, on the wall, a fat parcel of flesh, hairy, sweating, lonesome, while he waits, the hours pass, the riots growing in the country all around,¹⁷³ he begins to think in numbers again, in things and necessities, as he has for years. The farmers needed grain and cattle, the marriage laws needed improvement. In the south the hungry masses have the farms by the throat,¹⁷⁴ in the north there were no roads for shipping wood. They had

---

167. Brecht puts *'Dieser Mensch!'* in quotation marks, perhaps suggesting a catchphrase.

168. Solomon is not mentioned in the *BFA* fragments.

169. While the biblical record does not record Solomon himself killing anyone, he is not squeamish about giving orders for others to do so (1 Kings 2).

170. *Jedermannsherr* carries the sense of 'everyone's man' and is not a common expression. This translation picks up on the earlier use of 'guy' to suggest the cloying/ inauthentic informality/accessibility of Brecht's Solomon.

171. In explaining Solomon's apostasy from Israelite traditions, 1 Kings 11 notes that Solomon had many foreign wives including 700 princesses in addition to 300 concubines (11.3).

172. *Lustknabe* is a term with strong sexual overtones, akin to 'catamite' in English (translated here with more contemporary verve). Brecht coins the term *Thronbeschwerer*; the root verb *beschweren* (when transitive) refers to weighing down, while the reflexive verb *sich beschweren* means 'to complain'. Willett translated this as 'throne-filler'.

173. *Der Aufruhr wächst im Land rings*. *Aufruhr* carries the sense of commotion, fracas or uproar, and is translated by Willett as 'insurrection', but this is a different word from the later word *Aufstand*, which carries a stronger sense of revolt.

174. *Im Süden lagen die Hungernden den Höfen auf dem Hals*. The idiomatic sense of something laying across the throat is clear here; Willett is more free with 'the hungry were a burden to the farms'. Brecht does not use 'masses' in his line; its inclusion here is tied in with the preference for 'riots' (*Aufruhr*) leading up to the final 'insurrection' (*Aufstand*).

to be brought up there, with the children, the women, all. Sometimes the tormented man blinked, over the tips of the green trees, thought quickly of the riots that were gathering there, somewhere in the south, that would mean wasted time and wasted lives,[175] wiped it away. The aqueduct crept forward too slowly, the contracts with the Phoenicians were expiring. (The riot grows in the country...) Far too many idiots everywhere, secret resistances, vicious abductions, sabotage, system errors. One couldn't find peace. (The riots in the country...) Realities were good. They soothed, in spite of everything. One could stand by them. People had too many and too few faces, they had double heads, double feet, there was no counting on them. Made senseless revolts, costly in time and material. Aqueducts decayed, mouldered, or didn't line up, but they were visible, unambiguous, reparable.[176] Got water to the troughs, didn't grumble, never even drank themselves. Knew that it was the best: getting water to the troughs. (The insurrection...)

23 March 1921[177]

But under the abuse
showered with accusations
he went sluggishly away
and did not cleanse himself
nor raised his hands against stones.
But he went lighter under the stones
and raised no hand
and the abuses appeared to him too little
because he now knew:
how he was.

---

175. *Zeitverlust und Menschenopfer* would be more literally translated as 'loss of time' and 'human sacrifice', respectively.

176. *Wasserleitungen vergingen, zerfielen oder stimmten nicht, aber sie waren sichtbar, deutlich, reparierbar.* There are many choices of synonyms in the line, but *vergingen* in particular has been freely translated: it usually suggests simply 'passed on' or 'went by' and is often said of time.

177. This poem, rich in imagery from *David* and invoking the *Absalom* poem from B5, appears in BBA E 21/164. The remainder of the diary entry from that day does not reference *David* explicitly, however.

Chapter 2

BRECHT'S *DAVID* AND THE BIBLICAL DAVID: URIAH, BATHSHEBA, ABSALOM AND JESSE

Brecht and David: A Question of Character

While David is by no means the only character in Brecht's *David* fragments (any more than he is in the books of Samuel), whatever play or plays Brecht's fragments adumbrate do seem to have largely and eventually revolved around David. What is certainly clear is that the two lengthiest and most developed fragments exhumed from Brecht's notebooks have David at their heart, as do Brecht's diary entries from 1920–1921 which concern the fragments.[1] As we will see, Brecht was not the only dramatist of his age to find the story and character of David fascinating, but advance notice of the young Brecht's particular interest in David is furnished by a journal entry from 20 October 1916:

> I read the Bible. I read it aloud, chapter by chapter, but without interruption: Job and the Kings. It is incomparably beautiful, strong, but an evil book. It is so evil that one becomes oneself evil and hard, and knows that life is not unfair but fair, and that this isn't pleasant, but terrible. I believe that David killed the son of Bathsheba himself – of whom it was said that he was killed by God (who could do nothing about the sins of David) – [He killed the son] because David feared God and wanted to soothe the people. It is evil to believe; but the Bible may well believe it; it is full of deceit, as true as it is.[2]

---

1. In his diary entry (*BFA* 26, 131) for 30 July 1920 Brecht refers to 'a play, *Saul and David*'; on 20 August, he refers to what is probably a scene from *David Amid the Eagles*, which may be B10 given its reference to Saul and Jonathan as 'eagles'; on 6 September, Brecht refers to the play as simply *David* and does so again in entries dated 13 and 14 September and finally in the one from 4 March 1921. For more on the range of titles and possible projects reflected in the *David* fragments, see pp. 5–9 above.

2. *BFA* 26, 107.

Not least because some two years later, one of the earliest of the *David* fragments (A1) to appear in Brecht's notebooks has Bathsheba's son strangled, these musings of the teenage Brecht above offer a useful point of entry for reflecting on the relationship between Brecht's *David* and the biblical one.

First, and unsurprisingly, Brecht's diary entry from 1916 indicates that he is fully aware of the 'biblical' David and the insistence of 2 Sam. 12.14, 15 and 18 that the fruit of David's adultery with Bathsheba was struck down by God – whose gentleness with David (also noted by others) suggests to Brecht divine impotence rather than divine mercy. At the same time, in confessing his own belief that David killed the child himself to appease both God and the populace – and that the Bible may well share his belief – Brecht recognises the consequent dissonance which this would seem to imply between what the Bible says (God killed the infant) and what Brecht believes (that the Bible may believe): David killed the infant. While Brecht interprets this dissonance as deceit, interestingly, he does not see this deceit as precluding the 'truth' of the Bible, which he appears to finally admit.

Extraordinary in their own right, Brecht's comments here anticipate in a remarkable way the hermeneutic of suspicion which would come to be deployed so regularly by academic commentators on the Bible much later in the twentieth century in relation to David – not least in relation to whose blood the historical David did or didn't have on his hands.[3] Brecht does not of course specifically deny the divine involvement in the child's death (to which 2 Sam. 12.15 testifies), but Brecht's insistence on his own ability to discern what the 'Bible believes' for himself at such a tender age belies, we would suggest, the sort of extraordinary confidence which would allow him to produce the *David* fragments a few years later. While these fragments touch, but do not dwell at great length, on God's ways, we will see that Brecht's refusal here to view David through rose-tinted glasses will find a striking resonance in the interrogation of the character of David found in the fragments penned from 1919–1921. Indeed, while the fragmentary nature of Brecht's *David* makes it all but impossible to discern fully how the plot of Brecht's intended or potential *David* play(s) might relate to the biblical narratives, Brecht's interest in David's character, in both the literary sense and the moral one, offers an open invitation to consider Brecht's *David* in light of the stories of David we meet in the pages of the biblical books of Samuel.

3. See, for instance, Steven McKenzie, *King David: A Biography* (Oxford: Oxford University Press, 2002), 113–26, and Baruch Halpern, *David's Secret Demons: Messiah, Murderer, Traitor, King* (Grand Rapids: Eerdmans, 2001), 73–84.

While David is clearly central to both Brecht's play fragments and the biblical narratives of Samuel, he is by no means 'an island' in either. Indeed in her study of the latter, Adele Berlin – building on Shimon Bar-Ephrat's pioneering discussion of 'character' in Hebrew Bible narratives generally[4] – illustrates and complicates distinctions between primary and secondary characters in Samuel in her discussion of David and the women with whom he was involved.[5] Devoting attention to each female character in turn, Berlin sees Michal and Bathsheba (the latter in 1 Kings 1–2) as 'full-fledged' characters, realistically drawn and knowable to the reader; by contrast, Abigail is a 'type', specifically the perfect wife, while Abishag is merely an 'agent', part and parcel of the setting itself and/or a functionary of the plot. That Bathsheba appears to fulfil this lesser 'agent' function on her first appearance in 2 Samuel 11–12 before becoming 'full-fledged' in 1 Kings neatly illustrates the fact that characters may be drawn differently in different episodes. The most fully drawn character of all is of course David, and while he does not always carry the action (and in some episodes in 1 and 2 Samuel does not appear at all), he arguably remains the main concern of the wider narrative and the main character as well.[6] Such a conclusion reflects and is reflected in Berlin's final observation that even when David does not carry the action and the focus remains on the women, the presentation of David's character continues indirectly.[7] In sum, Berlin's discussion effectively highlights the value of considering so-called minor characters both in their own right and in relation to so-called primary ones.

Further encouragement to compare Brecht's treatment of not only his David but also his wider cast of characters with that of the books of Samuel is supplied by the work of Alex Woloch on characterisation and the recent application of his work to a 'minor character' in the David stories. In *The One vs. the Many*, Woloch attends to the amount of space (the character-space) apportioned to both protagonists (the 'one') and 'minor' characters (of which there are often 'many') within the novel. Amongst the questions posed by Woloch are the following:

---

4. Shimon Bar-Efrat, *Narrative Art in the Bible* (Sheffield: Almond Press, 1989), 86–92.

5. Adele Berlin, *Poetics and Interpretation of Biblical Narrative* (Sheffield: Almond Press, 1983), 24.

6. Ibid., 32–3, draws a distinction between David as the main concern but not always the main character of episodes which include these women.

7. Ibid., 33.

How often, at what point, and for what duration does a character appear in the text? How does she enter and exit specific scenes? How are her appearances positioned in relation to other characters and to the thematic and structural totality of the narrative? Why does a particular character suddenly disappear from the narrative or abruptly begin to gain more narrative attention? How does the text organize a large number of different characters within a unified symbolic and structural system?[8]

In Woloch's view, the relationship between character-space and system is central:

[A]ll character-spaces inevitably point us toward the character-system, since the emplacement of a character within the narrative form is largely comprised *by* his or her relative position vis-à-vis other characters. If the character-space frames the dynamic interaction between a discretely implied individual and the overall narrative form, the character-system comprehends the mutually constituting interactions among all the characters-spaces as they are (simultaneously) developed within a specific narrative. None of these characters get elaborated in a vacuum.[9]

While the nineteenth-century European novel offers Woloch especially fertile ground for theorising how minor characters are elaborated in relation to protagonists, there are various reasons to believe that his approach may be instructive for our own comparison of the cast of characters offered up by the biblical narratives of David with that of Brecht's *David* fragments.

First, the potential fruitfulness of Woloch's approach is suggested by William Buracker's recent application of Woloch's approach to the narratives of Samuel and to the minor character of Abner, the military commander who serves three kings: first Saul (1 Samuel) then his son Ish-bosheth and finally, briefly, David himself (both in 2 Samuel). While Buracker's analysis of Abner offers insights into the presentation of Abner as a character in his own right, perhaps even more illuminating is the way that Abner's character-space is shown to intersect with those of the respective protagonists (first Saul, then Saul and David together, and then David) and other minor characters (Joab).[10] The intersection of Abner's

---

8. Alexander Woloch, *The One vs. the Many: Minor Characters and the Space of the Protagonist in the Novel* (Princeton: Princeton University Press, 2003), 13–14.

9. Ibid., 18.

10. See William Buracker, 'Abner Son of Ner: Characterization and Contribution of Saul's Chief General' (PhD diss., Catholic University of America, 2017), 262–4, and now David J. Shepherd, 'Knowing Abner', in *Characters and Characterization*

character-space with that of Joab, David's own general, highlights the contrast between the two minor characters as on one hand, peace-seeking if naïve (Abner) and on the other, violently cunning (Joab). However, Buracker's analysis also highlights the way in which Abner's passivity during the reign of Saul gives way to his domination of the narrative (despite Abner's 'minorness') after the king's death (2 Sam. 2–3). This in turn foregrounds the passivity of both Saul's official successor Ish-bosheth in these chapters as well as his eventual successor/usurper David, who is the erstwhile protagonist of the wider story.[11] Long in the shadow of Saul, Abner's 'minorness' is confirmed by the fact that his *bona fide* emergence and ill-fated moment in the sun as king-maker is eclipsed as soon as David is made king.

Second, Woloch's observation that his analysis of 'minorness' is relevant to a broad spectrum of literature and specifically to cinematic art suggests its potential applicability to the theatre as well.[12] Indeed, the fact that one of Woloch's analytical questions above is framed in terms of how major and minor characters 'enter and exit specific scenes' more than hints at the applicability of such analysis to theatrical works.[13] Unsurprisingly, we will see that Brecht's greater dependence on dialogue for characterisation will differentiate his fragments from the David stories we find in the books of Samuel, but Brecht's proliferation of minor characters alongside David, especially in the street scene (B10), suggests the value of Woloch's approach in considering 'the one vs. the many' in the *David* fragments.

As useful as a focus on characterisation will turn out to be in considering Brecht's *David* in relation to its biblical antecedents, one caveat must be offered at the outset. At first glance, it would seem that the fragmentary nature of the evidence of Brecht's *David* bequeathed to us by his notebooks foregrounds their 'unfinished' character to a greater extent than do the books of Samuel. Certainly, our assessment of Brecht's interpretation and presentation of any character in the fragments, including David, must

---

in the Book of Samuel, ed. Keith Bodner and Benjamin J. M. Johnson (London: Bloomsbury, 2020), 205–25. For a discussion of still more 'minor' characters in 1 Samuel see Samuel Hildebrandt's 'The Servants of Saul: "Minor" Characters and Royal Commentary in 1 Samuel 9–31', *JSOT* 40 (2015): 179–200.

11. Buracker, 'Abner', 275–7, notes the similarity to this phenomenon in Dickens highlighted by Woloch.

12. Woloch, *The One vs. the Many*, 30. His own brief illustration of its applicability (345 n. 23) is limited to characterisation in the cinema.

13. It is all the more curious then that while Woloch's approach has been noted in discussions of the theatricality of the novel (so David Kurnick, *Empty Houses: Theatrical Failure and the Novel* [Princeton: Princeton University Press, 2011], 226), it has yet to register in work on character within the theatre.

be seen as permanently provisional or at least severely qualified by the partial nature of the evidence. However, it is worth noting that the long compositional history of the books of the Hebrew Bible and questions in certain circles at certain times regarding how (un)finished books like Samuel were understood to be, suggests that the evidence they too offer of their characters must be seen as provisional in its own way.[14] In other words, in both cases, we may only speak of David and other characters as they have been drawn, without knowing how any given characterisation might have been different if either Brecht's *David* or the biblical one had been 'less fragmentary'.

While Brecht's *David* includes characters of Brecht's own creation, anonymous and otherwise, to which we will refer in passing, his fragments also reference a variety of characters well-known from the ancient biblical traditions associated with David. In what follows we explore Brecht's treatment of Bathsheba (originally Uriah's wife and eventually David's), Uriah (Bathsheba's husband until his death), Absalom (David's third son) and finally Jesse (David's father).

Uriah (and Bathsheba)

Of Bathsheba and Uriah the fragments offer tantalisingly little, and indeed these characters appear only in what Brecht appears to refer to in his diaries as 'synopses of scenes',[15] rather than in the more developed dramatic fragments which contain dialogue. One such plan, A1, outlines a series of scenes involving David, Uriah, Bathsheba (all of whose character-spaces intersect in 2 Sam. 11–12) and Absalom, who doesn't appear in chs. 11–12 but in the one immediately following (2 Sam. 13). Perhaps Absalom is included here by Brecht because of this textual proximity, though the action described in the scenes themselves seems to reflect Absalom's rebellion against his father from still later in 2 Samuel along with elements of 2 Samuel 11–12 and its account of David's affair and its aftermath. Brecht says more (as will we) about Absalom, but A1's collapsing of Absalom's rebellion with the Uriah–Bathsheba affair offers Brecht's Uriah quite literally a new lease of life, in comparison with 2 Samuel 12 which narrates Uriah's death by the 'sword' of the Ammonites with the complicity of Joab, but most nefariously at the instigation of David. While the characterisation of Uriah within the biblical tradition

---

14. For a focused but accessible discussion of the history of scholarship on the story/ies of David, see John Van Seters, *The Biblical Saga of King David* (Winona Lake: Eisenbrauns, 2009), 1–52.

15. 'Szenenübersicht' (20 August 1920), *BFA* 26, 136.

is itself curiously ambiguous, not least in respect of how knowing Uriah is regarding David's affair with his wife,[16] it is widely agreed that the honourable refusal of Uriah to go home and sleep with his wife while his fellow soldiers are in the field is presented to foreground the reprehensibility of David in taking first Uriah's wife and then eventually his life.[17] As David Jobling has noted, however, Brecht's presentation of his Uriah in A1 is rather more complicated:

> Something is going on between Absalom and Uriah, who at one point go off arm in arm. Something is going on between David and Uriah: 'Uriah comes and David flees with him'. Uriah creates the hardest problems. His role is certainly negative: 'he does not believe in the good' (whatever this means) and near the end he is 'unmasked'. He is 'marked for death' as the Bible relates ('the enthusiasts' might be the 'valiant men' of 2 Sam 11:16) but he does not die! My best guess is that Brecht boldly infuses the Ammonite war and Absalom's revolt, and has Uriah play a double game, assisting Absalom's revolt (or pretending to), but also helping David escape. In a journal entry, Brecht has an aged David recall how he was ready to surrender to Absalom, and was waiting for him to take over, when 'Uriah...came to him, and he didn't succeed in seeing it through, but ran away again'. This, surely, is the same as 'Uriah comes and David flees with him'. Uriah's duplicity is what gets 'unmasked' in Absalom's tent. This account makes some sense, at least, of the scene outline, but it leaves Uriah's motives obscure.[18]

While I cannot improve upon it, Jobling's ingenious construal of A1 is not fully persuasive: it is, as Jobling himself acknowledges, difficult to know what Brecht means by suggesting that Uriah 'does not believe in goodness'[19] – the goodness of Absalom, or David perhaps, or simply the quality itself? – and it is equally unclear in what way and for the benefit of whom Uriah is unmasked at the end. If *Todeskeim* does indeed mean 'seed of death',[20] this at least chimes with the biblical tradition in which Uriah

---

16. See Meir Sternberg, *The Poetics of Biblical Narrative: Ideological Literature and the Drama of Reading* (Bloomington: Indiana University Press, 1985), 195–213.

17. Interestingly, the name Uriah recurs in Brecht's later work. For instance, in *Mann ist Mann*, one of the first soldiers that Galy Gay meets while seeking to buy fish in Scene 1 is named 'Uria Shelley'. So too, in a single page of the *Brotladen* notebooks (NB 25, 1929) Brecht lists 'Uriah' along with 'Sirens' and 'Trojan Horse', though what he may have had in mind is unclear since the play remained a fragment.

18. Jobling, 'David on the Brain', 232.

19. Nearly, but not quite, identical to Jobling's translation (see above).

20. See discussion of the translation (p. 26) above. A much later reference to Uriah appears in Brecht's notebooks from the 1940s in connection with an idea labelled *der pestkaufmann* [sic]. In the *BFA*, the line is filed under *Der Salzburger Totentanz* as

carries his own death warrant in a letter from David to his commander Joab (2 Sam. 11.14-15), and somehow makes sense of Uriah pleading for his life.[21] But if the biblical Uriah does know that he is marked for death, he gives no indication of it, nor does he take action to avoid it. Indeed, there is a still more notable difference between Brecht's Uriah and his biblical incarnation, namely, that the former has been drafted as a much fuller character – appearing in scenes 3, 4, 5 and 6 of A1's scheme – than the mere foil offered by the biblical tradition. Moreover, Brecht's Uriah is a character who is very much present and engaged with Bathsheba in these scenes. In the second scene, Bathsheba cries out for him; in the third he is first with Bathsheba and then embraces Absalom. In the fourth, he is again with Bathsheba, again with Absalom and then sent from Bathsheba to David, while in the fifth he comes to David and Bathsheba, is about to be sent away and then goes with David. Brecht's bringing of Uriah and his wife together in A1 highlights the extent to which the biblical Uriah is, by contrast, pre-eminently and persistently *not* with his wife, Bathsheba. Indeed, the biblical Bathsheba never cries out for her husband, and the biblical Uriah stubbornly refuses the king's command to go home (and

part of A1: 'The plague-merchant: The brother (nephew) is back from Florence. He has infected himself, since he wanted to make a business with the plague, didn't know anything about it [...] [the brother] is not there. When he comes and learns that Uria is back, he is terrified and flees. Brings death with him' (*BFA* 10.2, p. 958). This final sentence appears as follows in the notebooks (NB 51, 24v): *wenn er kommt und erfährt, daß er zurück ist, erschrickt er und flieht*. The first 'er' has been elaborated on the line above: *der Onkel, der den Neffen nach Florenz schickte, obwohl er wußte, daß dort die Pest herrscht*, while the second 'er' is crossed out, with *der Urias* written in as a correction. The plot outline of the Uriah story is visible in this situation, much more clearly than in the *BFA* version: someone is sent to the front lines carrying a secret death sentence. This small note suggests that Brecht had Uriah and his story 'on the brain' to some extent into the late 1940s.

21. That Uriah and his letter continued to hold a fascination for Brecht years later is suggested by a film he worked on or at least talked about working on in 1929–1930 under the title *Uriasbrief* (Uriah's Letter); while the project does not appear in the *BFA*, it is listed in the *GW Supplementband II* (654) and the archival text from BBA 235/53 links the concept of a film entitled *Desdemona* to this material, but has the later date of 1940. A single sentence of the project survives, all typed in lower case (retained here): 'the wife of uriah discovers the letter. she has fallen for david's charm. she fights against it, loses often, wins in the end.' An alternative theory, put forward in the electronic edition annotations for Notebook 25, is that the mis-dated fragment that entered the *David* fragments in B5 (BBA 503/47-48) was part of a later American offer for a Hollywood *Uriasbrief* from the 1940s, and (like Desdemona) was an excuse to tell a titillating tale of adultery that might sell well.

hopefully have sex with his wife to obscure David's adultery) not just on one occasion but twice. More similarities and differences between the biblical Uriah and Brecht's character would undoubtedly emerge had we Brecht's scenes themselves instead of merely A1's synopsis.[22]

Absalom

Absalom's presence in A1 along with Uriah and Bathsheba illustrates the liberty Brecht exercised in creating intersections between Absalom's character-space and others' which are unimagined by the biblical tradition, but elsewhere in the fragments there is ample evidence of Brecht's interest in a more recognisably biblical portrait of Absalom as well. Apart from Solomon, in whom the fragments show virtually no interest,[23] it is Absalom, the third son of David, who commands more attention in the biblical tradition than any of David's other sons. Indeed, while 2 Samuel 13 begins with the focus firmly fixed on David's firstborn, Amnon, and his rape of his half-sister Tamar, Absalom quickly takes centre stage in the narrative, first by comforting Tamar (v. 20) and then by plotting Amnon's murder, which he successfully orchestrates (v. 30), before fleeing to avoid blood vengeance being executed upon him.[24] That the threat of blood vengeance against Absalom is what keeps him in exile in Geshur and away from the Davidic court is confirmed by Joab's efforts to secure his recall with the assistance of a woman from Tekoa (ch. 14), who approaches the king to plead that her fictitious son be spared blood vengeance from her clan (v. 11) after he has killed his brother in the field (v. 6). When David is finally persuaded to spare her fictitious son, the woman presses David to do the same for Absalom (despite learning that the woman has been enlisted by Joab). David's unwillingness to offer Absalom an explicit

---

22. Thus A5 has 'Uriah, standing on his rights as a general (certificates of honour), while David fucks his wife', which seems to reflect David's adultery with Bathsheba and Uriah's honourable abstention from her, but it is difficult to know how it relates to A1.

23. He goes entirely unmentioned in the *BFA David* fragments, but see 'Previously Uncollected David Fragments' above, pp. 68–70.

24. While it has been regularly assumed and recently argued that the text wishes to present Absalom's killing of his brother Amnon as an act of justice (see e.g. Richard Smith, *The Fate of Justice and Righteousness during David's Reign: Narrative Ethics and Rereading the Court History According to 2 Samuel 8:15–20:26* [New York: T. & T. Clark, 2009], 146–63), it seems clear that Absalom's killing of Amnon incurs bloodguilt. See David J. Shepherd, *King David and the Problem of Bloodguilt* (Oxford: Oxford University Press, forthcoming).

exemption from blood vengeance *per se* sits comfortably with the fact that while Absalom is allowed to return (v. 21), he is not initially permitted to enter the king's presence (v. 24). Thus David is able to honour the commitment he has been lured into making by Joab and the woman, but to do so without either fully ending Absalom's exile or making final, at this point, his overlooking of Absalom's bloodguilt.

Absalom's own dissatisfaction at remaining exiled from the king's court culminates in 14.32 in both Absalom's demand that he be given a royal audience and his bold admission that if there is sin or guilt in him, he shall accept the death penalty. While it is possible that the NRSV and other English versions are correct to translate *wehĕmītánî* 'then let him (that is the king) put me to death', it is also possible to understand the Hebrew as suggesting that Absalom is inviting not the king, but Joab to kill him if Absalom is found to be guilty. If so, then the narrative here prepares us for chapter 18 in which Joab will show himself only too happy to take Absalom up on his offer.

Before that, however, 2 Samuel 15–17 recounts the returned Absalom's rebellion against his father David, including Absalom's initial success at ousting him (ch. 15), David's ignominious flight and Absalom's consolidation of power in Jerusalem (ch. 16), and then Absalom's planning and eventual military pursuit of David, who has fled to Mahanaim (ch. 17). Finally, in chapter 18 the forces of Absalom meet those loyal to David in battle, the climax of which is the account of the curious death of Absalom. Apparently torn from his mule and suspended in mid-air when his head (and possibly his hair) is caught in the branches of a large tree (v. 9), Absalom is then seemingly impaled by Joab with three sharpened staves (v. 14), before being set upon by Joab's ten armour bearers, who proceed to hack his body to the point of mutilation at best and dismemberment at worst (v. 15).[25] Insult is added to mortal injury when Absalom's body is denied a customary burial and is instead thrown into a pit and covered with large stones (v. 17). Unsurprisingly for the reader, who recalls David's earlier instructions to 'deal gently with Absalom' (v. 5), David is heartbroken by the news of his son's death (v. 33; 19.4), despite it signalling the end of the coup and his own restoration to the throne in Jerusalem.

---

25. In the absence of other cogent explanations for this cluster of curiosities in the account of Absalom's death, I have suggested (Shepherd, *King David*) that Absalom's impalement, hanging and mutilation are best explained as an attempt on the part of Joab and the narrator to present Absalom as dying the death of one who has incurred bloodguilt.

That Absalom featured prominently in Brecht's early interest in the dramatic potential of the David stories seems to be confirmed by Absalom's appearance in a variety of fragments. In a dialogue between David and an anonymous man (B1), for instance, Brecht has David confess not only that he loves Absalom best of all his children (because his hair reminds David of Absalom's mother [cf. 2 Sam. 14.25-26]), but also that it was David's love for Absalom which led him to forgive him for killing Amnon. While it is doubtful (or at least highly debatable) whether the final verses of 2 Samuel 14 indicate David's 'forgiveness' of Absalom rather than merely his ill-advised renunciation of blood vengeance against his son, Brecht's reading of the scene as indicating David's forgiveness is far from exceptional.[26] Moreover, given that 2 Sam. 13.4 has Amnon profess his love for his half-sister before he rapes her, the Brechtian David's endorsement of Amnon's love for her in B1 is a very plausible means of explaining (in addition to David's own love for Amnon), why the biblical David takes no action against Amnon despite the king's 'great anger' (13.21).[27]

How far back Brecht's interest in Absalom dates is indicated by Hans Otto Münsterer's recollections of Brecht's work in 1919:

> The first [play] originally bore the title *David* (or *Absalom?*), or *God's Chosen One*. Later it was changed to *Absalom and Bathsheba*. The story is taken from the Bible. Although in the play Absalom is the most sympathetic character, it is David who is 'God's favourite' – despite the immorality which is apparent even in the Scriptures. The opening scene shows Absalom in the courtyard listening to the guards' salacious anecdotes about the escapades of the ageing king. Suddenly the lowering silhouette of David appears on the battlements: 'I call on my son Absalom to account!' The curtain falls

---

26. See, for instance, Jože Krašovec, *Reward, Punishment, and Forgiveness: The Thinking and Beliefs of Ancient Israel in the Light of Greek and Modern Views* (Leiden: Brill, 1999), 284–5. Compare also the heading for 2 Sam. 14.25 furnished by the translators of the NRSV: 'David Forgives Absalom'. The possibility that the story of David and Absalom may offer something of relevance for considering the 'problem' of interpersonal forgiveness in the Hebrew Bible is allowed by David Reimer, 'Stories of Forgiveness: Narrative Ethics and the Old Testament', in *Reflection and Refraction: Studies in Biblical Historiography in Honour of A. Graeme Auld*, ed. Robert Rezetko, Timothy H. Lim and W. Brian Aucker (Leiden: Brill, 2007), 362–3, but he goes no further than this.

27. Why David takes no action against Amnon for his abuse of Tamar is a matter of debate. For discussion and secondary literature, see Gina Hens-Piazza, *Of Methods, Monarchs, and Meanings: A Sociorhetorical Approach to Exegesis* (Macon: Mercer University Press, 1996), 95–6.

on an ominous silence. It is an exposition Brecht might have been proud of even in his maturity. Amongst the high points were Absalom's conversation with the trees, and a tender love-scene when Bathsheba escapes from David and flees to her beloved Absalom in the field. The structure of the play was enormously involved, because of the central importance given to the lovers' relationship and David's cunning ruses to implicate Uriah in Bathsheba's pregnancy.[28]

If Münsterer's memory is reliable at this point, whatever Brecht produced which answered to his friend's description would appear to have been lost, for A1 bears only a general resemblance to the surviving fragments in that it too brings together Absalom with David and Bathsheba in a way that the Bible does not. That the action described above by Münsterer might indeed have something to do with A1 may, however, be suggested by the fact that in both, Absalom seems to manifest a particular interest in David's seduction of Bathsheba. Indeed, it is easy to see how the 'salacious escapades of the ageing king' which Münsterer's Absalom hears from the guards might correspond to the 'story of David and Bathsheba' (including the detail that she is pregnant), which Absalom proceeds to tell to those in the tavern in the second scene as Brecht sketches it in A1. Yet the fact that A1 displays little evidence of an Absalom 'beloved' by Bathsheba which Münsterer recalls, complicates any assumption that the two have much to do with each other. Moreover, while A1's Absalom seems to have plenty to do with Uriah (in scenes three and four), he does not appear to have anything at all to do with Bathsheba.

Despite Brecht's obvious innovations in A1, resonances with the biblical Absalom may nevertheless be discerned. Thus, while it might be possible to interpret the third scene's 'With Absalom many soldiers' in various ways, scene four – '(Absalom newly back with the treasonous soldiers!) Bathsheba and Uria. Absalom. Insurrection' – strongly hints at Brecht's acquaintance with and interest in the biblical Absalom's ill-fated rebellion against David remembered in 2 Samuel, as of course do the final words of A1's last scene, which are simply: 'Death of Absalom'.

Further evidence that it was Absalom's rebellion and death which most excited Brecht's dramatic imagination is supplied by the remaining fragments, including B5 (*Von Absalom*) which resonates with another piece, 'Absalom rides through the wood' or 'The public man' (*'Absalom reitet durch den Wald' oder 'Der öffentliche Mann'*) which appears to have been written by Brecht in the summer of 1920, when he turned his

---

28. Münsterer, *The Young Brecht*, 80.

dramatic attentions to the younger David.[29] In 'Absalom rides', references to drums (*'die Trommeln hinter sich'*, 49.5)[30] and red banners hint at Absalom's rebellion, while the work's title, along with the opening and concluding lines, situate it as an account of Absalom's fateful, lonely ride to his doom and the events leading up to it. That the journey of 'Absalom rides' is indeed ill-fated is suggested by references to the impossibility of escape (48.21), to the fact that he is not yet dead (48.27), to his flesh growing cold (49.1), to his thoughts of his *'Ende'* (49.6) and to the notion of one dying for many (49.10-11). That Absalom's fate is specifically bound up with the forest is intimated not only by generic references to it, but also by the mention of the 'trees' (48.21; 49.2, 12) which are ominously red (*'Zinnober'*, 48.22, cf. 49.2) and offer Absalom no help when he asks (49.1, 2). Even more premonitory are the references to Absalom's neck (*'Hals'*) and the pain in it about which he thinks toward the end of the piece (49.7, 10).

It is perhaps not surprising that various of Brecht's *David* fragments appear to offer echoes of 'Absalom rides through the wood'. B3 consists of a line of dialogue attributed to David and then one attributed to Absalom, but given that David speaks of Absalom in the third person, it is unclear to what extent this should be understood as an exchange or dialogue *per se*. In it, David finds himself wondering how it is that his son has become so immoderate 'That one has to kill him like a rabid dog?'. Brecht's David does not understand why Absalom wants 'to go into the dark ground', why he wants to die and to do so in the heat of the day.[31] But what is most intriguing is David's reference to the means of Absalom's death; David is incredulous that despite the softness of his hands, Absalom will strangle 'necks' (*Hälse*) and have his own 'neck' (*Hals*) strangled. If, as seems likely, the resonance here in the fragment with Absalom's pain in the neck in 'Absalom rides' is not a coincidence, then it may suggest the possibility

---

29. *BFA* 19, 48–9 (and line references). As the editor notes, the title of this and one other piece also include a reference to a collection, 'The Visions of Berthold Brecht', which Brecht appears to first moot in a journal entry from June 1920. Of this collection only these two pieces remain or perhaps were ever penned in the first place. The poem is reproduced with slightly different formatting in *BFA* 13, 154; for an alternative English translation to the one offered in the present volume, see Bertolt Brecht, *The Collected Poems of Bertolt Brecht*, ed. and trans. Tom Kuhn and David Constantine (New York: Norton Liveright, 2019), 89.

30. References are to the lineation of *BFA* 19, 48–9.

31. See p. 36 above.

that it is not the trees who will be responsible for it. Whereas the biblical David orders his commanders to deal gently with Absalom despite his rebellion, here in B3 Brecht's David seemingly accepts that his son must die, but is apparently bewildered at how it has come to this. The explanation offered by Brecht's Absalom (if it is an explanation) is laced with rage against heaven, an inclination toward self-destruction and above all ambition: 'I want to throw away what my hand can grasp. It's too small. I don't want what I can have: because it's too little' – sentiments which seem to resonate with the biblical narration of his *coup d'état*.

Other fragments offer their own resonances with 'Absalom rides'. In A2, we find either stage directions or the narrator's voice warning 'But behind (*hinter*) the scenes is stamping and drumming (*Trommeln*), as well as a barbaric song to be heard, coming ever nearer. This is Absalom.' So too, in 'Absalom rides', the reader is seemingly offered Absalom's view that it is nice to leave the 'drums behind' ('die Trommeln hinter sich'). Much more obvious, however, is A3's note of Absalom's death: 'The red tree, brown, in which Absalom is hanging in the end, brown sky, pastures, glistening eyes. Wind.' While not vermillion like the trees of 'Absalom rides' – which 'will not help' Absalom as he rides to his death – the redness of the 'Rotbaum' from which Absalom finally hangs in the fragment surely bespeaks a kinship of sorts between it and the fatal vermillion trees of 'Absalom rides'.

In addition to the anticipation and description of Absalom's death, the *David* fragments also seem to contain a lamentation of it (*Von Absalom*) in B5. While the end of 2 Samuel 18 (v. 33) reports David's mourning of his son's death ('the king was deeply moved...and wept'; 'O my son Absalom, my son, my son Absalom! Would I had died instead of you, O Absalom, my son, my son!'), the nearest biblical analogue to B5 would appear to be David's lamenting of Saul and Jonathan at their deaths (in 2 Sam. 1.19-27). Indeed, just as his lament for them begins and ends with reference to the stricken Saulides (v. 19: 'Your glory, O Israel, lies slain upon your high places! How the mighty have fallen!'; v. 27: 'How the mighty have fallen'), so too B5 begins and ends by referring to the 'stretched out' Absalom (*ausgestreckt*). Both biblical and Brechtian laments do also refer to the circumstances ('battle', v. 25; 'fulfilled is the revolt', *Aufstand*) and the respective places of death (Saul and Jonathan on Gilboa [v. 21] and Absalom 'in the wood' [*im Gehölz*]), but it is clear that the two are otherwise quite different. Whereas the biblical lament eulogises Saul and Jonathan's martial and physical prowess and Saul's generosity and concludes with David's expression of love and loss for Jonathan (v. 26), the tone of Brecht's poem is less obviously emotional.

Indeed, while the lament for Absalom acknowledges that he 'towered'[32] and the revolt was fulfilled, its primary interest is less in what Absalom did in life, than in what he did not: 'never cursing, never helping', 'never grasps, never resists'; hands laying folded in the lap and leaving this life with a 'shrug'; as tranquil in life as in his death, which does not require him to ever rise up or to give any orders.

Whereas the heights to which the biblical Absalom rises in his mercurial career are undeniably heady, the Absalom lamented in B5 feels rather more Brechtian than biblical. In, fact, one might argue that the Absalom lamented in Brecht's poem is, in his inactivity, a direct inversion or even subversion of the one remembered by the biblical tradition, who seems always to be reaching, always resisting, often helping and occasionally, one might imagine, cursing. As we have seen, the biblical Absalom comforts his raped sister, then avenges her by killing his brother and then flees to avoid death himself. Having burned Joab's field in order to gain an audience with the king and having been restored, Absalom then plots against and usurps his father, taking his capital city and his women. Finally, having lived by the sword, the biblical Absalom dies by it, massacred and mutilated. By contrast – and unlike the other Brechtian fragments which follow biblical sentiment in imagining Absalom's disfiguring death – here in B5's lament, Absalom remains as attractive in death as in life:

> The dying / in the wood a
> Beautiful corpse, stretched out –

Like the biblical Absalom, the Absalom of Brecht's lament also revolts, but he does not overreach nor does he die ugly; instead he rebels effortlessly and falls as easily as he rises.

Because the lament in B5 is clearly *Von Absalom* in the sense of being about him rather than attributed to him, the lament is technically unattributed. Indeed, Brecht may not have got that far or may well have imagined it voiced by a narrator. However, in light of the biblical David's lament of Saul and Jonathan and the noting of his grief and its expression in 2 Samuel 18 on hearing of the death of Absalom, one might be forgiven for assuming that Brecht imagined this lament too on the lips of David. Such an assumption might be strengthened by an awareness that Brecht will supply David with a song to sing for Saul (in B9), but most especially by the fact that some of the very characteristics for which Absalom is

---

32. For these references to B5, see pp. 204, 206 above.

eulogised here appear to be traits Brecht's David congratulates himself for possessing in B10 but which prompt more criticism than congratulation from David's own father Jesse, as we will see below.[33]

Jesse

In the Hebrew Bible, Jesse, the father of David, eventually sends David to serve Saul and later sends him to the Israelite front lines (1 Sam. 17.17) with supplies for his brothers who are bearing arms for Saul against the Philistines. But Jesse's first appearance is at the beginning of 1 Samuel 16, when the prophet Samuel comes to Bethlehem to anoint one of his sons to be king in Saul's place. Which of Jesse's sons will be anointed is the question which animates the narrative and encourages the reader's reflection on both the qualifications for kingship and the parts played in the process by both the prophet Samuel and Jesse. Samuel's initial assumption that Jesse's firstborn, Eliab, is to be king is shown to be misplaced by the narrator's reporting of the divine rebuke of the prophet: 'Do not look on his appearance or on the height of his stature, because I have rejected him; for the LORD does not see as mortals see; they look on the outward appearance, but the Lord looks on the heart' (1 Sam. 16.7).[34] As the narrator will shortly admit that David too is handsome (v. 12), the reader is invited to conclude that Samuel has been deceived by Eliab's stature, which also marked out the first king, Saul (9.2; 19.23), but could not save him from subsequent rejection as king. Samuel's repeated insistence that the Lord had not chosen any of the sons which Jesse subsequently calls before the prophet has been seen by some as a condemnation of Jesse's judgement.[35] However, given the cultural significance of birth order (however often it is subverted) and given the fact that it is Samuel himself who begins with the first-born Eliab, Jesse can hardly be blamed for following suit and calling his other sons in order of their age. Moreover, even if the reader had been offered an indication of the relative physical stature of Jesse's sons, the narrative gives no indication that Jesse has been made privy to the divine

---

33. For the latter, see pp. 113–15. For more on the relationship between Brecht's and David's Psalms, see pp. 122–4.

34. The irony generated by the narrator's insistence (v. 12) that David was himself physically attractive is obvious.

35. See, for instance, Martin Kessler, 'Narrative Technique in 1 Sam 16:1-3', *CBQ* 32 (1970): 550. Cf. James Muilenburg, 'A Study in Hebrew Rhetoric: Repetition and Style', *VTSup* 1 (1953): 99.

rejection of its relevance, so he cannot be held accountable for not bearing it in mind. Neither is it likely that the employment of the youngest, David, as shepherd should be seen as a subtle 'hint at the folly of Jesse and his family' for failing to recognise David's true talent and future vocation as royal shepherd of Israel.[36] Indeed, had David been present from the outset, the divine warning against attention to outward appearances might have led to the 'handsome' David (v. 12) being overlooked by Samuel until the end in any case. Thus, if Jesse's earlier failure to summon David, and Samuel's insistence that they will not sit down to table until he does so (v. 11) is intended as a rebuke of Jesse's underestimation of his youngest's son's royal prospects, it is surely a very gentle one indeed. Moreover, it should be noted that once prompted by Samuel, Jesse summons David without hesitation.

The biblical Jesse's next involvement in his son's story is to be found later in the same chapter when Saul hears of David's laudable qualities (16.18) and asks for Jesse to send his son to Saul and then to allow him to remain in Saul's service. While one might wonder how much scope Jesse has to refuse such royal requests, the narrator reports Jesse as obliging and indeed not merely sending his son to Saul, but also a variety of foodstuffs with him (v. 20). Such a gesture may well have been expected, but may not have been required, and would in any case hardly have hurt David's prospects any more than Jesse acquiescing to Saul's request for David to remain with the king, which is presumably what is signalled by Jesse's lack of response to the king's request.

Finally, Jesse is mentioned in the next chapter where his redundant re-introduction along with his son ('Now David was the son of an Ephrathite of Bethlehem in Judah, named Jesse', 1 Sam. 17.12) suggests an alternate origin for the Goliath pericope which follows, as does the fact that here it is now the three eldest sons – Eliab, Abinadab and Shammah – who are serving Saul against the Philistines (v. 13) and David who is back with Jesse looking after the sheep (v. 15). In addition to being reminded that Jesse has eight sons, the reader learns here that their father is 'old' ($z\bar{a}q\bar{e}n$) – the relevance of which is unclear, unless it explains his need of David and the four other brothers not serving with Saul. With the previous chapter in mind, the fact that Jesse again sends David to Saul and again sends him with foodstuffs, but now requires David to return with news of the brothers and to tend to the sheep might give the impression that David has been rather 'reeled in' by his father, even if this is an accident of the compositional history of these chapters. This is especially true if

---

36. So suggests Kessler, 'Narrative Technique', 550.

the reader feels inclined to validate Eliab's suspicions, voiced when David reaches the battlefront, that his younger brother's presence there reflects David's frustrated ambitions (even though the text sees the impetus for David's visit as resting with Jesse).

Following Jesse's departure from the narrative stage as a character in his own right, he appears only in name and, indeed, almost exclusively as part of the patronymic 'Son of Jesse' as a term of reference to David. In the books of Samuel, it has been suggested by some commentators that when 'the Son of Jesse' appears on its own, on the lips of Saul and some others within his orbit, it should be understood as 'derogatory'.[37] Thus for example:

> But on the second day, the day after the new moon, David's place was empty. And Saul said to his son Jonathan, 'Why has the son of Jesse not come to the feast, either yesterday or today?' Jonathan answered Saul, 'David earnestly asked leave of me to go to Bethlehem; he said, "Let me go; for our family is holding a sacrifice in the city, and my brother has commanded me to be there. So now, if I have found favor in your sight, let me get away, and see my brothers." For this reason he has not come to the king's table.' Then Saul's anger was kindled against Jonathan. He said to him, 'You son of a perverse, rebellious woman! Do I not know that you have chosen the son of Jesse to your own shame, and to the shame of your mother's nakedness? For as long as the son of Jesse lives upon the earth, neither you nor your kingdom shall be established. Now send and bring him to me, for he shall surely die.' (1 Sam. 20.27-28)

Here and elsewhere (see 1 Sam. 22.7, 14), there is no doubt that Saul's use of 'son of Jesse' instead of 'David' (v. 27) is far from affectionate or favourable. Indeed, one clue to the rhetorical significance of Saul's insistence on referring to the 'son of Jesse' is that Jonathan refuses to do so, referring instead to 'David' in the very next verse (v. 28) in responding to Saul's question regarding David's whereabouts. In fact, as Saul's re-use of the patronymic in his angry rejoinder to Jonathan's defence of David indicates, the king wishes to emphasise that the 'son of Jesse' (v. 30 and v. 31) is no 'son of Saul' insofar as a claim to Saul's throne goes.[38] Thus,

---

37. So H. J. Stoebe, *Das Erste Buch Samuelis* (Gütersloh: Gütersloher Verlagshaus Gerd Mohn, 1973), 378.

38. Whether Saul's subsequent references to David as 'my son' in 1 Sam. 24.16 (Heb. v. 17) and 1 Sam. 26 (vv. 17, 21, 25) reflect a change of heart or simply that these episodes belong to a different tradition than those found in ch. 22 is difficult to determine.

while the expression 'son of Jesse' is not derogatory *per se*, it is clear that Saul's use of this patronymic alone does serve to put David in his place and underline Saul's negative assessment of his status vis-à-vis Saul and his house.[39] While it is true that the persistent reappearance of Jesse in the dismissive patronymic 'son of Jesse' allows David's father to linger in the narratives of Samuel, Adele Berlin is surely right to conclude that Jesse is a 'peripheral character at most' in 1 Samuel.[40] Such a conclusion, however, makes it all the more fascinating that in comparison with Samuel, Brecht's *David* offers us a rather fuller portrait, of a rather different Jesse.

Indeed, this contrast is signalled by Brecht's placing of the phrase 'son of Jesse' not on the lips of Saul or others inclined to take a dim view of David, but instead in the street scene (B10) in the mouths of minor characters. Near the beginning of the scene, three beggars witness a man being bullied by another and proceed to collar the bully (**The Man**), who then appeals to David perhaps in part as a distraction but also in the hope that he will vouch for him:

The Man

It was just a bit of fun. Of course it was better in the old days. It's a misunderstanding. There's David, the son of Jesse, who you know, he knows me. Good day, David!

Later in the same scene, the same naming convention appears when the protagonist is recognised by a new set of characters:

A Pack of People (*coming slowly onto the stage*):

Hoho, there's David, the son of Jesse, who threw Joseph in the ring. He has a big mouth. He'll have something to say about the war!

The fact that the patronymic 'son of Jesse' is accompanied by 'David' on both occasions makes it unlikely that it is being used in a derogatory fashion or indeed to indicate David's status. Instead, Brecht appears to be using it purely descriptively, in much the same way the full naming formula, 'X, ben Y' is typically used within Hebrew narrative; that is,

---

39. So Robert Gordon, *I & II Samuel* (Exeter: Paternoster Press, 1986), 169, and David Firth, *1 & 2 Samuel* (Nottingham: Apollos, 2009), 227. On naming conventions in Hebrew narrative including in relation to David, see David J. A. Clines, 'X, X BEN Y, BEN Y: Personal names in Hebrew Narrative Style', *VT* 22 (1972): 266–87.

40. Berlin, *Poetics*, 37.

as a simple means of introduction.⁴¹ Accordingly, near the beginning of the scene, Brecht has **The Man** use this formula to allow David (who has been present on stage but silent) to enter the action and dialogue. Later, the entering crowd reuses the formula to do the same. Brecht's concession to 'biblical' style/convention here is noteworthy in part because he is so little bound by it in the dialogue of the *David* fragments generally.

Far more striking than the appearance of the 'son of Jesse' on the lips of minor characters is the fact that it heralds Brecht's otherwise unexpected introduction of Jesse as a character at the climax of B10. David has just finished telling his 'hard fable' of the pine tree and the briar when Jesse's off-stage approach is signalled by his whistling. Here then is the first clue that Brecht's Jesse will be unlike the biblical one in various ways: in the biblical account, Jesse goes nowhere. He is very much ensconced in Bethlehem and as the patriarch, he is the one who sends David or sends someone to fetch him (1 Sam. 16.12). By contrast, in Brecht's B10, Jesse is apparently forced to come and collect David himself from wherever this scene is set, clearly neither the battlefront, nor with the sheep, nor Bethlehem. The dialogue between Jesse and David makes it clear that the reason Brecht's Jesse has gone to collect David is because he wants him to go to war ('there is a war going on in your homeland'; 'In rain you don't go to war, eh?'; 'your mother is waiting for you with your iron armour, boy'). In 1 Samuel, it is true that Eliab suspects – and David's actions eventually confirm – that David's trip to the Israelite battlefront is not merely to deliver victuals and return with news. However, according to the text, these are the expressed purposes for which Jesse has sent David (though his ultimate or ulterior motives are more difficult to determine). Thus Jesse's active facilitation of his son's enlistment in Brecht's fragments would seem to constitute a departure from the biblical tradition, where the biblical Jesse may be seen as keeping his son, David, away from the war which has taken his three elder sons away from Bethlehem.⁴²

---

41. As Clines, 'Personal Names', 266, notes, the full formula is used to introduce both a new character within a narrative and a character's appearance in a new scene, but also when a speaker mentions a character for the first time.

42. Admittedly, it is impossible to judge the enthusiasm of Brecht's Jesse for the recruitment of his son (perhaps, indeed, Saul's men are requiring Jesse's sons of him).

In Brecht's *David*, Jesse is not merely concerned at David's disinterest in the battlefront, he is also irked by David's absence from the homefront.

Jesse

You even want to eat my roof and the stove too? Should I slaughter the lamb for you, that you let fall into the gorge? Eh? Should your old, sick father muck out the stables with his old hands, with your dirt under his nails, my dear son? Should your father walk through the fields in the slush, until there's blood in his shoes? Eh?

Clearly David's absence irritates Jesse at least in part because he perceives David to be neglecting his domestic duties. While Jesse's claims to have to 'muck out the stables' and 'walk through the fields in the slush' might be more suggestive of twentieth-century Germany than ancient Judah, Jesse's point is clear. Indeed, it is rather pressed home by Jesse's accusation that David has let a lamb 'fall into the gorge' – an indictment which takes aim at David's 'shepherding', the only domestic duty (apart from acting as envoy) with which David is associated in the biblical tradition. That the biblical David takes his shepherding seriously seems to be underlined first by the biblical narrator – who notes that David leaves the sheep with a keeper (*šōmēr*) before embarking for the battle lines (1 Sam. 17.20) – and especially by David's own efforts to persuade Saul that he possesses the necessary courage and combat skills to tackle Goliath:

But David said to Saul, 'Your servant used to keep sheep for his father; and whenever a lion or a bear came, and took a lamb from the flock, I went after it and struck it down, rescuing the lamb from its mouth; and if it turned against me, I would catch it by the jaw, strike it down, and kill it.' (1 Sam. 17.34-35)

If, as seems likely, Brecht has David's biblical reputation for shepherding in mind, then Jesse's accusation that David has let a lamb fall into a gorge may suggest an allegation of cowardice, but more likely simply one of incompetence. The sting in the tail of Jesse's accusation is his sarcastic offer to go ahead and kill the very lamb which has been injured through David's neglect. The language here – 'Should I slaughter the lamb for you?/*Soll ich das Lamm für dich schlachten?*' – bears a striking resemblance to that of Luke 15.27 where the older brother of the prodigal son learns that 'your father has slaughtered the fatted calf/*dein Vater hat ein gemästet Kalb geschlachtet*' (Luther's Bible, 1912). However, the sarcasm of Jesse's offer suggests that while Brecht's David may be a prodigal, his Jesse is by no means the *pater* of the Lukan parable.

If, as we've noted above, the biblical tradition may report Jesse's old age to imply his need of David's help, Brecht's reference to Jesse's old age may well do the same in part, but seems also to be doing considerably more. Jesse's own insistence that he is 'old' in the speech cited above is echoed by others later in the scene who refer to Jesse as an 'old honoured skin'.[43] The Brechtian David's clear refusal to acknowledge Jesse as either old or perhaps merely honoured sits uncomfortably with the biblical exhortation to 'honour one's father and mother'. However, what David's dishonouring of Jesse does sit much more comfortably with is the characterisation of David by others in this scene as 'teaching the old ones', which appears to be seen by them in terms of 'mocking the greybeards'.

While the intersection of Jesse's character-space with David's within B10 highlights a disrespect for Jesse for which the reader is unprepared by the biblical tradition, the sarcasm and general attitude of Brecht's Jesse toward David himself is equally noteworthy. Having become aware of David's attempt to hide himself when he heard his father coming, Jesse launches a blistering condemnation of David:

Jesse

Will I see you soon, eh, you pig? Were you just coming home? You had a few things to take care of, eh? Arrange yourselves around me, eh? You bloody bag of lies.

In having his Jesse denounce David as a 'pig', Brecht reveals his ignorance of (or simply disinterest in) the biblical preference for 'dog' as the insult of choice (2 Sam. 16.9). Nevertheless, the heart of Jesse's accusation is that the Brechtian David is lying to both his friends and his father in order to avoid Jesse. Interestingly, the angry accusation of his brother Eliab that David's delivery of food is merely a pretense for seeing the battlefront (1 Sam. 17.28) similarly alleges David's disingenuousness. While this latter tradition may have inspired Brecht at this point, it is worth noting that the allegation here is levelled by David's father rather than his brother, and that the substance of it is that David is avoiding home, rather than rushing to the war. If Brecht's Jesse here disparages his son's integrity, he also casts aspersions on his character by calling him a 'gobshite', even

---

43. For the German idiom which lies behind this translation, see above p. 66.

if an 'exceptionally clever' one.[44] Not satisfied with hurling invective at David, we see the Brechtian Jesse also resorting to throwing a stone at him. When the latter fails to find its mark, David in turn has the opportunity to ridicule his father, and Jesse the chance to wish that his own aim with the stone had been truer. We are perhaps meant to appreciate the irony that while Jesse fails to find the mark with his stone, David will shortly become famous for launching stones which will lay Goliath low (to which David's concluding reference to his slingshot alludes).

If Brecht's portrait of Jesse is considerably different from, and fuller than, the one offered by 1 Samuel, we have already seen that Jesse's interactions with David also contribute significantly to the characterisation of the latter. While a full picture of Brecht's David (even in B10) depends on an analysis of his interactions with others, a picture begins to emerge of David as reluctant to go to war but also desperate to be away from home, at loggerheads with his father, but still perhaps dependent in some ways on Jesse's support. Indeed, the state of their relationship is summed up nicely by its final exchanges:

Jesse

Don't suck up to them, young man! Don't start any funny business here, I'm not letting you out of my sight, don't even try it! You can't resist, your mother is waiting for you with your iron armour, boy.

He turns right around and goes to the rear. David follows him lazily and reluctantly from some distance. He mumbles.

David

I'm not putting on any armour. But I'll take my slingshot with me!

They disappear. The crowd laughs.

Evidently David seeks to get the last word and perhaps the last laugh, but it is unclear whether the crowd's laughter is at David's attempt at a joke or the infantilising of David in these final exchanges. Indeed, however reluctantly and lazily and at whatever distance David follows Jesse, and however much he mumbles his dissent, the fact that David is brought to heel by his father and disappears out of sight suggests that in terms of the power dynamics, the last laugh in this scene belongs not to David, but Jesse.

44. For the German underlying this relatively free translation, see above p. 66.

While Brecht's Jesse and his interactions with David suggest the young playwright's awareness and adaptation of biblical traditions in 1 Samuel, the distinctive way in which the figures are drawn and the relationship rendered may suggest that Brecht's imagination here was fired by more than simply the Bible. The eulogistic tone of Brecht's 'Ode to my father' and a letter from November 1919 have persuaded some biographers to offer a glowing portrait of Brecht's relationship with his father,[45] but the congratulatory tone of the letter can hardly be separated from Brecht's reason for writing, namely: to persuade his father to take Brecht's young son into the family home; and even then, the letter still acknowledges political differences between him and his father. While there is little doubt that Berthold was supportive of his son in numerous ways, the picture of their relationship which emerges from the diaries in 1920–1921 suggests something slightly more (though not abnormally) tense than is sometimes allowed. For instance, in April of 1921, Brecht reports a 'great row' with his father over the Eberle libel affair,[46] while the following month, an entry appears to voice what is presented as his father's view of him: 'And here am I with my hands among papers or in my pockets, scribbling stuff no-one will buy, smoking, thinking about my child and not earning anything. Just loafing around.'[47] Less than a month later, a conversation he reports between him and his father again on the subject of Frank leads Brecht to the conclusion that in his father's view, all he does is 'cook up films and fritter myself away'.[48] Indeed, Brecht's perception of his father's frustration with his own failure to contribute and his continuing dependence on him may already be detected in an entry from the previous Autumn (11 September 1920) while he was working on *David:*

> He'd like to know what I've done for the community so far, absolutely nothing at all. In five years' time I'll still not have my first medical degree. High time I did a proper job of work. My literary achievements in his personal view amount to nothing at all… So far I haven't earned anything. We are spongers, the last human beings not to be servants. Baal and Karamazov are of our company.[49]

45. While Parker, *Bertolt Brecht*, 129, does note the letter's acknowledgement of differences between father and son, his clearly positive evaluation of the relationship seems unduly influenced by his juxtaposition of it with the poisoned relationship between Franz Kafka and his father, made famous by the former's letter to the latter at almost exactly the same time.
46. *BFA* 26, 203; Eng.: Brecht, *Diaries*, 87 (17 April 1921).
47. *BFA* 26, 213; Eng.: Brecht, *Diaries*, 97 (15 May 1921).
48. *BFA* 26, 229; Eng.: Brecht, *Diaries*, 111 (4 June 1921).
49. *BFA* 26, 167; Eng.: Brecht, *Diaries*, 49.

Brecht's inclusion of himself with Baal in the company of spongers discloses his own view of the blurred lines between his own life and those of his characters. Moreover, the accusations which we have seen Brecht's Jesse make against his son David – of neglecting domestic duties, expecting his father's charity and generally misspending his youth – all suggest that Brecht's David might easily have been included in this company of spongers, at least in his father's view.

However similar their views of their sons may be in some ways, where Jesse and Berthold part company decisively is with respect to their sons' involvement in the 'war effort'. While Jesse's belated appearance to collect David in B10 appears to be motivated by his desire to ensure his participation in the war against the Philistines, it is well known that Berthold actively intervened not once but twice to seek the deferral of his son's conscription in World War I based on his medical studies.[50]

If this chapter has pointed toward a Brechtian willingness to re-write – at times radically – comparatively minor characters in the biblical traditions associated with David, we will see in the next chapter that Brecht feels equally free to do so when tackling the protagonists of the latter chapters of 1 Samuel: Jonathan, Saul and David himself.

---

50. Werner Frisch and K. W. Obermeier, *Brecht in Augsburg: Erinnerungen, Dokumente, Fotos* (Berlin and Weimar: Aufbau, 1998), 173; also see discussion in Parker, *Bertolt Brecht*, 108–10.

Chapter 3

BRECHT'S *DAVID* AND THE BIBLICAL DAVID:
JONATHAN, SAUL AND DAVID

Jonathan

In comparison with Jesse, the character of Saul's son Jonathan enjoys a rather fuller development in the pages of 1 Samuel, beginning in chapter 13. Given command of a thousand men in Gibeah by his father, Jonathan proceeds to launch an attack on a garrison of Philistines. The public 'credit' for the military intervention is given to Saul, but when it leads to Israel being a 'stench' to the Philistines, and when Saul's mustering of a larger force eventually leads to a confrontation with the prophet Samuel that costs Saul the crown, the reader may wonder whether Jonathan's bold intervention should be understood as being welcomed by his father after all, let alone sanctioned by him.[1] Despite the erosion of the military forces under Saul's command, however, Jonathan is depicted as remaining with his father, and the beginning of 1 Samuel 14 sees him launch yet another attack against the Philistines, with the narrator noting explicitly this time both that Jonathan 'did not tell his father' (14.1) and that the rest of the people were similarly in the dark (v. 3) regarding his initiative. Jonathan's careful invocation of the divine in the process (vv. 6, 10, 12), the apparently daring and improbable success of the assault and the people's recognition that it served as a catalyst for a great victory over the Philistines, are undoubtedly meant to leave the reader with a very fine

---

1. For a reading of 1 Sam. 14 which sees Jonathan compared favourably with his father, see David Jobling, 'Saul's Fall and Jonathan's Rise', *JBL* 95, no. 3 (1976): 367–76; for a contrary approach which finds in Saul's near-killing of his son a favourable comparison with Abraham's near-sacrifice of his own son Isaac, see Marsha White, 'Saul and Jonathan in 1 Samuel 1 and 14', in *Saul in Story and Tradition*, ed. Carl Ehrlich and Marsha White (Tübingen: Mohr Siebeck, 2006), 119–38.

impression of Saul's son as a military leader. While the end of the chapter will emphasise Saul's own military exploits, the rather paler impression left by Saul in this episode is suggested by the judgement – shared by the narrator (v. 24), Jonathan (vv. 29-30) and the people (v. 45) – that Saul's oath forbidding the people to eat until he was avenged on the Philistines (v. 24) was ill-advised. Moreover, Saul's insistence that Jonathan should die for violating his vow, despite Jonathan's ignorance of it, offers a further indication that the relationship between father and son is far from ideal and plagued by poor communication.[2]

Such difficulties are laid bare and undoubtedly exacerbated by the introduction of David into the narrative of 1 Samuel. At the beginning of chapter 18, after Saul has summoned David following his defeat of Goliath, the reader is informed that Jonathan loves David and binds his soul to David's (vv. 1, 3), to the extent that he makes a covenant with him (v. 3) and marks it with the gifting to David of his robe, armour, sword, bow and belt (v. 4). At the beginning of the following chapter (19), Jonathan's delight in David (v. 1) leads him to mount a spirited defence of David in the face of his father Saul's attempts to eliminate him (vv. 1-7). But the 'reprieve' Jonathan secures for David (v. 7) is short-lived and eventually serves to expose David to Saul's further efforts to kill him. Jonathan's covenant with David and commitment to serve him and thwart his father is underlined at the beginning of the following chapter (20) where he agrees to David's request to test Saul's feelings toward David. Perhaps suspecting that Saul's murderous intentions and the ascent of David in spite of them will eventually put Jonathan and his descendants at risk, the narrator notes Jonathan's success in eliciting a vow of David's commitment to him, in keeping with his own to the son of Jesse (vv. 14-17).[3] Saul's anger at his son's devotion to David and efforts to kill Jonathan for it prompts Jonathan's own anger: 'for he was grieved for David, and because his father had disgraced him' (v. 34). Indeed, the narrator signals a similar strength of emotion and the depth of their mutual devotion when Jonathan meets David to confirm Saul's hatred of him.

> As soon as the boy had gone, David rose from beside the stone heap and prostrated himself with his face to the ground. He bowed three times, and they kissed each other, and wept with each other; David wept the more. (1 Sam. 20.41)

---

2. See Gordon, *I & II Samuel*, 136 and 140.

3. The narrator's earlier observations of Jonathan's love for David (18.1, 3) makes it likely that the further note in 20.17 that 'he loved him as he loved his own life' should be read as Jonathan's love for David (though the converse is not impossible).

A renewing of their covenant in a final brief meeting in chapter 23 (vv. 16-18) and David's lamenting of the death of Jonathan, as one whose love 'was wonderful, passing the love of women' (v. 26), cements the reader's perception of the depth and emotion of Jonathan's bond with David and has led to considerable scholarly discussion of the nature of their relationship, especially in recent years.

Prompted by resonances between the description of David and Jonathan's relationship and the language of the erotic (albeit heterosexual) poetry found in Song of Songs, some have been persuaded that David and Jonathan's relationship is presented in Samuel as implying a homoerotic, or indeed homosexual, relationship.[4] There is no doubt that, taken together, the intensity of the emotional language and demonstrations of affection/ devotion encountered in descriptions of David and Jonathan's relationship are not typical of relationships between males in the Hebrew Bible. Moreover, it is also true that David's relationship with Jonathan seems to be closer and more meaningful to David than David's relationship with his own wife (and Jonathan's sister) Michal.[5] Yet, as has been observed by others, comparison with other texts within the Hebrew Bible suggests that taken singly, such emotion and demonstrations are compatible with an unusually close or intense friendship between men.[6] Indeed, that David and Jonathan's friendship might be portrayed as needing to be especially close or intense seems entirely plausible, given the mortal danger posed

---

4. See, for instance, Tom Horner, *Jonathan Loved David: Homosexuality in Biblical Times* (Philadelphia: Westminster Press, 1978), 26–39 and Silvia Schroer and Thomas Staubli, 'Saul, David und Jonathan – eine Dreiecksgeschichte? Ein Beitrag zum Thema "Homosexualität" im ersten Testament', *Bibel und Kirche* 51 (1996): 15–22 (Eng. trans., 'Saul, David and Jonathan – the Story of a Triangle?', in *A Feminist Companion to Samuel and Kings*, ed. Athalya Brenner [Sheffield: Sheffield Academic Press, 2000], 22–36).

5. This is a point noted by many, including Susan Ackerman, *When Heroes Love: The Ambiguity of Eros in the Stories of Gilgamesh and David* (New York: Columbia University Press, 2005), 177–81, who interprets it as reinforcing an eroticised interpretation of David's relationship with Jonathan, and Markus Zehnder, 'Observations on the Relationship between David and Jonathan and the Debate on Homosexuality', *WTJ* 69 (2007): 157–60, who acknowledges several parallels but does not come to the same conclusion.

6. See most prominently, Zehnder, 'Observations'. For a more recent reading of the relationship between David and Jonathan which comes to this conclusion see Jonathan Rowe, *Sons or Lovers: An Interpretation of David and Jonathan's Friendship* (London: Bloomsbury, 2012).

to both of them by Saul's murderous efforts to come between them. While the Hebrew Bible's generally disapproving view of male–male sexual activity and its lack of other examples of sanctioned same-sex relationships make it quite unlikely that David and Jonathan's relationship in 1 Samuel was written (or read) in antiquity as implying homoeroticism, let alone homosexuality, there is no doubt that the relationship between David and Jonathan offered in 1 Samuel sits very comfortably with examples of homosociality in the literature of the ancient world.[7]

Whatever the precise nature of David's relationship with Jonathan within 1 Samuel, given Brecht's primary interest in David, it is not surprising that Jonathan's military career prior to his introduction to David finds no place in Brecht's surviving fragments. However, the synopses of scenes offered in A7 and A8 offer illustrations of Brecht's thinking about Jonathan's place in the narratives about David. In one such scheme, A7, 'Jonathan tells Saul of David, who is returning from his victory over Goliath. Covenant between him and Jonathan.' While in 1 Sam. 17.55-58, it is Abner rather than Jonathan who facilitates the post-Goliath encounter between Saul and David, Brecht's preference for Jonathan over Abner here may well be explained in part by a desire to focus on David and the main players (Jonathan and Saul) at the expense of comparatively 'minor' characters like Abner, who is left unmentioned.[8] Indeed, Brecht may also have been encouraged to focus on Jonathan here rather than Abner by 1 Sam. 18.1's insistence that Jonathan was present at this point and that this was the catalyst for their covenant, narrated in the verses which follow, as we have seen above. That Brecht characterises this covenant between David and Jonathan as a *Bund* ('Covenant') reflects Luther's interpretation of the Hebrew *bĕrît* ('Und Jonathan und David machten einen Bund miteinander', 1 Sam. 18.3; Luther's Bible, 1912) in language which emphasises the formal/legal/political character of the agreement between David and Jonathan – a feature that has been widely appreciated by many

---

7. The parallel to the David and Jonathan relationship of 1 Samuel cited most often is that of Gilgamesh with Enkidu from the Mesopotamian epic tradition. Ackerman, in *When Heroes Love*, offers an insightful reading of both traditions, but seems to overestimate the eroticisation of the David and Jonathan relationship in 1 Samuel and thus the dissonance between it and what she rightly acknowledges is the wider biblical tradition's antipathy toward homoeroticism. For more on the homoerotic reception of Jonathan and David in German-language adaptations of the late nineteenth and early twentieth centuries, see Chapter 4 below, pp. 142–58.

8. For more on the character of Abner in the biblical tradition, see Shepherd, 'Knowing Abner'.

readers of the biblical tradition.[9] Of course, the synopsis of scenes gives little indication of how the forming of such an alliance might have been realised by Brecht within the dramatic action.

While the fourth scene projected in A7 – 'David's farewell from Jonathan' – might reflect the account of their final meeting and covenant noted briefly in 1 Sam. 23.16-18, the fact that Brecht's scene comes hard on the heels of a third listed only as 'Saul's spear-throw' strongly suggests that Brecht has in mind the much fuller and more emotionally inflected account of Jonathan and David's covenant-making offered earlier in 1 Samuel 20. Yet again, there is little indication of how such a scene might have been worked out, nor of the penultimate scene of A7 listed as 'Jonathan goes into battle' (the final one being: 'David becomes king'). That it is Jonathan who enters the fray in Brecht's penultimate scene rather than Saul (who accompanies him in the biblical tradition) certainly reflects A7's earlier interest in Jonathan, though the absence of any specific mention of David's lament (2 Sam. 1.17, 27) for Jonathan (let alone Saul) warns against assuming too much from the unexpected focus on Jonathan's going into (and presumably dying in) battle.

If Jonathan's inclusion at the beginning, middle and end of A7 (and in the opening of A8) hints at Brecht's appreciation of the dramatic potential of Jonathan's character-space intersecting with David's, it is clear that both synopses of scenes are dominated by Saul's relationship to David and hew relatively close to the biblical tradition. It is thus all the more interesting that whereas in B10, Saul is mentioned but does not appear as a character, Jonathan enjoys considerable prominence.

The initial reference to Jonathan is made by the First Man early in B10, when he refers (evidently admiringly) to both Saul and his son as 'eagles'.[10] After David is called upon to pass judgement on the assault on the beggar, Brecht's Jonathan arrives on the scene with an officer and soldiers in tow. Responding to his officer's hasty and mistaken assessment of the situation, Jonathan turns to David and asks him 'What happened?' – the first of a series of questions posed by Jonathan to David in the dialogue which follows. In the biblical tradition, while the Jonathan of 1 Samuel 14 is undoubtedly a man of action, he is certainly not lost for words, most of which he uses to issue commands to his armour-bearer

---

9. For the political character of this covenant, see the literature cited by Zehnder in 'Observations' (162–6), where he offers a succinct, if rather polemical, summary of the evidence.

10. For Brecht's probable awareness of 1 Sam. 1.23, see the note on the translation (Chapter 1, p. 48) above.

(1 Sam. 14.1, 6, 8, 12) prior to the appearance of David and the concluding of their covenant.[11] Having first informed David of his father's plans to eliminate him and then promised to keep him informed in 19.2-3, the biblical Jonathan in the following chapter (20) asks David a variety of questions as they hatch their plan for Jonathan to confirm Saul's feelings toward David (see above). What is immediately obvious from Jonathan's questions is that they are rhetorical. Thus, in responding to David's own rhetorical question regarding what wrong David has done to deserve Saul's murderous ire (v. 1), Jonathan responds in kind:

> He said to him, 'Far from it! You shall not die. My father does nothing either great or small without disclosing it to me; and why should my father hide this from me? Never!' (1 Sam. 20.2)

While the biblical Jonathan here marks the rhetorical character of his question by answering it himself, his further questions in vv. 9 and 12 are no less rhetorical.[12] Indeed, in the face of David's considerable doubts regarding his own survival, Jonathan's rhetorical questions underline the passion of his effort to persuade David of Jonathan's ability and inclination to gauge his father's attitude toward David and disclose it to his friend.

That the dynamics are rather different in Brecht's scene is made clear by the questions posed by Jonathan to David in B10. First, the already liberal use Jonathan makes of questions in the biblical narrative pales in comparison to what we see in B10. Indeed, all but one of Jonathan's contribution to the dialogue end with (and often consist solely of) a question, the first of which ('What happened?') frames those that follow as Jonathan's investigation of the initial fracas between the man and the beggar, as well as his interrogation of David as a witness to it. Yet Jonathan's efforts to get to the bottom of things are immediately complicated by the cryptic nature of David's answers. In response to the question of what happened, David stares at the sky, and when pressed by Jonathan's officer, asks whether

---

11. He also criticises his father's vow in 14.29-30 and admits in v. 43 that he has violated it.

12. 1 Sam. 20.9: 'Jonathan said, "Far be it from you! If I knew that it was decided by my father that evil should come upon you, would I not tell you?"' and 1 Sam. 20.12: 'Jonathan said to David, "By the LORD, the God of Israel! When I have sounded out my father, about this time tomorrow, or on the third day, if he is well disposed toward David, shall I not then send and disclose it to you?"' Indeed, even Jonathan's question of the boy is rhetorical: 'When the boy came to the place where Jonathan's arrow had fallen, Jonathan called after the boy and said, "Is the arrow not beyond you?"' (1 Sam. 20.37).

Jonathan has ever studied a flying dove. This prompts two questions from Jonathan about doves, before Jonathan returns to the matter at hand by asking 'What kind of man is this beggar?' Finally, Brecht's David appears to offer a straightforward answer: 'He is quarrelsome, lazy, greedy and philosophical', but in response to Jonathan's query regarding the violence, David offers a curious story about a 'friend, Joshua' and a vineyard which proves amusing to the crowd and apparently persuades Jonathan to send his officer back to Saul and release the beggar. Jonathan, however, remains and continues his investigation of what sparked the confrontation in the first place, by resuming his questioning of David, who suggests that he corrected the 'old man' because he had the wrong opinion. Jonathan then solicits David's opinion regarding the 'warlike people' and, prompted by his perception of David's ambivalence, proceeds to interrogate David's disinterest in military service (armour is 'too heavy. It's iron.') and resentment of the bother of fighting Philistines. When Jonathan queries what David does apart from (in David's own words) 'sound strong', it is the beggars who insist that David is lazy, and when David admits to Jonathan that one shouldn't be, they insist that David said just the opposite the previous day, at which point Jonathan exits, responding to his father's call to arms to fight the Philistines.

In sharp contrast to 1 Samuel 20, the questions asked by Brecht's Jonathan are clearly not rhetorical but intended to elicit information, in part about the fracas, but increasingly about who Brecht's David is and why he does what he does. Indeed, whereas 1 Samuel 20 offers a glimpse of a well-developed and passionate relationship between David and Jonathan, in B10 the third beggar's belated introduction of 'David, the son of Jesse' to Jonathan makes clear that this is their first encounter in the Brechtian drama.[13] If the project had progressed, Brecht might well have developed Jonathan's character and his relationship with David further, but on the basis of the extant fragments, Brecht's Jonathan displays little of the passionate commitment to David demonstrated by his biblical counterpart. Indeed, while the biblical Jonathan does remain in the shadow of David after the latter's emergence and plays a much more minor part in the narrative than his father Saul, the role of Brecht's Jonathan in B10 is more minor still. Moreover, while Brecht's Jonathan issues commands, his insistence that he and his father need silence to think about how to respond to the Philistine incursion, as well as his evident need to remind the crowd that 'I am Jonathan!', may hint at Brecht's deprecation of

---

13. This scene does not appear to correspond to those listed in A7 or A8. Certainly the titles of A8's first scene, 'David and Jonathan', hardly seems adequate for a scene of the complexity of B10.

Jonathan. If so, then the crowd's response 'Hail, Jonathan! Hail, Jonathan, who has killed 500!' may well have been intended by Brecht as ironic, given that in the biblical tradition the women of Israel sing that 'Saul has killed his thousands and David his tens of thousands' (1 Sam. 18.7). In any case, Brecht's casting of Jonathan in the role of investigative officer encountering a rather curious witness in David highlights the extent to which, in comparison with the biblical tradition, Brecht's Jonathan serves as 'agent' in service not so much of the plot, but rather of Brecht's characterisation of David in B10. Like David's interactions with the Brechtian Jesse, his exchange with Brecht's Jonathan suggests a perception of David by others as not only work-shy and war-shy, but also full of opinions (wise and otherwise) as well as contradictions, general cheekiness and outright impudence.

Saul

The story of Saul's anointing, reign and demise occupies the bulk of 1 Samuel, running as it does from Saul's introduction in 1 Sam. 9.2 to the account of his death in the final chapter of the book (31). As with Jonathan, however, Brecht's dramatic interest in Saul arises in conjunction with the intersection of his character-space with David's beginning in ch. 16, where, as we've noted above in our discussion of Jesse, King Saul finds himself beset by a troubling/evil spirit and sends for David to come and play for him (16.19), the latter having been recommended by the king's courtiers (v. 18). As vv. 21-23 makes clear, David the musician proves an immediate hit with Saul:

> And David came to Saul, and entered his service. Saul loved him greatly, and he became his armor-bearer. Saul sent to Jesse, saying, 'Let David remain in my service, for he has found favor in my sight'. And whenever the evil spirit from God came upon Saul, David took the lyre and played it with his hand, and Saul would be relieved and feel better, and the evil spirit would depart from him. (1 Sam. 16.21-23)

While neither the Hebrew grammar nor the syntax of v. 21 makes it clear who loves whom, most commentators conclude that it is Saul who loves David (so the NRSV above).[14] Such a conclusion is perhaps encouraged

---

14. So, for example, Firth, *1 & 2 Samuel*, 188, and J. P. Fokkelman, *Narrative Art and Poetry in the Books of Samuel: Interpretation Based on Stylistic and Structural Analysis, Vol. 2: The Crossing Fates (I Sam. 13–31 and II Sam. 1)* (Assen: Van Gorcum, 1986), 139.

by the narrator's insistence elsewhere that love for David seems to run in Saul's family.[15] Thus David is not only loved by Saul's son Jonathan (as we have seen, 18.1, 3 cf. also 1 Sam. 20.17; 2 Sam. 1.26), but also by Saul's daughter (and David's sometime wife) Michal (18.20, 28).[16] What is rarely commented upon, however, is that while Saul's son and daughter may love David, their father Saul loves David greatly (*wayye'ĕhābēhû mĕ'ōd*, v. 21).[17] Despite the 'greatness' of Saul's love for David noted here, commentators have shown little inclination to speculate regarding whether Saul's love was amorous or not,[18] perhaps because Saul's love for David is mentioned only here and lacks the emotional overtones found in relation to Jonathan. Or indeed perhaps it is because Saul's love for David gives way to murderous jealousy, when David's slaying of Goliath and eventual appointment over the army leads to military success and adulation beyond that afforded even the king:

> And the women sang to one another as they made merry, 'Saul has killed his thousands, and David his ten thousands'. Saul was very angry, for this saying displeased him. He said, 'They have ascribed to David ten thousands, and to me they have ascribed thousands; what more can he have but the kingdom?' So Saul eyed David from that day on. The next day an evil spirit from God rushed upon Saul, and he raved within his house, while David was playing the lyre, as he did day by day. Saul had his spear in his hand; and Saul threw the spear, for he thought, 'I will pin David to the wall'. But David eluded him twice. Saul was afraid of David, because the LORD was with him but had departed from Saul. (1 Sam. 18.7-12)

The fact that Brecht's only other developed scene among the fragments, 'Saul and David' (B9), not only opens with Saul's references to killing 'a thousand' and David killing 'ten thousand' (v. 9) but also closes with Saul throwing his spear at David, strongly suggests that Brecht associated

---

15. Keith Bodner, *1 Samuel: A Narrative Commentary* (Sheffield: Sheffield Phoenix Press, 2008), 174.

16. Indeed, he is also loved by all Israel and Judah (1 Sam. 18.16).

17. Fokkelman, *The Crossing Fates*, 139, renders 'Saul loved him dearly'. Given his translation ('and he loved him greatly') Firth's omission of 'greatly' (*1 & 2 Samuel*, 188) in his comments on the ambiguity of 'and he loved him' seems unlikely to be intentional.

18. J. A. Thompson, 'The Significance of the Verb *Love* in the David–Jonathan Narratives in 1 Samuel', *VT* 24 (1974): 335, who argues for the political import of the verb *'ahab* in these narratives generally, only suspects that the narrator here is 'preparing us for the later political use of the term'. See, however, the demurral of Gordon, *I & II Samuel*, 153.

it with the narrative moment described in verses 10-11 above. As we will see below, in this scene the bulk of Brecht's characterisation of Saul may be found in Saul's own words. By contrast, in B10, which was evidently intended to precede B9, it falls to others to characterise Saul, who does not appear himself at all. Indeed, in the opening exchanges of B10, Saul's military handling of the Philistines becomes a point of dispute, with the opinion being offered that things (including Saul) were better in the old days than now. In fact, while Brecht doesn't reference any of them, differences of opinion regarding Saul's merits are easily found within the biblical tradition.[19] Indeed, if Brecht's scene includes the comic deprecation of Jonathan (see above), then it may do so of Saul as well when Jonathan insists on silence so that Saul can 'think'. Finally, we recall at the end of the scene that Brecht's Saul is reported as seeking to muster the people for war against the Philistines. While the biblical tradition witnesses to Saul's difficulties in gathering troops at other points (see 1 Sam. 13), Saul has no difficulties in 1 Sam. 17.1 in marshalling Israel to fight the Philistines (before the spectre of Goliath is raised). By contrast, the efforts of Brecht's Saul to do so in B10 are wilfully obstructed by Brecht's David (see below).

Given how little B10 offers in relation to Saul, the uninitiated reader of the fragments is ill-prepared for the king's pre-eminent role in B9, in which David's sings to Saul. Whereas 1 Sam. 18.10 merely describes David's playing of the lyre in passing, Brecht's 'corresponding' scene runs to several pages, in part because it includes the lyrics of the song sung by Brecht's David. Of course, the biblical tradition in 1 Samuel offers no suggestion that David *sang* to Saul in private, in addition to, or while, playing for him. However, the young Brecht was very much aware of David's fame as a composer of Psalms and also seemingly of David's lament *for* Saul (and Jonathan) following their deaths (2 Sam. 1.17-18) – if the ninth and final scene of A8 'Saul dying and David' is any indication. As we will see below, the song which Brecht's David sings has more in common with his own 'Psalms' (as he referred to some of his own songs composed at this time) than those found in the biblical Psalms.

In Saul's opening speech in B9, while he acknowledges that David is the 'victor' and that the public is crediting David with ten times the military triumphs of the king, the response of Brecht's Saul is not rage, but a kind of resignation:

19. See for instance and most obviously, the affirmation of and devotion to Saul reported in 1 Sam. 10.19, 26 followed immediately by his denunciation by others (v. 27).

Saul

And about the victory: I don't care. They say I killed a thousand. You have ten thousand, they say, a thousand are nothing anymore, times move on. But I think: it's better to kill a thousand and have peace, than if you have to kill ten thousand to win. That'll give you a lean face and bad sleep, too.

Whether the peace which Saul claims to enjoy is still in his possession by the end of the scene may be doubted, but even here his claims to not care are gently undercut by his insistence that he is better off than David. If Brecht's Saul appears to take less umbrage than his biblical counterpart at the celebration of David's military success, it is nevertheless not long before Brecht's David also feels the need to emulate his biblical counterpart by offering Saul a song.

Before David can begin, however, Brecht's Saul interrogates his motives: 'But I want to know why you sing. Tell me!' In keeping with the biblical narrator's judgement, Brecht's David insists that he sings to soothe the king's spirit: 'Your face changes and your hands get calmer'. Yet, Saul's response to the song in Brecht's scene is noteworthy, characterised as much by incomprehension as by calm: after interrupting the song to claim that he doesn't understand it and that it makes no sense, Saul returns eventually to his initial judgement that David's song is in fact good, but concludes that the middle is weak. That the verbal sense of a song is largely dispensable and beside the point in fact squares with Saul's insistence earlier in the scene that he doesn't listen to the words, that the song itself, or perhaps merely the words, in Saul's own words, 'don't matter at all' to him – an ironically apt conclusion given that 1 Samuel offers no evidence, as we have seen, that the biblical David accompanied his music with lyrics.

Confirmation that Brecht saw Saul as making the running in this scene would seem to be supplied by his own description of it in his diaries: 'Saul delivers his potpourri and covers all the high and low points, and during the entire switchback ride David is sitting there cutting his nails'.[20] While David Jobling is satisfied with Brecht's assessment of his Saul in the scene, he argues that Brecht here underestimates his own David:

---

20. *BFA* 26, 130; Eng.: Brecht, *Diaries*, 13 (28 July 1920). Brecht uses the word *Berg-und-Tal-Bahn* which can refer to switchback trails, but it can also refer to a rollercoaster, possibly a more likely metaphor in the context; 'switchback ride' seems to be Willett having it both ways.

> Brecht intuitively makes David into a therapist with a convincing technique. He replies with Freudian brevity to Saul's long rambles. He encourages Saul not to analyse everything but to take what life offers. The longest and most 'directive' of these interventions reads: 'I don't know what you mean. Can't you lie in the sun or swim or kill enemies? Perhaps that would help' (10.131).[21]

There is no doubt that Brecht's David does wish to help Saul by singing to him, by offering him occasional suggestions and indeed by simply listening ('I think: it lightens your burden'), but Jobling's construal of Brecht's David in terms of a modern therapist (whether Freudian or otherwise) does underestimate the power dynamics between the two characters – dynamics signalled in the opening stage directions: '**Saul and David** enter. **Saul** has his arm on **David's** shoulder, and **David** has a lyre in his hands'. That Brecht's Saul as king will seek to possess David and that David will seek refuge in his lyre finds confirmation in the action at the end of the scene when David's parting sentiment – 'I am glad that my song revived you' – prompts Saul's attempt to harpoon the fleeing David with his spear. While Brecht's portrayal of Saul's mounting emotional and psychological instability is admittedly impressive, in light of the scene as a whole, the brevity of David's responses seems less a sign of therapeutic skill or instinct (so Jobling) than a symptom of David's profound discomfort and incomprehension.

Indeed, the theme of Saul and David's mutual incomprehension is reinforced repeatedly in the scene, as much by what David doesn't say as by what he does, as the scene continues to its conclusion. Saul's earlier insistence in the middle of the song that he doesn't understand what David is singing about finds an echo in the king's perception of David's own incomprehension, as Saul himself becomes increasingly impassioned. This in turn finds a further resonance in David's own insistence that he doesn't know what Saul wants, which accompanies his conspicuous silence when Saul declares his love for David. That Saul's love for Brecht's David is an erotic one seems evident, given that it not only makes Saul miserable (he is love-sick), but also requires secrecy and evidently makes David so uncomfortable that he flees. The homoerotic quality of Saul's feelings is reinforced by his insistence that his admission of love for David is daring because, in his words, 'I am a man and I said this'. It is also reinforced by Saul's admission that undressing himself before David somehow revived him, despite David's lack of response. When David does respond by

---

21. Jobling, 'David on the Brain', 236.

suggesting that it is not Saul's 'uncovering' of himself, but David's song which has revived the king, Saul's rage suggests that he prefers David's silence. Indeed, in seeking to justify either his rage or his love for David by quoting a line from David's own song as he throws his spear ('Strong are those who do there, you say, what they...MUST... You say!'), Saul suggests that he was listening to the words after all (despite his earlier assertions to the contrary). If so, David's silence and flight from Saul and his spear may well be read as reflecting his wish that Saul should have listened more closely to how the line of his song ends: 'Strong are those who do just what they must, and stronger those who make nothing of it'.

While we will have more to say about Brecht's characterisation of Saul and David's interaction later on in this volume, it is worth reflecting on how Brecht's scene relates to the biblical tradition.[22] First, it may be observed that while 1 Samuel is insistent that the spirit which besets Saul is divinely inflicted, the only other information furnished for the reader is that the spirit is a 'troubling/evil' one for Saul (1 Sam. 16.14, 15, 16, 23). If the eroticisation of the scene described above reflects a reading of the biblical tradition – and this is by no means certain – it certainly suggests a much more specific reading of this 'spirit'. Rather than 18.10-11, where Brecht seems to have imagined this scene to fit, the eroticisation of the scene itself seems more likely to depend on the initial and close conjunction of the arrival of the spirit in 1 Samuel 16 (see the passages above) with the narrator's comment in the immediate vicinity that 'Saul loved David very much' (1 Sam. 16.21). In the biblical tradition, it is clear that the troubling of Saul's spirit precedes the arrival of David and invites (though does not absolutely require) the interpretation that Saul's 'great love' for David might have arisen in part because of the latter's musical ability to banish the troubling spirit.

In Brecht's scene, by contrast, the binding together of Saul's mounting instability with his desire for David may suggest Brecht's pathologising of Saul's homoerotic desire, and perhaps even his theologising of it, if it implies that it is divinely instigated. Alternatively, Saul's increasing instability over the course of the scene may be, and is perhaps better, read as a symptom of unrequited homoerotic desire. In the presence of such desire, it is hardly surprising that while David's presence may offer a temporary balm, his reluctance and then eventual rejection of Saul's confession of erotic love pushes Saul over the edge.

22. While Nebel, *Harfe, Speer und Krone*, 254-5, notes both Saul's vulnerability and increasing agitation and David's presentation of David as knowing and dispassionate by comparison, this is the extent of the analysis which is offered.

While we will see in the next chapter that Brecht was not alone in reading homoerotic desire into the biblical tradition at this point, it is worth considering B9 briefly in light of the depiction of homoeroticism/sexuality seen in Brecht's other writings of the time, including 'The Ballad of Friendship', which appears to have been written either the same day or the day before he wrote his 'David before Saul'.[23] To a far greater extent than B9, the 'Ballad' is suffused with a homoerotic sensuality, introduced already in the first stanza's references to the two male characters' 'love for each other', 'with averted eye' and remaining 'as one many nights together', the latter of which serves (with variations) as the first of a two line refrain which is repeated throughout.[24] This homoerotic focus of the poem is underlined by a further reference to the intertwining of their bodies, but its allusion to the friends' experience of brothels in which they share the same woman suggests a sensual enjoyment of both sexes of which B9 predictably offers no hint, focused as it is on Saul's desire for David. While the 'Ballad' portrays a fondly remembered homoerotic/sexual 'friendship' which eventually runs its course (with one leaving the other behind on the desert island they have enjoyed together), the tonality of the poem is very different from Brecht's scene of 'David before Saul', in which the homosexual relationship is pre-empted entirely by the fact that Saul's homosexual desire is unrequited by David. Thus, if the 'Ballad' seems to be about homoerotic desire sated, B9 is about homoerotic desire frustrated.[25]

---

23. *BFA*, 11, 95–7; Eng.: Bertolt Brecht, *Poems, 1913–56*, ed. John Willett and Ralph Manheim (London: Eyre Methuen, 1976), 52–6. Brecht's diary indicates that the poem was written on 27 July 1920, when Zarek read his version of the 'David before Saul' scene to Brecht and the day before the latter wrote his own version of this scene (see below, pp. 147–9). It is a curious coincidence that Brecht's 'Ballade von der Freundschaft' was composed on the same day he heard Zarek's scene, a key motif of which is 'Freundschaft' (see pp. 145–8 below). What makes the coincidence still more curious is that Zarek was gay and Brecht knew it, as his diary entry from 3 March 1921 makes clear: 'And in the evening called on little Zarek, who's ill; male midwife to the Kammerspiele, boyfriend to that rubber-merchant (Neuhofer), who uses a french letter to masturbate. I took *David* along as he's quite "nice" and I'm fond of flowers, of whatever sort' (*BFA* 26, 181; Eng.: Brecht, *Diaries*, 66).

24. The operative term here is *vereint/vereinen* 'unite/d', whilst the reference to 'nights' seems to hint at an intimate and perhaps sexual union (cf. Gen. 2.24 and its reflexes in the NT [e.g. Mt. 19.5-6]).

25. While Brecht's short story 'Bargan gives up', published in 1921, is sometimes cited with 'The Ballad of Friendship' as further illustrating Brecht's interest in homosexual relationships, the lack of sensuousness or any sense of eroticism in

In *Baal*, which Brecht had been working on since 1918 and had not yet been published or performed in 1920–1921, homosexuality appears instead as one amongst many tokens of the eponymous protagonist's dissipation.[26] Of course, the poet's dissolute journey to self-destruction also includes encounters with women including Johanna, who commits suicide after Baal seduces her and Sophie, his mistress and bearer of his child, whom he abandons. But, like the friends of the 'Ballad', Baal's erotic appetites also include men, and here too the action is dominated by Baal's relationship with a male friend, Ekart.[27] Despite the eroticisation of their relationship, here neither man sails off into the sunset, and there are no fond memories. Instead, their love–hate relationship comes to an end in scene 18, which is strongly reminiscent of B9 in ways which do not appear to have been detected previously. Toward the end of the preceding scene (17), Ekart voices his suspicion to his friend, that Baal's prodigious poetic output suggests that he has not had a woman for a long time. In scene 18, Ekart is drinking with Johannes and Watzmann and confesses that despite Baal's evident failings, Ekart still loves the 'child' Baal.[28] Saul's use of similar language in B9 initially suggests Baal as a kind of David figure, and indeed when Baal enters the scene he proceeds to sing for Ekart and the others as David does in B9, even finding the tuning of his instrument wanting twice over, precisely as David does in B9. Just as David's song is judged 'good' by Saul, so too is Baal's song declared 'good' not by Ekart, but by Watzmann.[29] Indeed, at this point, Baal's behaviour begins instead to resemble Saul's behaviour toward

---

the story perhaps makes this more a case of homosociality (so Gerald Weales, in his review of Willett and Manheim's English edition of the stories in *The Sewanee Review* 92, no. 3 [1984]: lxv–lxviii).

26. We cannot discuss here Brecht's depiction of homosexuality in *In the Jungle* and *Edward II*, which were written slightly later. However, for discussion of them (though not *David* in any detail) in light of the wider treatment of male homosexuality in German theatre of the period see Wolf Borchers, 'Männliche Homosexualität in der Dramatik der Weimarer Republik' (PhD diss., Universität zu Köln, 2001), 233–45, 293–9. For discussion of these plays in light of queer theory, see K. Scott Baker, 'The "Nature" of Pleasure: Homosexuality as Trope in Early Brecht', in *Nach der Natur – After Nature*, ed. Franz-Josef Dieters et al. (Berlin: Rombach, 2010), 195–210, and for a still fuller treatment in this vein of both the plays and the poetry, see Ján Demčišák, *Queer Reading von Brechts Frühwerk* (Marburg: Tectum Verlag, 2012).

27. For the German versions see *BFA* 1, 18–173.

28. *BFA* 1, 131; Eng.: Bertolt Brecht, *Brecht Collected Plays: 1*, ed. John Willett and Ralph Manheim, trans. Peter Tegel (London: Bloomsbury, 1994), 52.

29. *BFA* 1, 133; Eng.: Brecht, *Brecht Collected Plays: 1*, 55.

David: after querying Ekart's feelings for him, Baal rises to his feet when Watzmann's lighting of the lamp reveals Ekart with the waitress on his lap and arm around him. Sensing Baal's displeasure, Ekart seeks to disentangle himself from the woman, dismissing it as nothing. As Baal's anger mounts, an increasingly desperate Ekart now seeks to pacify him with questions 'You're not jealous of her?', 'Why shouldn't I have women?', 'Are you my lover?'[30] Baal's only answer is to launch himself at Ekart and kill him with a knife. The differences are of course marked, but Baal's perception that his homoerotic feelings for Ekart are not reciprocated, and the violent assault which results, clearly has much in common with Saul's efforts to kill David with a spear when his own feelings for David are unrequited. While there is nothing to save Ekart from Baal's knife, Brecht may have felt at less liberty to dispatch David in B9, given 1 Samuel's insistence that David evades Saul's spear rather than falling victim to it.

What makes Brecht's realisation of 'David before Saul' in B9 all the more interesting is the way in which it may be seen to flesh out the skeletal synopses of schemes which also reference David's singing and Saul's spear. While A8's synopsis of scenes/action includes merely '4. Saul and David' and '5. David flees', in A7, the other synopsis relating to David's rise and Saul's demise, Brecht offers fuller details. In the latter, we find the following:

1

2
Jonathan tells Saul of David, who is returning from his victory over Goliath. Covenant between him and Jonathan. Saul grows fond of David. ('When I stretch a few guts over a piece of wood, it gives a strong sound and I can sing to it. Perhaps you'll fall asleep, when I sing to the guts?')[31]

3
Saul's spear-throw.

From the references to both David's return after defeating Goliath and his pact with Jonathan, it is clear that Brecht has the action found in 1 Samuel 17 and 18 in mind. While there it is not Jonathan who tells Saul of David, the fact that Brecht has him do so here is, again, likely to be explained by Brecht's abovementioned tendency to reduce the biblical cast to its main players.

30. *BFA* 1, 133; Eng.: Brecht, *Brecht Collected Plays: 1*, 55–6.
31. See note on A7 (pp. 28–9).

Here in A7, as in B9, David understands and articulates the therapeutic value of his music for Saul, and here too, as in both B9 and the biblical tradition, David's music gives way to Saul's violence. What is of course missing from the biblical tradition, but developed at considerable length in B9, is a dramatisation of *how* and *why* David's music yields to Saul's violence, with Brecht interpreting the latter as arising not because of David's music, but rather David's rejection of Saul's great (erotic) love for him (1 Sam. 16.21). Indeed, when it is recognised that David's music is as parenthetical here in A7 (indeed, literally so) as it is in B9, it becomes all the more clear that here too Saul's violence ('Saul's spear-throw') arises from his feelings for David ('Saul grows fond of David'). While A7's *Saul gewinnt David lieb* may well express merely platonic affection, the more frequent use of it to express romantic or erotic attraction suggests that we have in A7, *in nuce*, the erotic desire of Saul which is more fully developed by Brecht in B9. What Brecht also includes in B9, as we have seen, but leaves unarticulated here for whatever reason, is the idea that it was David's unwillingness to requite Saul's love, which prompts the violence that ensues. Whence this idea comes will be explored in the next chapter.

David

While the above discussion of various characters in Brecht's *David* fragments has offered glimpses of the relationship between the Brechtian David and the biblical one, it is worth considering Brecht's treatment of his title character in its own right first in B10 and then in B9, the sequence in which Brecht seems likely to have intended them to be read.

When considering the David of B10 and its related fragment (B11), one theme which emerges clearly is that of David's 'indolence'. After the first beggar begins to explain to Jonathan the fracas at the beginning of the scene, the third beggar seeks to divert Jonathan's attention to David by noting his indolence ('he's much too lazy, isn't that so, David?'), and later in the same scene the first beggar will agree: 'Lazy. Lazy's what he is. He is lazy. Otherwise nothing. That's his career.' After David makes a speech about the war, the first beggar reiterates his accusation, in terms which make it clear that he sees it as an irritating vice ('This laziness has annoyed me, to the limit!'). While this characterisation of Brecht's David by others is seemingly confirmed by Brecht's stage direction ('lazy David') as he makes his entrance, it is then subsequently complicated by the following exchange:

Jonathan

Should one be lazy?

David

No.

The Third Beggar

He says something different every day. It's bad with him! Yesterday he said: I must be as lazy as a quail. Then I'll know from the white clouds whether it will rain or not.

Taken together, the impression given here by David and the third beggar appears to be that David's own mind on indolence is far from made up, or perhaps that he considers indolence a virtue at one moment and something other than that at other times – an impression which is compatible with Ismael's confirmation in B11 that while Brecht's David may praise and embrace laziness, he nevertheless also 'works in the Autumn'.

While the biblical David is not obviously idle, it is interesting that Brecht's other writing at this time does reflect a certain interest in the human trait of indolence. Thus, for instance in scene 4 of *Baal*, when the two sisters come in to have sex with him and Baal is put off by their mention of Johanna's fate, Baal dismisses them on the basis that he feels lazy, and when they are thrown out of his room by the outraged landlady, he consoles himself with a reminder of his own laziness. The theme is resumed in scene 10, when the second woodcutter accuses Baal of putting their boots into the water so that they couldn't go into the forest, because 'he was lazy as usual'. Finally, in the fateful scene 18 in the Inn, as Watzmann and Johannes discuss Baal before he arrives, Watzmann reminds the group: 'He only does what he has to. Because he's so lazy.'

Perhaps even more apposite when considering David's indolence, however, is Brecht's writing about his own tendencies. For instance, in the summer in which he wrote B9 and B10, in a diary entry from late June, Brecht admits, 'I've been lounging around on the sofa and playing guitar. Lots of thoughts but the flesh is weak and nobody's strong enough to get me going.'[32] Indeed, while his diary entries from the summer of 1920 offer ample evidence of his writing in the summer months, two days after admitting lounging, he further insists, 'I can never work

---

32. *BFA* 26, 122; Eng.: Brecht, *Diaries*, 4 (21–26 June, 1920).

properly in the summer. I can't keep glued to my chair.'³³ Two months later (having written both B9 and B10 and much else in the meantime), Brecht confesses: 'Paper has lost its power to stimulate me. I hang like a bit in the turret of idleness: mouth downwards.' Yet, in the very same entry, he voices his conviction that his summer of 'idleness' would soon be over: 'Thoughts are impurities. That's why they start up in the winter'³⁴ – a sentiment which clearly resonates with Ismael's abovementioned acknowledgement in the fragments that the otherwise lazy David 'works in the Autumn'.³⁵

That the David of B10 is not merely indolent or perceived as such but also impudent at times is made clear in a variety of ways, including in his initial failure to respond to Jonathan's question and then in his response when it is finally offered (stage direction: 'looking at him impudently') and in the officer's perception of it as 'impudent'. Indeed, later in the scene, the stage direction specifies David's response ('Sound strong') to Jonathan ('What do you do all the time?') as 'impudent'. This tone continues, as we have seen, in David's response ('cheekily') to his father about not eating pebbles or dates and in his mocking of his father's poor aim. We see it too in David's refusal of his father's assumption that he will put on armour and indeed, elsewhere in the scene, others judge David to be mocking of 'greybeards' in general.

While Brecht's David is impertinent in B10, it is also clear that he is perceived by others as opinionated. The third beggar makes the point explicitly in dismissing him ('He just has opinions on everything, my lord! Just opinions!'), Ismael shares this view in B11, and it is clear throughout the scene that David is full of ideas and thoughts which he wishes to share. Jonathan is, as we have seen above, presented as

---

33. *BFA* 26, 123; Eng.: Brecht, *Diaries*, 5 (27 June 1920). See also Brecht's 19th Psalm in which the Davidic/Brechtian voice (for which see below) claims 'I do no work at all in summer, I travel around and run into the country, but by September my face is a landscape and I am calmer than at any other time of the year' (*BFA* 11, 28; Eng.: Brecht, *The Collected Poems*, 66).

34. *BFA* 26, 139–40; Eng.: Brecht, *Diaries*, 21–2 (25 August 1920).

35. See also Brecht's diary entry the following week in which, amongst the lines he wishes for his imagined clowns to deliver, is found the following: 'The way he said "One must be idle as a dormouse". Excellent!' *BFA* 26, 150; Eng.: Brecht, *Diaries*, 32 (1 September 1920). Münsterer's account of both their 'summer of compulsive sloth' together in 1919 (Münsterer, *The Young Brecht*, 79) and Brecht's dismissal of workaholism in others offers further vantage points from which to assess the young Brecht's attitude in this respect.

especially keen to solicit David's ideas and thoughts, but he is not alone. Indeed, after 'the people' have first asked for David's thoughts on the war with the Philistines and then for him to tell the 'truth' about it, a second group appears later in the scene and, spotting David, insists: 'He has a big mouth. He'll have something to say about the war!' Brecht's David does indeed have something to say, as we will see, but what is particularly striking is the way in which he uses stories/parables at various points to say what he does. The first is presented as a personal anecdote ('My friend Joshua had a house and a vineyard') in response to a query about 'art'. Told by David with a smirk, the anecdote prompts a laugh. The second is a fable about a war between a pine tree and a briar, and a tortoise who responds to the latter's requests for advice but eventually drowns himself in the process. This story divides the hearers' opinion, with some finding it wise and good and others incomprehensible. Apart from its impenetrability, David himself hints at why his 'wisdom' here and elsewhere polarises opinion in B10, when he explains to Jonathan that the reason David helped the old man was 'Because he needed it. He had the wrong opinion', to which the first beggar responds: 'That's his old nonsense! He gives old people advice! He sits there and makes up wise sayings for old people!' Despite accusations of presumptuousness, the young David's sharing of his wisdom is grounded in an unshakeable conviction that others' wrong opinions require correction by his right ones (a theme which we will see resumed in the next chapter).

In 1 Samuel, Eliab's accusation of David's presumption/ambition and neglect of domestic duties in bringing victuals from Bethlehem to the Israelite battlefront (1 Sam. 17.28) may suggest that the biblical David himself was remembered as impertinent. In any case, there is little doubt that David's request that Nabal cater for his feast (1 Sam. 25) on the grounds that David has 'protected' Nabal's sheep-shearing activities is seen by Nabal as impertinent at best and even presumptuous:

> But Nabal answered David's servants, 'Who is David? Who is the son of Jesse? There are many servants today who are breaking away from their masters. Shall I take my bread and my water and the meat that I have butchered for my shearers, and give it to men who come from I do not know where?' (1 Sam. 25.10-11)

While we don't have any evidence that this latter episode attracted Brecht's attention in his musings about David, it is not impossible that Brecht took inspiration for B10's David from one or both of these traditions. But the particular species of impertinence seen in B10, the prominence of 'opinions' and their mixed reception and the Brechtian David's appetite for performing does also resonate strongly with the picture offered by Brecht and others of Brecht himself in these years, as the description offered by a fellow student at the university suggests:

> Of course none of us could even begin to suspect what would later become of Brecht, but even then there was no doubt at all that he was self-willed and obstinate, resolute in his disregard of both praise and criticism, and self-opinionated to the point of arrogance.[36]

While Münsterer's account of Brecht's circle and Brecht's own diaries confirm that his friends were regularly favoured with the young Brecht's wisdom, stories and songs, the perceived impertinence and opinionated arrogance are exemplified in two well-known episodes from the Brecht hagiography.[37]

In November 1917, Brecht's first contribution to the revered professor Arthur Kutscher's theatre seminar consisted of an excoriating dissection of Hanns Johst's play, *Der Anfang* (*The Beginning*) delivered in such a way that it made an indelible impression on those present, for reasons a fellow student makes clear:

> He barked out his seminar paper in a clearly articulated voice, impassively, and never once looked up at his listeners. Applause, laughter, hissing and shuffling all left him unperturbed… He reaped a certain amount of applause, and a great deal of criticism; but compared to the run-of-the-mill academic seminar paper, his was a veritable grenade in our midst.[38]

The experience made a permanent enemy of the professor, who dismissed the paper not only for its 'indefensibility' but its 'perverse attitudes' and 'adolescent vitriol'.[39] Nor was Kutscher alone in taking umbrage at Brecht's opinions and the way in which he chose to express them – especially when they found their way into his reviews of local productions in the Augsburg theatre, which were published regularly in the city's

---

36. Cited in Frisch and Obermeier, *Brecht in Augsburg*, 120–1. Eng.: Münsterer, *The Young Brecht*, 159.

37. Helpfully discussed by Kuhn and Leeder ('Further Perspectives') in Münsterer, *The Young Brecht*, 159–62, from which the English translations above and below are drawn.

38. Frisch and Obermeier, *Brecht in Augsburg*, 120–1.

39. Kutscher, *Der Theaterprofessor*, 73.

Der Volkswille. Indeed, Brecht's review of Hebbel's biblical play *Judith* was so scathing in its criticism of director and actors that one of the latter, Vera-Maria Eberle, pursued a court action for libel, which was settled at some cost to Brecht's local reputation and his father's pocketbook. While the Brechtian David's impertinence, opinions and stories do not prove quite so costly to him in B10, those reading the scene alongside Brecht's early personal history cannot fail to note a passing resemblance, in these respects at least, between the young Brecht and his young David.

Of course, the subject on which Brecht's David has the most opinions in B10 is the conflict between the Israelites and the Philistines. While our discussions of David's interaction with Jesse and Jonathan have pointed in this direction, the thematic importance of the war is signalled from the outset of the scene, when a difference of opinion regarding the Saulide capacity to deal with the Philistine military threat leads to a physical altercation. It is, however, only after Jonathan makes his entrance and a crowd later brings news that the Philistines have invaded 'Gad'[40] that the war becomes the focal point of the action and dialogue. When asked for his opinion on a warring people, Brecht's David not only suggests that war distracts a nation from investing in the younger generation; he also dismisses the prospect of serving himself, because the trappings of war ('armour') are too burdensome. Pressed about the problem of the Philistines' incursion, David recognises but laments the need to 'chase them off' as a waste of time.

As already noted, a second group of people arrive on the scene, reiterating news of the invasion, adding that Saul has called up 'all the men' and asking David this time for the 'truth' about the war. When David's encouragement to 'Go anywhere where you can catch flies' is interpreted by the second beggar as an incitement to refuse Saul's mobilisation, David boldly insists both that 'No one in Judah can command us anything' and that 'No one in this patch of earth can call us anything', which may reflect an assertion of exceptionalism or suggest that the scene is set in a city on the margins of Saul's sovereignty.[41] While the third beggar's response that they are not beyond the reach of King Saul is dismissed by David ('King Saul won't chase sand fleas'), David appears at this point to be persuaded

---

40. Brecht's cipher for Germany, which capitalises on the similarity of the name of the biblical tribe of 'Gad' to 'Gath', the Philistine city famously associated with Goliath.

41. So too Jesse's reference to war in David's 'homeland'. An assertion of excepetionalism might well be based on the notion of a community on the outskirts of the social order.

by the prospect of war 'cripples' (perhaps including himself) to flee with them until Saul has defeated the Philistines.

Before they take flight, however, yet another crowd of people arrives and presses David repeatedly for his opinion about the war. When his initial prediction of their victory is cheered, David goes on to clarify that the corpses will (also) be theirs. Though he paints a harrowing picture of their deaths, he insists that the latter will be glorious, and that their women will be heroines for remaining chaste in their absence. Both David's and Brecht's tongues seem to be firmly in cheek here, and the crediting of him with a good speech by some is drowned out by the chorus of protests at his presumptuousness, inexperience, indolence and cowardice which culminate in the suggestion that 'A few kicks in the arse and he'll be glad to hold his tongue'. While David's insistence that he will head 'out there, where there are no soldiers' points toward a continuing refusal to be conscripted, he nevertheless delays his departure to tell his story of the 'war between a pine tree and a briar'.

If indeed David's parable relates to the war in view in the scene, and if the Philistines might be read as the pine and the Israelites as the briar, then the Brechtian David may be inviting the crowd to read himself as the tortoise, given that the latter, like David himself, is subjected to an interrogation relating to the war. If so, then the tortoise's eventual death by drowning in the river in seeking to assist the briar suggests that the tale is a cautionary one, not least since David appears to suggest that he himself will head down to the river shortly, and physical violence will be in the offing. Indeed, David's story may well be intended to pre-empt such a turn of events, but while his audience are still debating the merits and intelligibility of David's story, his father Jesse makes his arrival, interrogating his son's reluctance to return home before requiring him to do so to don 'your armour'.

The Brechtian David's resistance to conscription of himself and others finds little resonance within the biblical traditions about the young David. Indeed, Eliab's suspicions that it is the latter's appetite for combat and glory (1 Sam. 17.28) that explains his appearance at the battle-front with the Philistines seems to be confirmed by David's eagerness to fight Goliath and achieve further military successes (1 Sam. 17–18). While war between Israelites and Philistines is thus very much the context in which the biblical David rises to power at Saul's expense, it is hardly surprising that it would prove an especially prominent theme in B10, given the impact of World War I and its aftershocks on the young Brecht and his circle. Indeed, the conflict has left a visible trace in Brecht's earlier poems and newspaper contributions, some of which reflect a predictable patriotic fervour and invoke sacrifice as a lens for viewing the inevitable suffering of war.[42] Perhaps drawing on others' experiences of the war due to the lack of his own, the young Brecht sought to offer readers as vivid a picture as possible of the horrors of the battlefield: 'A picture emerges: The last rays of the sun stray over a battlefield strewn with corpses... Thousands are lying there: dead or with limbs twitching.'[43] Yet as the war dragged on and the horrific death toll mounted, not least amongst local boys whom Brecht had known, his writing about the war took on a quite different hue.

Already by 'Springtime', a poem published in May of 1915, the imagery of suffering ('Bodies lie in flowers / Steaming blood pours / From trembling flower spikes') is now accompanied by a despairing interrogation of sacrifice.[44] The following year, in an essay now lost, the schoolboy Brecht took square aim at Horace's *dulce et decorum est pro patria mori*, apparently dismissing it as propaganda that would hardly prevent anyone facing death in battle from fleeing in fear.[45] In a Germany now in desperate need of young men like Brecht to give their lives to and indeed for the war, it is hardly surprising that his essay might have been perceived as disloyal not only to king and country, but to his teacher, Dr Gebhard – who had taken Brecht under his wing – and perhaps even to the teacher's beloved Horace. Saved from expulsion from school by the intervention of a clerical acquaintance of the family, Brecht's attitude toward the war was to lose him friends, some of whom who were predictably suspicious that Brecht's criticism of it bespoke little more than cowardice.[46]

While they may not be simply equated, Brecht's evolving view and opinions of the war clearly bear a certain similarity to those of his David. As we have seen, David too paints a vivid picture of corpses on the battlefield which impresses some but provokes howls of protest (and perhaps threats of worse) from others. Moreover, David's resistance to his own conscription and participation in the Israelite war effort obviously parallels Brecht's own well-known efforts to avoid enlistment in the last two years of the war. Indeed, his attempt to disqualify himself at his recruitment medical in May of 1918 by overdosing on caffeine suggests

---

42. See texts and discussion in Parker, *Bertolt Brecht*, 60–1.

43. *BFA* 21, 15. Eng.: Parker, *Bertolt Brecht*, 62, who notes Brecht's indebtedness to Liliencrom.

44. See Parker, *Bertolt Brecht*, 63, for discussion of this poem along with others written the following year.

45. Recalled by Otto Müllereisert, cited in Frisch and Obermeier, *Brecht in Augsburg*, 86–7.

46. So Rudolf Prestel cited in ibid., 143.

the lengths to which he would go to avoid the draft, and may well support Münsterer's suggestion that Brecht chose to study medicine in 1917 because it offered the best prospect of escaping military service.[47] This suggestion is further strengthened by the fact that on the day of Brecht's medical examination, his father Berthold appealed to the importance of his son's medical studies in order to persuade the authorities to defer the young man's conscription.[48] Thus, very much unlike Jesse in B10, who gives the appearance of collecting David to enlist him in the war effort, Brecht's father clearly did everything in his power to save him, including submitting a further request for a deferral later that summer. Nevertheless, the result for their respective sons is the same: the reluctant soldier David is dragged off to fight Goliath, while the reluctant soldier Brecht was compelled to begin his military service in October of 1918.

Whereas we have seen that David is central to B10 as soon as he makes his entrance, we have also seen that B9 is dominated by Saul, with David very much the object of the king's ultimately frustrated desires. Indeed, in the latter scene, as in the biblical tradition which inspired it, David largely fulfils the role of court musician, in order to soothe Saul's troubled spirit. Brecht's insistence on having his David sing his song rather than simply play it, however, offers us a slightly fuller means of assessing David as poet/musician.[49] While the refrain's encouragement to 'laugh' and 'clap' in Judah clarifies the song as one of celebration or joy, what it encourages Saul to delight in is less transparent. In the opening section, the image is one of grass stomped down by a bull, which nevertheless proves its strength by seeing the sky. Grass, frequently used in biblical poetry as an image of both proliferation (Ps. 92.7) and destruction (Isa. 40.6-8), becomes in the Brechtian David's song 'stronger' than the animal which in the biblical economy either eats it (Ps. 104.14) or gambols about on it as a sign of delight or enjoyment (Jer. 50.11). It is, however, one of Brecht's own poems, 'The Seventh Psalm', written sometime during 1920, which furnishes the nearest parallel to David's song at this point: 'I had a woman, she was stronger than me as the grass is stronger than the

---

47. See Münsterer, *The Young Brecht*, 18 (and 'Further Reflections', 140) but also Parker, *Bertolt Brecht*, 97, who offers a helpfully nuanced discussion of Brecht's possible motivations.

48. Parker, *Bertolt Brecht*, 108, speculates that the unusual granting of the request may have had something to do with the fact that the civilian chair of the local recruitment committee sang in the same male choir as Brecht's father.

49. 'Stark ist der Stier' ('The Bull is Strong') is included in *BFA* 13, 177.

bull. The grass lifts up again.'⁵⁰ Here, Judah seems to be invited to delight in the resilience of the weak in the face of the strong. However, the cause for Judah's celebration in the second part of David's song is first that a 'stone' is 'stuck' and then that 'you're not blind' (as the stone turns out to be), while the third stanza offers a parade of images which eventually reference a resistance to hailstones and culminate in encouraging Judah to laugh simply because it can laugh.

Saul's view of the song as good, if weak in the middle, must be qualified by his confession of incomprehension halfway through: 'Hold on, I don't understand the song. It makes no sense, my child.' While in other respects, the David of B10 bears little resemblance to David here in B9, Saul's lack of understanding of David does resonate with the incomprehension expressed by some in response to David's story in B10. Another resonance between the two scenes may be found in David's insistence in the second part of his song that it is good to have a 'big mouth' (*voll Maul*)⁵¹ – the very thing which David is accused by the crowd of possessing to justify their seeking of an opinion from him about the war. Yet, if anything, the absence of David's 'big mouth' throughout the remainder of 'David before Saul' underlines how different the portraits of David found in B9 and B10 are. Whereas the indolent and impertinent David of B10 entertains, insults and befuddles the people with his anti-war wisdom and stories before being brought to heel by his father, the servant singer of B9 unintentionally befuddles his king with his song, offers what minimal advice he can, but ultimately enrages Saul by refusing to return his love and fleeing.

However different from each other the two scenes may be, the suggestion that they (and especially B10) offer us a portrait of a David who is, in various ways, rather like Brecht himself is hardly surprising. In, 1920, at the very time he was writing *David*, Brecht took to calling some of the poems he was writing 'Psalms'.⁵² While at least one of his poems was clearly inspired by the 1920 publication of a German translation of

---

50. *BFA*, 11, 20–1; Eng.: Brecht, *The Collected Poems*, 57. See too the poem 'Ballad of any man's secret' in *BFA* 11, 74; Eng.: Brecht, *The Collected Poems*, 201. For further evidence of Brecht's fascination with grass see, in the same volume, 'Grass and Peppermint' (99) and 'Let the grass too have meaning' (101).

51. See note in B9 on this idiom and its relationship to *gewaltiges Maul* in B10.

52. Brecht references the writing of 'Psalms' and the reading of them at Gabler's in his diary entry of 18 July 1920 (*BFA* 26, 129; Eng.: Brecht, *Diaries*, 11) and again on 31 August (*BFA* 26, 146; Eng.: Brecht, *Diaries*, 29).

Walt Whitman's modern psalmody,⁵³ the twenty or so 'psalms' penned by Brecht around this time draw upon the biblical psalmic tradition itself in various ways.⁵⁴ Clearly, Brecht's numbering, naming and formatting of his Psalms was specifically intended to evoke the biblical genre. More particularly, while the imagery of Brecht's psalms is ecclesial at various points, it is also explicitly biblical at others, referencing Ararat, the Song of Songs and the Decalogue. Indeed, some have even detected commonalities between the biblical Psalms and Brecht's compositions in terms of poetic technique and structure.⁵⁵

While of course the biblical Psalms are attributed to a variety of parties (including most prominently, Asaph and the sons of Korah), the association of so many of the Psalms with the biblical David known from 1 and 2 Samuel has ensured that the genre is strongly identified with the David of historical memory. Given this identification, there can be little doubt that in the very act of authoring 'Psalms' as such, Brecht, as a young musician and poet, transparently sought to identify and associate himself with David, the only character in the Bible who is portrayed as both a young musician and a poet. Yet if Brecht seeks to associate his voice with the author of the biblical Psalms by writing 'Psalms' of his own, it is clear from even a cursory reading of them that the voice we hear in the Psalms is also very much Brecht's own. For instance, while Brecht's Psalms are far from atheological, recent work on them has rightly drawn attention to how different the theology of these Psalms is from David's. In sharp contrast to the God of the Psalter, in Brecht's Psalms,

---

53. So conclude the editors of Brecht, *The Collected Poems*, 53, which seems to be confirmed by Brecht's borrowing of the title of his 16th Psalm, *Gesang von mir* [*Song of myself*] from Whitman's work of the same name, whose translation by Max Hayek appeared in 1920 (Brecht, *The Collected Poems*, 65, and related note).

54. The *BFA* includes 23 compositions in the category of 'Psalmen' while Brecht, *The Collected Poems*, translates 20 along with four 'poems belonging with the Psalms'. For a more inclusive collection, see Arnold Stadler, *Das Buch der Psalmen und die deutschsprachige Lyrik des 20. Jahrhunderts: Zu den Psalmen im Werk Bertolt Brechts und Paul Celans* (Köln: Boehlau, 1989), 22–102.

55. In addition to Stadler, see Cornelius Hell and Wolfgang Wiesmüller, 'Die Psalmen: Rezeption biblischer Lyrik in Gedichten', in *Die Bibel in der deutschsprachigen Literatur des 20 Jahrhunderts, Band 1: Formen und Motive*, ed. Heinrich Smidinger (Mainz: Mattias-Gruenewald, 1999), 158–204 and Inka Bach and Helmut Galle, *Deutsche Psalmendichtung vom 16. bis zum 20. Jahrundert: Untersuchungen zur Geschichte einer lyrischen Gattung* (Berlin: de Gruyter, 1989), 334–46.

> God is repeatedly and insistently figured as essentially oblivious to humanity and its concerns. The fears of the biblical psalmists have come true: God, if he exists at all, is indeed asleep, deaf, apathetic – unconcerned with immorality, caught napping in the late afternoon, blithely entertaining himself at the country fair for hour after hour.[56]

Of course there are a very few canonical Psalms (including Pss. 14 and 52) which acknowledge the practical atheism of those who say or behave as if 'there is no God' or at least no God whom they need heed or fear.[57] But while the biblical Psalms also frequently voice their frustration at God's *apparent* silence or worse, the God of Brecht's Psalms is in fact regularly and conspicuously absent, at other times superfluous and at still others, merely inconspicuous.[58] An even more striking contrast is offered by the respective reactions to the divine absence and disengagement: for the biblical Psalmist(s) it prompts despair or further supplication, whereas for the Brechtian Psalmist it is largely an encouragement to *carpe diem*.

While the young Augsburg poet-musician's desire to associate himself with his Israelite counterpart, David, by writing his own 'Psalms' seems clear, Tom Kuhn and David Constantine's observation that Brecht's Psalms annex 'a traditional Jewish Christian form for a new purpose in a new voice' would also seem to offer a useful vantage point from which to consider Brecht's *David*.[59] No less than the Psalms, the biblical stories of David and Saul offered Brecht a 'traditional jewish Christian form' – narrative rather than lyrical – for him to infuse with a new voice, and use for a new purpose. Nowhere is this infusion more visible than in B9 where we hear David's song, but Brecht's voice.

This chapter and the preceding one have highlighted the dissonances and resonances between Brecht's voice in the fragments and both the biblical tradition and Brecht's own experience as it is reflected in his own writings and those of his circle. In what follows, we listen for resonances and dissonances between the voice and purpose of the *David* fragments and those of others in which the David–Saul form has also been annexed for the stage.

---

56. Jennifer Bjornstad, '"Damit der liebe Gott weiterschaukeln kann": The Psalms of Bertolt Brecht', in *Der junge Herr Brecht wird Schriftsteller/Young Mr. Brecht Becomes a Writer*, ed. Jürgen Hillesheim and Stephen Brockmann, *Das Brecht Jahrbuch / The Brecht Yearbook* 31 (2006): 173.

57. See for instance, the helpful discussion of Ps. 14 in Richard J. Clifford, *Psalms 1–72* (Nashville: Abingdon Press, 2002), 89–90.

58. Bjornstad, 'Psalms', 170–81.

59. Kuhn and Constantine, in Brecht, *The Collected Poems*, 53.

Chapter 4

BRECHT'S *DAVID* AND OTHER ADAPTATIONS: FEUCHTWANGER, ZAREK AND GIDE

David and Saul on Stage

While the setting of Brecht's adolescent Augsburg experiment *Die Bibel* in the Thirty Years' War shows his early interest in the Scriptures as a source of themes and motifs for dramas set in other contexts, his *David* fragments display a different polarity: in them it is the biblical narrative (largely) which supplies the characters and setting for themes and motifs of Brecht's own making.[1] In this respect at least, Brecht was no great innovator even in his own circle, as we shall see. Indeed, the dramatic adaptation of biblical narratives has a long and well-established history stretching back into (and well before) the medieval period.[2] Moreover, amongst the biblical narratives favoured by dramatists, those of David featured prominently from the sixteenth century onward for a host of reasons, including his christological importance, his association with psalmody and the multi-faceted portrait of him and others offered up by the books of Samuel.[3] Plays of David and Saul appeared regularly in

---

1. For the resumption of Brecht's interest in the David narratives in his unfinished opera *Goliath* (with Eisler), see the Concluding Reflections below.
2. For the genesis and evolution of the genre in the medieval period, see Lynette Muir, *The Biblical Drama of Medieval Europe* (Cambridge: Cambridge University Press, 1995), and for an earlier treatment of English plays from that period to the middle of the twentieth century, see Murray Roston, *Biblical Drama in England: From the Middle Ages to the Present Day* (Evanston: Northwestern University Press, 1968).
3. See, for instance, the discussion of David's treatment in French drama of the sixteenth and seventeenth centuries in Alexandre Lorain, 'Les protagonistes dans la

the French theatre of the eighteenth century, thanks to the flourishing of 'biblical tragedy' inspired in part by Racine's *Athalie* (1689).[4] They also reappeared in sizeable numbers in the late nineteenth and early twentieth centuries in English – a phenomenon which has been attributed by some to 1 and 2 Samuel's comparative disinterest in the spectacle of the supernatural,[5] but which is surely also related to the sustained complexity of the narrative and character development seen in these books but seldom elsewhere within the biblical tradition. As we will see, David and Saul were popular in French drama of the nineteenth century, but most relevant for our study is the remarkable fascination with David and Saul displayed by those writing for the stage in German in the late 1800s and early decades of the twentieth century.[6] While German-language plays focussed on the Saul and David stories appeared at an average rate of only three per decade between 1840 and 1890, the last decade of the nineteenth century and the first two of the twentieth century witnessed a dramatic increase, with fully a dozen Saul/David dramas published and/or performed between 1890 and 1900, a further 13 appearing between 1900 and 1910, and another 11 between 1910 and 1920.[7]

In a useful study of these plays, Inger Nebel seeks an explanation for their popularity in the ecclesial and political currents swirling within German culture toward the end of the nineteenth and beginning of the

---

tragédie biblique de la Renaissance', *Nouvelle Revue du XVIe Siècle* 12, no. 2 (1994): 197–208. For an admittedly slender sampling of two millennia of interpretation of David in 'literature' see Raymond-Jean Frontain and Jan Wojcik, *The David Myth in Western Literature* (West Lafayette: Purdue University Press, 1980), which references the theatrical David regularly in its introduction (2–4, 8) but fails to feature him in its contents.

4. Mireille Herr, *Les Tragédies bibliques au XVIIIe siècle* (Paris: Champion; Geneva: Slatkine, 1988), 101–53, who notes that playwrights of this period were particularly attracted to the 'tragic' quality of Saul's loss of his kingdom to David, and David's (admittedly temporary) loss of his to his son, Absalom.

5. So Roston, *Biblical Drama*, 254. While the books of Samuel are admittedly happy to credit the untimely deaths of Nabal (1 Sam. 25.38), Uzzah (2 Sam. 6.7) and David's child by Bathsheba (2 Sam. 12.18) to divine intervention, these books do lack the spectacular manifestations of divine power seen for instance in the miracle-working of Moses in the Pentateuch, or Elijah and Elisha in the books of Kings.

6. Nebel, *Harfe, Speer und Krone*.

7. Ibid., 27–9 and Appendix A for a list of plays published between 1880 and 1920, including Brecht's *David* fragments and Feuchtwanger's *König Saul* and *Das Weib des Urias*, but not Zarek's *David*, which was published in 1921.

twentieth century.⁸ While Nebel notes the controversy associated with Julius Wellhausen's scholarship on the Old Testament in the latter decades of the nineteenth century and detects specific points of influence in two of these plays,⁹ whether this suggests Wellhausen's ideas were a significant stimulus for the dramatic interest which burgeoned in these and later decades may be doubted. Better evidence may be drawn from the plays themselves for Nebel's suggestion that the clash between Saul (as king) and Samuel (as prophet/priest) was seen as symbolic of the tension between secular and ecclesial power exercising German society in the latter decades of the nineteenth century.¹⁰ Entirely plausible, but less provable, is Nebel's observation that questions of royal accession and succession in the narratives of Saul and David will have had a particular resonance in the late 1880s, when German society was exercised by the issue of the succession of Wilhelm I.¹¹ Indeed, while these and other factors may well help to explain the unusual enthusiasm for Saul and David on stage in the late nineteenth century, Nebel's theories leave unexplained both the persistence of their popularity in the first two decades of the twentieth century and the dramatic dwindling of interest in them following 1920.¹²

While our focus here on Brecht's *David* fragments and selected other adaptations means we cannot pretend to offer any comprehensive answers to such questions, the following chapter's treatment of one play in German from the turn of the century (Feuchtwanger's *König Saul*), another from just after this period (Otto Zarek's *David*) and a third from beyond the German-speaking world (André Gide's *Saül*) may point toward additional reasons for their popularity.

Lion Feuchtwanger's König Saul

When Brecht moved from Augsburg to study medicine and humanities at the Ludwig Maximilian University in Munich in the Autumn of 1917, his own theatrical and cinematic ambitions drew him toward the city's

---

8. It is not impossible that some plays written during this period may have escaped Nebel's attention and indeed some from before it, but the spike in play production in these decades is noteworthy.

9. Nebel, *Harfe, Speer und Krone*, 268–9.

10. Ibid., 269.

11. Ibid., 270.

12. For ample evidence of German Expressionism's engagement with the traditions of the Hebrew Bible, see Lisa Marie Anderson, *German Expressionism and the Messianism of a Generation* (Leiden: Brill/Rodopi, 2011), 53–80.

leading artistic personalities, including Frank Wedekind (before his death the following year), Karl Valentin and Lion Feuchtwanger. Feuchtwanger was, like Valentin, a native son of Munich (b. 1884), but born and raised in a devout, indeed Orthodox, Jewish household, in which (according to his brother Martin's recollections) the walls were hung with paintings of biblical tales with which their father Sigmund apparently enjoyed regaling his children.[13] Despite chafing under the yoke of his parents' conservative sensibilities, Feuchtwanger's fascination with the ancient past, including the stories of the Old Testament, remained a feature of his teenage years. Following his studies in Munich where his academic ambitions were nurtured and then a year in Berlin, Feuchtwanger returned to the city of his birth in the latter months of 1906 to pursue a doctorate on the subject of Heinrich Heine's *Der Rabbi von Bacharach*. Yet despite completing the latter in short order and embarking upon the required *Habilitationschrift*, his academic career was soon overtaken by a literary one. Already by 1903, Feuchtwanger had published a couple of sketches – under the title *Die Einsamen* (*'The Lonely'*) – and perhaps more significantly had co-founded a literary society, Phoebus, which produced plays (Hauptmann's *Elga* and *Pippa tanzt*) and sponsored lectures (by Alfred Kerr and others) which promoted a new and liberated theatrical aesthetic. While Phoebus' own short-lived semi-monthly publication *Der Spiegel* had little impact, Feuchtwanger's installation in 1908 as the Munich critic for the *Schaubühne*, one of the country's most distinguished dramatic reviews, undoubtedly contributed to his growing reputation as a knowing (and often cutting) critic of the theater.

Following a two-year period abroad in the company of his new wife, Martha, and a brief stint in the army from which he received a medical discharge, Feuchtwanger set about writing plays in earnest, and by 1916, with two successes under his belt (*Die Perser* and *Warren Hastings*), he had begun to reap the rewards, including an apartment in Munich's fashionably artistic neighbourhood of Schwabing. Amongst those living in the vicinity was, for instance, the sculptress Lottie Pritzel, in whose circle Lion and his wife Martha were included. Firm supporters of the avant-garde theatre, the Feuchtwangers entertained Wedekind regularly in the years before his death, during which time Feuchtwanger was not only continuing to write his own plays, but also serving as 'Lektor' for Munich's progressive theatre, the Kammerspiele, reading and recommending the plays of others for production there. Thus, it was hardly

---

13. Lothar Kahn, *Insight and Action: The Life and Work of Lion Feuchtwanger* (Rutherford: Fairleigh Dickinson University Press, 1975), 27.

surprisingly that when the young Brecht appeared at the Café Stephanie, a favourite haunt of artists in Schwabing, and approached the well-known actor Arnold Marlé to ask him what he should do with his play *Spartakus*, Marlé's response was 'Go to Feuchtwanger'.[14] It was advice that would prove crucial for Brecht's early career in Munich, for in Feuchtwanger Brecht found not only a willing reader of what would be the first of his plays to reach the professional stage in 1922 (as *Drums in the Night*), but also someone with whom he would collaborate on *Edward II*,[15] directed by Brecht himself at the Kammerspiele, where he would work as dramaturg from 1922–1924.[16] But in 1920, in addition to his many other projects, we have seen that Brecht had 'David on the brain', and in this he was not alone amongst German playwrights of the period, as we have seen above, nor even amongst his close associates like Otto Zarek, as we will see below.

What has not been widely credited in this connection, however, is that Feuchtwanger himself had once had David and Saul very much on his mind as well. Some fifteen years earlier, when he himself was twenty and still a student at the university, Feuchtwanger's own earliest dramatic efforts also included several one-act plays, three of which were focused on biblical characters: *Joel*, *Das Weib des Urias* and *König Saul: eine dramatische Studie*. Of these, only about *Saul* can anything be said, for only it is preserved (and only four pages of it) and it alone seems to have been performed (and only once), appearing on the stage of the Münchner Volkstheater on 25 September 1905.[17]

What may be said based on both the fragment which survives and reviews of the production is that Feuchtwanger's one-act Saul takes its biblical inspiration from 1 Samuel 28, the chapter discussed briefly in our introduction, in which King Saul, faced with the threat of the Philistines

---

14. Frisch and Obermeier, *Brecht in Augsburg*, 152.

15. For more details on this collaboration, see Faith G. Norris, 'The Collaboration of Lion Feuchtwanger and Bertolt Brecht in Edward II', in *Lion Feuchtwanger: The Man, His Ideas, His Work: A Collection of Critical Essays*, ed. John M. Spalek (Los Angeles: Hennessey & Ingalls, 1972), 277–306.

16. For a history of the Kammerspiele and the contributions of Feuchtwanger, Zarek and Brecht, see Wolfgang Petzet, *Theater: Die Münchner Kammerspiele, 1911–1972* (Munich: K. Desch, 1973).

17. In his review of *Saul*, Hanns Gumppenberg, 'Rezension, "Koenig Saul – Dramatische Studie in einem Akt von Lion Feuchtwanger" und "Prinzessen Hilde – Romantisches Drama in einem Akt von Lion Feuchtwanger"', *Das Literarische Echo* 8, no. 2 (1905): 132–4, seems to suggest that Feuchtwanger's *Joel* may have been performed or at least recited.

and deprived of divine guidance, visits a medium in Endor to consult the spirit of the recently deceased prophet, Samuel. After the prophet is conjured up by the medium and announces the imminent death of Saul and his sons and defeat for Israel, the medium presses Saul to accept the hospitality of a meal from her before going to his doom.[18] Feuchtwanger's main innovations in relation to the biblical tradition are, first, to make the medium Saul's former lover, with their relationship eventually thwarted by his royal ambitions. Second, Feuchtwanger has David, in his flight from Saul, hide out in her house for some three weeks prior to the arrival of Saul. While Nebel illustrates how frequently German stage adaptations from the period interpolate non-biblical love interests into the stories of Saul and David,[19] the medium of Endor appears in only 10 of the 36 plays he catalogues between 1890 and 1920,[20] is rarely developed as a character in her own right, and in only one other instance in relation to an unhappy love story (which, however, does not involve Saul).[21]

According to what may be reconstructed of the rest of Feuchtwanger's play from reviews of it, the medium's houseguest, David, has already been safely removed from the scene to sleep in an adjoining room of her hut by the time Saul arrives to ask his former lover to summon up Samuel. As Feuchtwanger's Saul laments God's abandonment of him and embrace of David, the woman's former affection for him is stirred to the point that she presses him repeatedly to become the king he once was, by taking matters into his own hands and killing his enemy David, asleep in the next room. When Saul fails to summon up the wherewithal to do so, the woman sends the doomed king off to meet his fate at the hands of the Philistines on Mt. Gilboa.

18. For a recent discussion of this episode in 1 Sam. 28 in light of the wider narrative context of 1 Samuel and the Former Prophets, see Matthew Michael, 'The Prophet, the Witch and the Ghost: Understanding the Parody of Saul as a "Prophet" and the Purpose of Endor in the Deuteronomistic History', *JSOT* 38 (2014): 315–46.
19. See Nebel, *Harfe, Speer und Krone*, 34.
20. Ibid., Appendix B.
21. Ibid., 34. The medium is unlucky in love in Heinrich Grosch's *König und Zauberin* (1912), while in Karl Siedler's *Saul* (1913), it is her daughter who is caught up in a love triangle with Saul and the (unbiblical) grand-daughter of the prophet Samuel. For a helpful comparison of the medium's treatment in Charpentier's seventeenth-century *David et Jonathas* with that found in Carl Nielsen's 1901 opera *Saul and David*, see Theresa Angert-Quilter and Lynne Wall, 'The "Spirit Wife" at Endor', *JSOT* 25 (2001): 55–72, and for a discussion of the place of 1 Sam. 28 in controversies associated with Spiritualism of the nineteenth century, see Christopher James Blythe, 'The Prophetess of Endor: Reception of 1 Samuel 28 in Nineteenth Century Mormon History', *JBR* 4, no. 1 (2017): 59–62.

That the four-page fragment which has been preserved is the opening of Feuchtwanger's play is suggested both by the absence of Saul from it and the extended set and stage directions at the top of the first page, locating the action in a dilapidated hut in which a fire burns. In his dialogue with 'Jezabel' – the name Feuchtwanger borrows for his medium from Israel's later history – David very much makes the running both in terms of dialogue and action, scurrying about to stir the fire, checking on a noise outside and offering a damning report of the state of Saul's army, upon which he has recently spied. Jezabel, whom David himself accuses of being 'So stumm und duester und versonnen!' (so mute and gloomy and pensive!), has already been described at the outset as 'ein alterndes Weib, verwittert, duester!' (an aged wench, weathered, dreary!) and she does little to dispel this impression with her laconic reply to David's query about whether she feels cold: 'Jezabel (muerrisch): Was kuemmert's dich?' (**Jezabel** [*cantankerously*]: What's it to you?)

Neither Hanns Gumppenberg, the critic for the *Literarische Echo*, nor the Munich journalist Gustav Adolf Müller were greatly impressed with David's verbosity (of which the surviving fragment admittedly shows some evidence),[22] with Müller insisting that David's penchant for repeating himself fully justified Jezabel's grumpiness. But Müller's greatest reservations related to what he saw as the weakness of Feuchtwanger's Saul, best exemplified, in his view, by both the king's pathetic plea, 'Rette mich, Jezabel' (Save me, Jezabel), and his inability to kill the sleeping David, despite Jezabel's repeated encouragements. Gumppenberg also appears to take issue with what he sees as Feuchtwanger's excessive interest in and approach to describing the biblical setting.[23] Unless the rest of the play surfaces, the latter criticisms are difficult to evaluate, but Feuchtwanger's own response to his critics, penned some three weeks after the opening and published alongside Müller's review, offers an

---

22. Gumppenberg, 'König Saul'; Gustav Adolf Müller, 'Rezension, "König Saul – Dramatische Studie in einem Akt von Lion Feuchtwanger" und "Prinzessen Hilde – Romantisches Drama in einem Akt von Lion Feuchtwanger"', *Münchener Schauspielpremièren* 1, no. 1 (1905): 33–5. The latter was an organ of Phoebus and apparently published by Lion's brother Martin. Müller speaks of David as a 'phrasengeschwollener Jüngling' (literally, 'phrase-swollen lad', but both the root words carry a similar additional valence of pretentiousness: *Phrasen* is often used to mean not just any phrase, but specifically a 'platitude' or 'cliché', and *geschwollen* can be used metaphorically as an adjective for bombastic, pompous individuals).

23. Gumppenberg, 'König Saul', 134, laments Feuchtwanger's 'Hang zu äußere lich-affektierte Manier, das Milieu anzudeuten' (propensity to indicate the milieu in an outwardly affected manner).

insight into Feuchtwanger's dramatic objectives and interests.[24] He begins by setting out his aims:

> With my 'Saul' I wished to write a royal drama. Neither Saul, nor David, nor Jezabel were intended to stand at the heart of the work, but rather the will to power which rules these three people. The drama was devised as a hymn to royal glory and royal humanity. The longing for the crown, which both intoxicates and destroys Saul, which makes David's eyes clear and his hands strong, and allows the old Jezabel, frozen with loneliness and weathered by bitterness, to become young again and rise above herself – this hot, drunken, unruly longing runs through the play like a red thread. This with regard to the much-maligned 'idea' of the drama.[25]

Here Feuchtwanger, still a student, disavows a primary interest in the characters, whether David or his witch, or even the eponymous king of the play. According to Feuchtwanger, the end to which they are all merely a means in his play is the illustration of an 'idea', namely, the 'Will to Power' made famous by Friedrich Nietzsche, which runs, he says, 'through the play like a red thread'. While neither Gumppenberg nor Müller take aim at the 'idea' of *Saul* or lack thereof in any obvious way, Feuchtwanger may here be responding to criticism from other quarters. Certainly in seeking refuge in the notion of a drama of 'ideas', Feuchtwanger was in good company in the German theatre of the end of the nineteenth century.[26] Likewise, Feuchtwanger was far from the only playwright of his time to reflect an awareness of Nietzschean ideas.[27] Yet the young playwright's insistence that Saul was not his primary interest is belied somewhat by the amount of ink he spills in responding to the criticism that his Saul was weak. Mounting a rather eloquent defence of the play's characterisation of Saul and his emotional complexity, Feuchtwanger disclaims 'critics' (and

---

24. Lion Feuchtwanger, 'Einige Worte über meine Dramen "König Saul" und "Prinzessin Hilde"', *Münchener Schauspielpremièren* 1, no. 1 (1905): 37–40.

25. Ibid., 37.

26. For ample evidence see, for instance, the collection of seminal German writing on the theatre from the eighteenth to the twentieth century (including essays by Nietzsche and the mature Brecht amongst many others) in Margaret Herzfeld-Sander, ed., *Essays on German Theater: Lessing, Brecht, Dürrenmatt, and Others* (New York: Continuum, 1985).

27. For a useful discussion of the influence of Nietzsche on August Strindberg's *Miss Julie* (1888) and George Bernard Shaw's *Major Barbara* (1905/1907), see David Kornhaber, *The Birth of Theater from the Spirit of Philosophy: Nietzsche and the Modern Drama* (Evanston: Northwestern University Press, 2016).

here he would appear to have Müller in mind) who 'encounter so little manliness in life, they want to populate the stage with loud gentlemen and woe to the author, who does not radiate "heroism" in every direction'.[28] While Feuchtwanger does not respond directly to Müller's criticism of Saul's weakness in being unwilling or unable to kill the sleeping David, the umbrage he takes at accusations of excessive interest in the context of the scene may contain an oblique response:

> But I would like to lodge a protest against the accusation of describing the social context in an incongruous and artificial way. It is not a question of taste but can only be determined by research/science (*Wissenschaft*). And here I dare say: not a single thought in my 'Saul' violates the spirit of the Old Testament, no comparison, no image, no word runs contrary to the sense of the Old Hebrew poetry.[29]

Even if the play had been preserved, it would be impossible to test such a claim, but Feuchtwanger's insistence on his fidelity to the biblical tradition (invoked both under its Christian name 'Old Testament' and in terms of 'ancient Hebrew poetry') points to one obvious reason for Feuchtwanger not to allow his Saul to kill the sleeping David: it would have radically contradicted the books of Samuel, which famously narrate David's rise to the throne following Saul's death. Moreover, Feuchtwanger's invocation of research/science (rather than, for instance, the category of faith/religion) in relation to the Old Testament offers further evidence of the extent to which the young playwright saw, or at least presented, his treatment of Saul and David as being shaped not by the faith of his parents, but rather by literary and antiquarian interests, and perhaps even academic ones, given that his undergraduate studies at the university in Munich included courses in biblical criticism.[30]

When Brecht wrote to Paula Banholzer in the spring of 1919 to report that his play, *Spartakus*, was being promoted by 'A doctor in Munich, who has a great deal of influence and himself writes good plays',[31] the good plays Brecht almost certainly had in mind were those Feuchtwanger had published since 1915, rather than his early biblical experiments like *Saul*. However, while the omission of *Saul* from Feuchtwanger's later bibliography of his own work suggests he was eventually happy to forget his

---

28. Feuchtwanger, 'Einige Worte', 38.
29. Ibid.
30. Kahn, *Insight and Action*, 39.
31. *BFA* 28, 77.

early biblical efforts in the light of later successes,[32] it seems unlikely that he had already forgotten them entirely when two of his protégés, Brecht and Otto Zarek, began working on their own plays featuring David and Saul at the very same age he once had, and while both studying at the same university. Indeed, Brecht's account of writing the two 'complete' scenes of the *David* fragments (B9 and B10) in late July of 1920 upon hearing Zarek's version of 'David before Saul' (for which see below) suggests Feuchtwanger had a front-row seat for their youthful endeavours:

> 30 July 1920
>
> In the afternoon Feuchtwanger and Zarek came to tea. Wrote the first scene of a play, *Saul and David*, which I propose to do on the side and without any previous plan, though the raw material is good.[33]

While it is quite unlikely that Feuchtwanger came to tea with his *Saul* (which had after all been performed for the first and last time when Brecht and Zarek were still in grade-school), it is certainly tempting to imagine what conversation might have passed between three authors of theatrical works on the same subject, on the very day when Brecht reports making further progress on his play. Indeed, it is certainly not impossible that the exchange of ideas about David and Saul between Zarek and Brecht three days earlier (again see below) was repeated, but now included their mentor Feuchtwanger, who of course had his own experience of adapting these very stories for the stage, and clear ideas, as we have seen, about how one should do so.

Despite the loss (thus far) of Feuchtwanger's play as a whole, the four surviving pages and the author's thoughts in response to his critics are worthy of reflection both in relation to the biblical tradition and to Brecht and his own *David* fragments. Unlike Feuchtwanger's David, the biblical David has joined the ranks of the Philistines in 1 Samuel 28 and is absent from the story of Saul's visit to the medium. Moreover, the biblical Saul needs to be told that there is a medium in Endor (1 Sam. 28.7), which hardly suggests to one acquainted with the Bible that the two were former lovers, as Feuchtwanger's *Saul* insists. Such innovations are obvious and may (or may not) have discomfited viewers who were particularly attached

---

32. Kahn, *Insight and Action*, 40. The fact that the MSS of these works do not appear to have been preserved seems to point in this direction, though Nebel, *Harfe, Speer und Krone*, 34, notes that the preservation of the four pages of *Saul* in Feuchtwanger's papers (now held at the Feuchtwanger Memorial Library at the University of Southern California) may suggest otherwise.

33. *BFA* 26, 131; Eng.: Brecht, *Diaries*, 13.

to this particular canonical story, which was of course less famous than some (e.g. the battle with Goliath or affair with Bathsheba), but must have been far from unknown to most. However, based on what may be reconstructed of the play, such departures should by no means be taken as a sign of Feuchtwanger's disinterest in the biblical tradition, as we will see.

Within the biblical tradition by this point, Saul undoubtedly cuts a rather desperate and ultimately pathetic figure, ignoring his own outlawing of mediums (1 Sam. 28.9) by seeking one out and then summoning up the prophet Samuel, whom the biblical narrator and Saul himself see as, if not the architect of Saul's demise, then certainly instrumental in both realising it and reminding Saul of it.[34] Indeed, one sign of Saul's mounting desperation in the chapters prior to 1 Samuel 28 is his obsessive pursuit of David in an attempt to eliminate the one who would take his crown (1 Sam. 22–24; 26).[35] Moreover, as David and the narrator seem intent on reiterating, and as Saul himself recognises (1 Sam. 24 and 26), what makes Saul's desperate desire to shed David's 'innocent' blood all the more culpable and dishonourable is the fact that when David is repeatedly presented with the opportunity to kill the king who seeks to kill him, David exercises restraint and spares him on the grounds that Saul is the 'LORD's anointed' (1 Sam. 24.6 [Heb. v. 7]; 26.9, 11, 23).[36] In fact, the extraordinary extent of both Saul's vulnerability and David's restraint is illustrated by the second of these two episodes: even when David and his cousin and comrade-in-arms Abishai manage to steal in under cover of night to where 'Saul lay sleeping within the encampment', the doomed king is still spared by David (1 Sam. 26.7) – who later confirms his reputation for protecting innocent blood by avenging those who murder Saul's son Ish-bosheth in his sleep (2 Sam. 4).

What makes all of this relevant to the present discussion is that in *Saul*, Feuchtwanger gives his eponymous king the opportunity to kill the sleeping David, and indeed has him tempted and even strongly encouraged to do so by someone close to him who appears to be acting in his interest (just as Abishai does in 1 Sam. 26). While Feuchtwanger appears to have

---

34. For an example of a reading which exonerates Samuel in relation to the 'Fall' of Saul see V. Philips Long, *The Reign and Rejection of King Saul: A Case for Literary and Theological Coherence* (Atlanta: Scholars Press, 1989), 75–95. For a reading which incriminates Samuel, see David M. Gunn, *The Fate of King Saul: An Interpretation of a Biblical Story* (Sheffield: Sheffield Academic Press, 1980), 33–40.

35. This theme is already reflected in Saul's famous and repeated efforts to spear David (1 Sam. 18.11; 19.9; 20.33).

36. For discussion of the importance of the theme of illegitimate/innocent blood in the traditions about David, see Shepherd, *King David*.

seen the dramatic value of Saul vacillating and agonising over whether to spare the sleeping David or not, the final unwillingness of Feuchtwanger's Saul to take the life of God's anointed (in this case, David) while he sleeps allows Feuchtwanger to belatedly credit the doomed Saul with a righteous restraint which in the biblical tradition qualifies David, rather than Saul, to rule. Feuchtwanger's medium does not of course see Saul's inability to kill David in this way, nor does Feuchtwanger make this point in responding to criticisms of Saul's weakness, but he surely might have, for when seen from the vantage point of the biblical tradition, his Saul's inability to kill David might have been presented by Feuchtwanger not as a sign of weakness, but of moral rectitude.

It is also worth observing that while Feuchtwanger's one-act play departs from the canonical tradition in the ways noted above, he nevertheless remains bound by the biblical chronology which has David and Saul as contemporaries. By contrast, as we have seen in the previous chapter, in both Brecht's synopses of scenes relating to the 'older' David (1919–1920) and in his eventual resumption of these efforts recorded in his later diary entries, Brecht is quite unafraid to have characters from the life of the 'young David' (e.g. Jonathan and Saul) appearing in scenes alongside those from the life of the 'older David' (e.g. Absalom and Uriah), despite the fact that these characters do not overlap or interact with each other in the biblical tradition.

Brecht's greater license vis-à-vis the biblical tradition, especially when juxtaposed with Feuchtwanger's forceful defence of his play's interest in the 'milieu' of the Old Testament and its lack of contradiction of the social context, gestures toward a further point of contrast between the theatrical impulses of the young Feuchtwanger in 1903 and the young Brecht in 1920. While Feuchtwanger's orthodox Jewish upbringing and primary and secondary education are not likely to have been much, if any, more 'biblical' than Brecht's Lutheran one,[37] the young Jewish playwright's greater (and according to his critics, excessive) fascination with the biblical milieu of the stories about Saul and David seems likely to be related to both his enduring interest in ancient history and his classes in biblical studies as an undergraduate. While Brecht's B10 does evince an interest in its biblical narrative setting, including especially the sociopolitical context of military conflict with the Philistines, there is little in his fragments to suggest Brecht was deeply interested in or indeed even meaningfully acquainted with the historical 'milieu' of the Old

---

37. For Brecht's biblical formation, see the Introduction, pp. 1–3 and 8–9 above, and Rohse, *Der frühe Brecht und die Bibel*.

Testament with which Feuchtwanger had surely become familiar during his university studies.

A further and surely more significant point of contrast is to be found in Feuchtwanger's professed interest in and defence of his *Saul* as having an 'idea' – namely, its exploration of the impact of a royal 'will to power' on the respective lives of David, who is not yet king; Saul, who is not the king he once was; and the medium, who loves Saul and wishes for him to be king again. It is not so much Feuchtwanger's interest in the Nietzschean idea itself which offers the point of contrast with Brecht and his David,[38] but rather Feuchtwanger's apparent subscription to the notion that a play, or his *Saul* at any rate, should have or be about an 'idea' at all.

As we will see below, Brecht's disparaging of Otto Zarek's *Karl V* performed in Berlin in the Autumn of 1920 is premised in part on what he saw to be the play's 'nonsense about ideas [*Ideen*] and ideals [*Idealen*]!'[39] While Brecht does not elaborate on this criticism of *Karl V*, his diary entry from the previous day further illustrates Brecht's resistance to the expectation that an 'idea' might be expected of *Drums in the Night*, the play on which he was continuing to work:

2 September 1920

Here is a man apparently at an emotional climax, making a complete volte-face; he tosses all passion aside, tells his followers and admirers to stuff it, then goes home to the woman for whose sake he created the whole mortal fuss. Bed as final curtain. To hell with ideas, to hell with duty [*Was Idee, was Pflicht*]![40]

Here it appears to be his character's volte-face and his dispensing with passion that Brecht sees as tantamount to a laudable dismissal of ideas and duty. But the suggestion that Brecht wishes to free not only his protagonists, but also his plays themselves, from the burden of 'ideas' seems to be supported by his reflection on *David* found in his diary entry thirteen days earlier:

---

38. For some indications of how Brecht was influenced (if not inspired) by Nietzsche with respect to the conception of the literary task, see Hans Reiss, *The Writer's Task from Nietzsche to Brecht* (London: Macmillan, 1978), 140, 166 (in relation to *Baal*). For a fuller exploration of the relationship between the two, see Reinhold Grimm, *Brecht und Nietzsche oder Geständnisse eines Dichters: Fünf Essays und ein Bruchstück* (Frankfurt am Main: Suhrkamp, 1979).
39. *BFA* 26, 152; Eng.: Brecht, *Diaries*, 34.
40. *BFA* 26, 151; Eng.: Brecht, *Diaries*, 33–4.

20 August 1920

I can manage to fit in the young David at some point (*David Amid the Eagles*) and write a kind of history, with no relevance, no point [*ohne Pointe*] to the story, no 'idea' [*ohne 'Idee'*], just the young David [*einfach den Jungen David*] and a slice of his life [*ein Stück aus seinem Leben*]. Then instead of a single interpretation [*einer Deutung*] there'll be hundreds and I won't have to distort anything. Moreover I'm sure that if the visions are really vivid it will acquire some element if not of reason at any rate of soul without my having to do anything about it.

I wrote the first scene right through and started the second. As for the whole I've barely sketched out a scheme of scenes. This evening it seemed the danger was that I might slide off in the direction of grotesqueness. I must make it more concentrated and provide blood and shit rather than intellectual stuff.[41]

Given that as we have seen above (and will revisit in greater detail below), Brecht reports writing B9 and probably B10 the previous month, his reference here, some three weeks later, to writing a first scene and starting a second is more likely a reference to these scenes already penned than to additional scenes. However, the resumption of Brecht's interest in the 'older David' witnessed in the fragments found in the later diary entries may well be anticipated here in Brecht's references to a sketch of schemes of 'the whole', into which the 'young David' – *David Amid the Eagles* – may be incorporated.[42]

Here we see Brecht reject the notion that his play about David should have an 'idea' (or perhaps 'Idea'), which he seemingly equates or at least relates to the story/history having a 'point'. According to the young Brecht, the advantage of freeing his play from the need to have an 'idea' or 'point' (of the playwright's own making) is that it radically democratises the interpretation of his 'young David', indeed exponentially so, allowing it to have not 'one meaning/interpretation' but hundreds. What sorts of 'ideas' Brecht wishes to juxtapose with (and jettison from) his 'piece' of the 'young David's' 'life' may be hinted at in the diary entry of the following day in which Brecht reflects on the deficiencies of Friedrich Hebbel, whose diaries he was reading at the time:

21 August 1920

What grips us is not the magnificent gesture with which Fate [*das Schicksal*] crushes the great man, but just the man himself [*allein der Mensch*], whose

---

41. *BFA* 26, 136; Eng.: Brecht, *Diaries*, 18.
42. This must surely include B10, based on David's reference to Saul and Jonathan as 'eagles', and possibly B9 as well.

fate merely displays him. His fate is his opportunity. So it's not a matter of creating great dramas of principle [*ideele Prinzipiendramen*] which will show the way the world works and the habits of Fate, but straightforward plays [*einfache Stücke*] depicting the fates of men, men who must be the real dividend of the plays [*Stücke*].[43]

In dismissing Hebbel, Brecht here rejects great dramas about principles such as 'Fate' in favour of what truly 'grips' the viewer, namely, 'the man himself' – which echoes his aspirations for *David* voiced in the previous day's entry. Indeed, it is Brecht's use of '*Stück*' (rather than *Drama* or *Spiel*) in the successive diary entries which allows him and us to connect his reflection on theory with his ambition in practice: for the young Brecht, just as the simple piece (*einfache Stücke*) is superior to the dramas of ideas, so will the latter, with its vain aspirations of relevance, be surpassed by Brecht's 'piece of David's life' (*ein Stück aus seinem Leben*) which is nothing more than 'simply young David' (*einfach den Jungen David*).

Whether the 'whole' *David* which Brecht seems to have been sketching would have managed to steer so completely clear of 'ideas' is of course impossible to judge. Nor is it clear even whether Brecht would have judged B9 and B10 (as he left them) to have fully realised such ambitions. Indeed, similar uncertainties apply to Feuchtwanger, not because he did not finish his play, but because so little of the one act he wrote has been preserved for posterity. Nevertheless, the foregoing discussion suggests that, when the young Brecht sat down to dramatise the stories of David and Saul, he had little time in theory at least for the drama of ideas so staunchly defended by the young Feuchtwanger in connection with his own efforts to dramatise David and Saul fifteen years earlier.

Otto Zarek's David

While Brecht gives no explicit indication of his awareness of Feuchtwanger's *Saul*, Brecht's diaries do disclose his familiarity with another adaptation of *David* being written by a mutual acquaintance, Otto Zarek, whilst Brecht was working on his own version.[44] Eventually better known as a writer of novels in the 1930s and of biographies in Budapest where he fled from the Nazis in 1933, Zarek continued his historical writing (including his own memoirs in 1941) in London, before eventually

43. *BFA* 26, 137–8; Eng.: Brecht, *Diaries*, 19–20.
44. For the recollection of the association between Feuchtwanger and Zarek at this time, see the discussion of Brecht's diary entry for 30 July 1920 below.

returning to Germany after the Second World War.[45] In the aftermath of the First World War, however, the young Zarek found himself in Munich, where his path crossed those of Brecht, Feuchtwanger and others in their circle, including Hedda Kuhn. Introduced by Kuhn to Brecht in the winter of 1918/1919 after a meeting of Kutscher's theatre seminar which they all attended, Zarek was, like Brecht, seeking to make his way as a playwright whilst studying a more respectable subject (in his case, law) at the same university. But while Zarek was the same age as Brecht (indeed, ten days younger), his first serious play, *Karl V*, had already been published by Georg Müller in 1918 and opened at Max Reinhardt's Deutsches Theater in Berlin on 29 August 1920.[46] Brecht's diary entry five days after *Karl V*'s premiere reveals Brecht's unguarded view of his rival and the play:

> 3 September 1920
>
> Zarek has been chucked out of 'Junges Deutschland' chez Reinhardt: (Young Germany, an outfit full of young Germans, that's to say not German all that long, their Germanness is young.) [Zarek's] *Karl V* is a vacuous botch up, full of 'glowing' ambition which of course people take for passion. But that chap is far too vain to be able to do anything worthwhile. You can massacre yourself, but not by flagellation. And all that nonsense about Ideas and Ideals.[47]

Here again, we see Brecht railing against the drama of ideas, as exemplified in Zarek's play. While Brecht was not alone in his dismissal of the 'Young Germany' series or the final instalment of it offered by Zarek,[48] he may have passed judgement on *Karl V* well before the play reached the Berlin stage, if he shared the views of Hedda Kuhn:

> In Munich, in my room in the Adalbertstraße, we – Zarek, Brecht, and I – staged a kind of song contest. Each one has to write a scene about Karl V. Zarek did it easily, because he just had to take something out of his play of that name. Brecht also wrote something, in which he tore the Kaiser apart.

45. Originally published as Otto Zarek, *German Odyssey* (London: J. Cape, 1941) and in an adapted form under the title of *Splendour and Shame: My German Odyssey* (Indianapolis: Bobbs-Merrill, 1941).
46. Otto Zarek, *Kaiser Karl V: Ein Drama* (Munich: Georg Müller Verlag, 1918).
47. *BFA* 26, 152; Eng.: Brecht, *Diaries*, 34.
48. See, for instance, the review of the play by Max Meyerfeld, 'Exit Junges Deutschland', *Neuen Zürcher Zeitung*, 5 September 1920, which highlights the lack of dramatic tension in Zarek's play (http://horst-schroeder.com/krit19-33.htm). Cf. also the review by Fritz Engel ('Verein Junges Deutschland Otto Zareks "Kaiser Karl V"', *Berliner Tageblatt*, 30 August 1920.

For that I wanted to judge him the victor, but we couldn't reach agreement. Where the scenes Brecht wrote at that time are now, I don't know.[49]

Given the complicated nature of Kuhn's relationship with Brecht, it would be unwise to draw too many conclusions from her favouring of his scene over Zarek's, but her contrasting of Brecht's excoriation of the emperor with Zarek's depiction certainly resonates with Brecht's unvarnished treatment of David in B10, as we have seen. While the absence of Brecht's own 'fragment' of *Karl V* from his writings, if it ever existed among them, prevents its comparison with Zarek's published play, Kuhn's recollection of Brecht's anti-heroic tendencies in reaction to the more conventional work of a rival also resonates with Brecht's writing of *Baal* in response to *The Loner (Der Einsame)*, by Hanns Johst, whose 1917 novel, *The Beginning (Der Anfang)*, Brecht had so ruthlessly dissected in Kutscher's seminar.[50] More specifically, Kuhn's memory of Brecht's creative clash with Zarek in relation to *Karl V* sits very comfortably, as we will see, alongside Brecht's own recollection of his reaction to Zarek's *David*.

The *David* fragments which appear in Brecht's notebooks appear to confirm Münsterer's recollections that Brecht had his *David* 'on the brain' prior to the summer of 1920. As we will see however, Brecht's diary suggests that Brecht was not as far along with his *David* as Zarek was with his when they met at the end of July in 1920. Indeed, while Brecht's *David* would never be finished, Zarek's play may well have been at quite an advanced stage at this point, given that it was published the following year, again by Georg Müller, not long after the publisher finally rejected Brecht's *Baal*.[51]

Quickly published, but seemingly never produced, Zarek's five-act *David* is a rather free adaptation of the biblical account of David's rise at the expense of Saul and his family beginning with David's triumph over Goliath (1 Sam. 17) and culminating in his crowning as king (2 Sam. 5).[52]

---

49. Frisch and Obermaier, *Brecht in Augsburg*, 128.

50. See, for instance, Ulrich Weisstein, 'The Lonely Baal: Brecht's First Play as a Parody of Hanns Johst's *Der Einsame*', *Modern Drama* 13, no. 3 (1970): 284–303. For Brecht's critique of Johst, see Chapter 3 above, p. 117.

51. Otto Zarek, *David: Ein dramatisches Gedicht in fünf Akten* (Munich: Georg Müller Verlag, 1921).

52. While Zarek's *David* does not appear to have a conventional production history *per se*, a reading of two scenes of the play is reported in connection with a private gathering of associates of Karl Meier, editor of the gay periodical *Der Kreis*, in which the scene of David's farewell to Jonathan was published. For this and further

The freedom of Zarek's treatment may be seen in his creation of novel characters (e.g. Asuba, a maidservant of Michal, who is in love with David and Hagar, a young boy in David's entourage); his elimination of others from the canonical tradition (Abner, Saul's general and Abigail, David's wife); and his enlarging of still other characters including Michal, but also notably Achish, king of the Philistines, and Saul's son Ish-bosheth. Indeed, Zarek's most notable structural innovation is to have Saul's son Ish-bosheth plot with the Philistines to create a war which will eliminate not only David, but Saul and Jonathan too, allowing Saul's younger son an unobstructed rise to power. While the latter thus becomes the primary antagonist of Zarek's *David*, one of the play's thematic interests is found in the tension between generations, exemplified in the exchanges between a 'young warrior' and an 'old warrior', but also in Jonathan's characterisation of David as 'youth' incarnate, over and against the old guard represented by Saul.[53]

At the same time, judging from the play itself, Zarek, like others, shared the biblical tradition's interest in David's relationships with Saul and Jonathan.[54] In his study of male homosexuality in the theatre of the Weimar Republic, Wolf Borchers rightly notes that Zarek's *David* foregrounds the relationship between Jonathan and David at the expense of the latter's relationship with Michal, a pattern which we have already noted is established in the biblical material itself.[55] Borchers suggests that Zarek's homoerotic colouring of Jonathan and David's relationship in the play may be seen in its references to physical displays of affection between the two.[56] It is true that Zarek's Jonathan does rhapsodise over a hug,[57] but it should be noted that elsewhere he feels only *like* one

---

indications of Meier's esteem for Zarek's play and other work, see Hubert Kennedy, *The Ideal Gay Man: The Story of* Der Kreis (Binghamton: Haworth Press, 1999), 26–8, 110.

53. As observed by Jobling, '"David on the Brain"', 233, and Borchers, 'Männliche Homosexualität', 133. See Zarek, *David*, 57.

54. While Borchers, 'Männliche Homosexualität', 35, acknowledges that evidence for a homoerotic reading of Jonathan and David in German-language adaptations around the turn of the century is slender, he argues that Friedrich Sebrecht's *Saul* (1919) and Johanna Wolff's *Die Töchter Sauls* (1919) both explore this more fully. Based on the textual support Borchers musters, however (35–7), the latter two would appear to offer very little of substance in this direction and arguably rather less than Zarek's *David*.

55. See Chapter 3, p. 99.

56. Borchers, 'Männliche Homosexualität', 139.

57. Zarek, *David*, 150.

who is kissed *by the sun* rather than kissed by David;[58] other references to 'kissing' are clearly couched in metaphor.[59] Indeed, in some ways, Zarek's play is less explicit than the biblical tradition itself which, as we have seen, happily represents Jonathan and David's displays of physical affection ('they kissed each other', 1 Sam. 20.41). Likewise, while Borchers observes that the relationship between Zarek's David and Jonathan is explicitly characterised as one of 'love',[60] this is little more than the biblical tradition (2 Sam. 1.26) happily admits, as we have seen. Moreover, given that as Borchers admits, there is no explicit enactment of homoeroticism in the play,[61] such colouring in Zarek's work is ultimately rather faint, accomplished largely by allowing the intimacy of David and Jonathan's relationship to be verbalised by the characters themselves in ways not seen in 1 Samuel.

That this colouring is less vivid than it might be is perhaps also due in part to David's eventual characterisation of his relationship with Jonathan in terms of 'friendship'. When Joab and Michal interrupt David's lament over the funeral bier of his 'beloved' Jonathan (236), Zarek's David expresses twice over that he has been left now with 'no friend in the world' (twice on 237), a refrain which he echoes a third time (240) and then a fourth time (241) as Joab seeks to extract David from his grief. While the public quality of David's profession of 'friendship with Jonathan' may perhaps be dismissed as a concession to cultural conventions of heteronormativity (both ancient and modern), the importance of 'friendship' for Zarek's David is also highlighted in the negotiation of his relationship with Saul, illustrated most clearly in Zarek's play when David plays and sings before Saul.[62]

58. Ibid., 65.
59. See e.g. ibid., 152.
60. Borchers, 'Männliche Homosexualität', 138, notes that the relationship is characterised in terms of 'love' not only by David and Jonathan themselves but also by others.
61. Ibid., 139.
62. Zarek and Brecht were of course not the only ones to see the dramatic potential of David's singing before Saul. Indeed, the cataloguing undertaken by Nebel (*Harfe, Speer und Krone*, 56–7) indicates that David's singing was the single most adapted element in the biblical tradition, appearing in no less than 28 of the 33 German-language plays devoted to David or Saul written between 1880 and 1920 – including one in which David's singing is sufficiently important that he is made to sing before Samuel instead of Saul, because the drama concludes with the election of the latter. While in many of these plays, David's singing serves little narrative purpose, in others the treatment of the scene reflects larger scale departures from the biblical storyline (resulting in the inclusion of other characters, including Michal or

In a scene (Act II, Scene 17) which effectively corresponds to Brecht's B9, Saul's response to a song which David has just finished playing on the harp includes the following:

Saul

Am I not good? I love you, David!
And what I am, I fought for myself,
And what I am not, must I never be![63]
In this hour, I am good. The earth
Often reaches me and pulls me deep into the dust.[64]
But now she fell asleep – and I am free!

David

Neither in morning nor in evening storm,
In autumn wind nor in summer rain
Does God divide sense into time and time![65]
O King! Who did not succumb to earth
And fearfully cast himself at the feet of its plunder.[66]
Hold back[67] what you suffer from Being,
And suffer: God![68]

Abigail), while in still others the scene is seized upon as a means of illuminating the relationship between Saul and David, as in the four plays discussed in this chapter. For fuller discussion and references to specific plays, see ibid., 250–3.

63. *Und was ich nicht bin, darf ich niemals sein!* The verb choice of *dürfen* suggests the idea of 'being allowed' to be, stronger perhaps than 'must' (or possible alternative 'may') in the translation. This could refer either to the self 'allowing' oneself to be a certain way, or it could imply an external entity (like God) 'allowing' one to be.

64. *Die Erde / Erreicht mich oft und zerrt mich tief in Staub.* A difficult line with unusual verb choices; *erreichen* is associated with achievement and accomplishment, rather than the active form of 'reaching' that is implied here, while *zerren* includes the sense of 'lugging' or 'dragging' as well as 'pulling', as translated here.

65. *Zerteilt der Gott den Sinn an Zeit und Zeit.* Makes little sense in the German. An alternative to this translation is the idea that God divides sense (*Sinn* in the sense of 'meaning') from time and time, rather than 'into'.

66. *Wer erlag der Erde nicht / Und warf sich angstvoll ihrem Raub zu Füßen.* The translation interprets the phrase *ihrem Raub* as relating to the Earth's plunder, rather than to the King's.

67. The verb used here is *verhängen*, which is typically used in the context of 'to impose' or 'to inflict' penalty. It could also carry the sense of a covering up; the context is insufficient to determine the playwright's intent.

68. Zarek, *David*, 92.

Saul is here responding to David's earlier assurances that despite Saul's own doubts, the king is indeed 'good'. There are no signs in the rest of the scene that Saul loves David for anything more than his reassuring words. Certainly, such love would seem to fall well short of the 'great love' (1 Sam. 16.21) the biblical Saul feels for David, and has nothing in common with the eroticised love Jonathan has for David in Zarek's play or that which Saul has for David in Brecht's scene (B9). Sensing instead that Saul's need is for spiritual companionship and that Saul still seeks a glimpse of the heavenly king, about which it is implied David has already sung,[69] Zarek's David agrees to sing another song, or perhaps the same one again, which highlights the 'friendship' of God:

David's Song

Mankind is tired!
But I am the King of the World!
For the King of the World is the lover.

There is no path between gods and the human.
Bridges build the fools and dreams the poor,[70]
So that they rise up, to the solitary divinity above.[71]
But between this and the people
Is no path.
For there is a God, who does not hide himself,
But is a friend to mankind!

There are secrets in our twisted vessels,[72]
They breathe the divine in tired lamps
Streaming out oil. – And there are solitudes,
That hold the tread of the eternal in their narrowness:
For there is a God, who is a friend to mankind.

The friend: is the God of mankind.
With naked eyes we run on
Against things and radiant form and giving hands

---

69. Ibid., 91, 93.
70. *Brücken bauen die Toren und Träume die Armseligen*. It is clearer in the German that the noun form of 'dreams' is intended, in parallel with 'bridges' in the grammar, rather than another verb.
71. *Gottheit* is used here, which is more like 'godliness' or 'deity' than 'God'.
72. *wirren Gefäßen* has few possible translations, but it is understood here that the vessels are 'twisted' rather than it referring to the mental action of 'confused' that normally applies to the adjective *wirr*.

And do not turn our sight away from light play
And active time and wisdom and word.
But wise and restless is not the friend of mankind
For mankind's friend: is God!

But neither in the eyes, nor in the senses
Is the friend of mankind visible.
And I said, he would be visible in the heart:
But I said nothing!
For the heart is the eye of the soul,
And the soul the essence of God,[73]
And God is unnamable.

But mankind built itself a throne
Above the clouds of the earth, near to the stars.
And there the clouds of the Lord asked of him:
'What is your dwelling near the Lord, for God,
And so proud is your being near the Lord, so near,
And no longer tired is mankind!' –

Thus I named mankind's dwelling at the heart of God,
Who is friend to men, and I said:
'The eye of man, that sees above the clouds,
And the heart of man, that beats near the throne of God,
And the spirit of man, radiating through space:
You know, what mankind's dwelling is: a soul.
But mankind's soul is: Love!'

Mankind is tired! The earth is not his place.
But the friend is the God of mankind,
And the eternal soul of man is: Love![74]

This friendship of God to mankind, evoked in various forms throughout the song, is clearly its *leitmotif* and is intended to reassure a forlorn Saul, whose spirit is beset by troubles both temporal and especially spiritual. Zarek's imagining of a song of this sort for David does not seem entirely out of place, given the biblical witness to Saul's sense of abandonment by

---

73. *Und die Seele das Wesen des Gottes* is a theologically freighted line, which has governed the translation of 'essence' for *Wesen*, instead of alternatives like 'nature of God' or 'being of God'.

74. Zarek, *David*, 94–5.

God, his sense of being replaced by David and his increasingly troubled spirit. In the absence of other signals, the song's reference to 'secrets in our twisted vessels' – an alternative to the translation might be 'confused' vessels – if it relates to homoerotic feelings at all (to which we will return below), can only relate to Jonathan's feelings for David, rather than Saul's. Indeed, David's ode to 'divine friendship' in Zarek's scene suggests that the ailment for which it is an antidote is Saul's spiritual isolation rather than a homosexual frustration.

What makes the above contrast between Zarek's scene with Brecht's all the more intriguing is the virtual certainty that Brecht was inspired to write his scene of 'David and Saul' (B9) after hearing Zarek's version. One month before *Karl V* was to open in Berlin, Brecht recalls meeting Zarek, who was perhaps back in Munich to take up his role as dramaturg at the Kammerspiele:

27 July 1920

Met Zarek, Bazarek.[75] He's not as clever as I'd expected, creatively speaking he has a conceptual block. On top of that he has a damned rigid style. I sang some of my songs and he described a scene from his *David* (David before Saul). Apparently it had turned sticky and he had made it work by means of plotting [*Intrige*]. I said offhand it should be done without plotting [*Intrige*]. And then I demonstrated it without that. He opened his mouth wide. It popped in, then he shut it again, gulped once or twice with his Adam's apple, and swallowed. He fancied he now felt like rewriting the whole thing. 'Zo?', he said.

28 July 1920

Wrote the Saul–David scene. Good stuff in it. It works without any plotting [*Intrige*]. Saul delivers his potpourri and covers all the high and low points, and during the entire switchback ride, David is sitting there cutting his nails.[76]

The first of these entries clearly reflects Brecht's not-so-thinly veiled contempt for a rival who had, despite his evident mediocrity in Brecht's

---

75. While Antony Tatlow (in private correspondence) points out that 'bazi' – with which Brecht conflates Zarek's name – seems in the southern dialect of the time to have had the connotation of nothing worse than 'scamp' or 'rascal' (cf. *BFA*, 26, 531), it fits comfortably with Brecht's dismissal of his rival here and elsewhere in the diaries.

76. *BFA* 26, 130–1; Eng.: Brecht, *Diaries*, 12–13.

eyes, achieved a measure of the artistic success which had thus far eluded Brecht himself. It is of course impossible to know whether Zarek actually expressed a desire to rewrite his own scene having heard Brecht's improvised effort, or if he did so, whether the scene was rewritten by Zarek before it was published. However, it seems quite probable that the 'Saul–David scene' Brecht claims to have written the day after hearing Zarek's version is none other than the one exhumed from his notebooks (B9), not only because Brecht's scene like Zarek's answers very well to the description 'David before Saul', but also because, as we have seen, Brecht's response at other times to what he perceived to be inferior or flawed work was to write something which improved upon or corrected it in some fashion.[77] But improved upon it in what way?

While Brecht's eroticisation of the older Saul's love for the younger David in B9 is nowhere to be seen in Zarek's scene, the above diary entries seek to juxtapose Brecht's efforts with Zarek's in terms of 'plotting' (*Intrige*) and perhaps also style. Brecht's use of *Intrige* confirms that the problem he detects in Zarek's scene is not one of plot (*Handlung*), but of 'plotting' in the sense of English 'intrigue', 'machinations' or 'scheming'.[78] In Brecht's scene, Saul's inability to contain his affection for David and David's inability to cope with it leave little room at all for 'scheming'. But the fact that there seems to be even less of it in Zarek's scene as published may well suggest that Zarek did indeed rewrite the scene following Brecht's advice and example, though that is far from certain.

Rather more transparent are the differences between Zarek's and Brecht's scenes in terms of 'style'. These are already visible when the respective songs of David in the two plays are compared. While Zarek's David sings in regular stanzas and poetic language of serious ideas (i.e. friendship of God), Brecht's David sings, as we have seen, in free verse, a boisterous and even bucolic ditty whose refrain captures its essence: 'Ha! Ha! Laugh in Judah, laugh and clap, Clap in Judah; that you can still laugh!' It is entirely possible that when Brecht laments the '*unplastischen Stil*' of the scene Zarek read for him on the 27th of July, he may

---

77. Contra Jobling, 'David on the Brain', 233, who dismisses too quickly Brecht's claim to have written his 'Saul–David scene' the following day as a 'typical Brechtian myth to advertise how quick and clever he is'. Evidence that the scene referred to in the diaries is none other B9 is also furnished by the dating of the MS of the latter (28.7.20) in his notebooks (BBA 10459/14r).

78. For Brecht's reflections on plot (*Handlung*) in relation to *David* and Hebbel, see his diary entry for 6 September 1920 (*BFA* 26, 157; Eng.: Brecht, *Diaries*, 39).

have had in mind not only David's song, but also the dialogue between king and courtier, illustrated by the exchange between David and Saul prior to David's song, to which we've already referred in the previous chapter.

Because Brecht in his diary entry above describes his own scene as dominated by Saul with David contributing little (apart from his song), his accusation of Zarek's rigid style may reflect Brecht's rejection of the conventional balance and pacing of the latter's scene, in which neither Saul nor David ever deliver fewer than three lines at a time, and frequently offer many more. Thus, not only is the language in Brecht's scene more colloquial and less exalted, the dialogue is also quicker and sharper, with Saul and David exchanging single lines especially toward the end of B9 as the tension between them grows. Indeed, whereas according to Brecht himself, in his own scene David is merely 'cutting his nails', in Zarek's version, David very much holds his own and indeed arguably ends up dominating proceedings.

Two days later, (as we've noted above), Brecht reports a further encounter with Zarek and more progress on his own David:

> 30 July 1920
>
> In the afternoon Feuchtwanger and Zarek came to tea. Wrote the first scene of a play, *Saul and David* which I propose to do on the side and without any previous plan, though the raw material is good.[79]

It is impossible to say for certain whether the scene which concludes with the appearance of Jesse (B10) is the 'first scene' Brecht refers to here, but circumstantial evidence points in this direction: while the allusions to David having killed his 'ten thousands' in B9 suggests that B9 presupposes David's triumph over the Philistines, B10's frequent references to imminent conflict with the Philistines and especially the allusion to David's sling at the end of the scene, seem to anticipate his monomachy with Goliath.[80] Unlike B9, which was evidently written in reaction to Zarek's own version, there is little in the remainder of Zarek's play to which Brecht's B10 may be compared, in part because Brecht's indolent and irreverent David, so full of opinions, is so far removed from Zarek's David.

---

79. *BFA* 26, 131; Eng.: Brecht, *Diaries*, 13.
80. For a discussion of Brecht's *Goliath*, see pp. 208–16 below. How, if at all, Brecht had planned to treat the character of 'Goliath' at this stage we do not know.

For all their differences, Brecht's B10 and Zarek's play do share a common, heightened interest in the military conflict with the Philistines. While the latter is very much the backdrop against which the narrative of Saul's demise and David's rise is played out in 1 Samuel, it is not altogether surprising that with the traumas of WWI fresh in the two young playwrights' minds, war moves to the foreground at various points in Zarek's play and in Brecht's scene, as discussed in the previous chapter. In Zarek's play, while the enthusiasm of an old warrior for battle is resisted by a young warrior, the insistence of the latter, on the morning of the battle with the Philistines, that he doesn't want to die,[81] is less a principled objection to war than a sentiment stemming from a fear that David is not yet with them. Indeed, the young warrior responds whole-heartedly to Zarek's Jonathan ('To the battle! Jonathan and Youth!')[82] when the latter eventually rallies the troops to do their duty – something which Brecht's Jonathan does too in B10 despite his deferential treatment of David.

When Zarek's David finds himself a vassal of the Philistine Achish, and Joab suggests it is his duty to attack the Amalekites after they have raided one of the villages in David's care, David's response is noteworthy: 'Two Amalekites? You kill them! Should a people bleed in war because of that?'[83] Note, however, that Zarek's David here objects not to war *per se* (nor clearly to killing), but to war as a disproportionate response to aggression which should be handled in a proportional way. While one might easily imagine how the circumstances surrounding the outbreak of WWI might have nudged Zarek's David in this direction, his David has little else to say about wars against the Philistines or indeed war in general. This is of course in sharp contrast to Brecht's David who has plenty to say about 'the war', as we have seen in the previous chapter.

It is clear that Otto Zarek's *David* played a significant role in Brecht's creative process, by, as was so often the case, demonstrating to Brecht what his *David* should not be. Indeed, further comparison of Brecht's *David* fragments with other 'Davids' written for the German stage in the early twentieth century might well prove fruitful, but to limit our focus to German literature is to forget both the breadth of the young Brecht's literary interests and the popularity of German translations of dramatic works originally written in other languages, including, of course, French.

81. Zarek, *David*, 211.
82. Ibid., 215.
83. Ibid., 198.

André Gide's Saül

Born in Paris nearly thirty years before Brecht, André Gide too was brought up as a Protestant – the only son of the notably devout Juliette Rondeaux and Paul Gide, a Professor of Law from a respectable southern Huguenot family. Just as Feuchtwanger's early experiences of the Bible were mediated by his father's fascination with them, so too Gide recalls the Scriptures featuring amongst the great works of literature read to him by his father. However, whereas Herr Feuchtwanger drew upon the stories illustrated on his walls, Professor Gide burdened his son with the beginning of the book of Job, where the latter's life is destroyed by Satan with divine permission in order to determine whether Job's piety is truly disinterested. Perhaps because of his mother Juliette's own piety and concern for her son's soul, Gide later recalled that she asked to join father and son for the reading of Job, which was relocated to a small-drawing room, more properly his mother's domain.[84] While Gide admits that some of Job's aesthetic virtues may have eluded his young mind, he notes the deep impression the reading of the 'sacred' text made upon him, not only because of the solemnity of the story, but also the gravity with which it was delivered by his father and attended to by his mother.

Some indication of the impression made by the Bible on Gide may be glimpsed in the frequency of references to it in his early writings, including his first book *Les Cahiers de André Walter*, published in 1891. Indeed, according to Gide, that the Bible was not referenced even more in the *Cahiers* was thanks only to the objections of his cousin, Albert Démarest, who upon reading a draft, objected both to an excess of pietism but also to the frequency of his scriptural citation.[85] While Gide claims to have excised two thirds of them in response, the fact that so many remain indicates just how steeped in the Scriptures the young Gide was. The *Cahiers*' portrait of a Walter besotted by his cousin Emmanuèle pointed rather obviously to Gide's chaste love for his own cousin, Madeleine, whom he would pursue until she married him, some five years later.[86] Before doing so, however, Gide spent time in North Africa, not in the company of his wife, as Feuchtwanger would with Martha some years later, but with others including Oscar Wilde and various locals – an

---

84. André Gide, *If It Die*, trans. Dorothy Bussy (New York: Penguin, 1950), 15.
85. Ibid., 205.
86. Gide had the name Emmanuèle replaced with Madeleine in several copies, and dedicated the book to her. See Alan Sheridan, *André Gide: A Life in the Present* (London: Penguin, 1998), 60–1.

experience which confirmed both Gide's platonic feelings for Madeleine and his sexual taste for young men. Such tastes may be detected in *Les Nourritures Terrestres* (*The Fruits of the Earth*), which is no less self-revelatory than the *Cahiers* in its own way, though more overtly didactic.

The anonymous narrator of *The Fruits* tells the story of his own teacher Ménalque for the benefit of the narrator's disciple Nathanaël, to whom the work as a whole is addressed. Both Ménalque and the narrator are clearly open to both homosexual and heterosexual experiences and indeed, the work is first and foremost a paean to desire (including but not limited to sexual desire) and its satisfaction. Not surprisingly, however, given Gide's own journey, the narrator's spiritual/pedagogical purposes are suffused with a pederastic sensuality:

> And as Elisha stretched himself upon the Shulamit's [*sic*][87] son to recall him to life – 'his mouth upon his mouth, and his eyes upon his eyes, and his hands upon his hands', so will I, shedding all the light of my radiant heart upon your still unilluminated soul, stretch myself upon you, my mouth upon your mouth, my forehead upon your forehead, your cold hands in my burning hands, and my burning heart... ('And', it is written, 'the flesh of the child waxed warm'...) so that you may awake in delight – *and then leave me* – for a thrilling and lawless life. Nathaniel, here is all the warmth of my soul – take it. Nathaniel, I would teach you fervour.[88]

For our purposes, it is not so much the sensualising of the teacher-pupil relationship itself which is remarkable, but the way in which Gide's narrator uses the even then relatively obscure passage from 2 Kings 4.34, in which the prophet Elisha resurrects a boy who has died, by first praying and then lying on him in an act of contagious magic. Gide's choice of biblical episode is clearly not accidental, nor in all likelihood is his omission of Elisha's prayer. Indeed, the comparable episode of Jesus raising the widow of Nain's son (Luke) by the power of his word alone might well have satisfied Gide's requirements, had he been interested purely in the revitalising power of pedagogy. However, it is clearly the physicality of Elisha's Old Testament episode (exceeding even the Elijah version found earlier in 1 Kings 17) which suggested itself to Gide's narrator as a profoundly sensual illustration of his point, despite the absence of eroticism in its biblical incarnation.

87. Comparison with the French (André Gide, *Les Nourritures Terrestres* [Paris: Mercure, 1897]) suggests Bussy has misread 'Shulamit(e)' (of Song of Songs fame) for Gide's expected and correct 'Sunamite'.
88. André Gide, *Fruits of the Earth*, trans. Dorothy Bussy (London: Secker & Warburg, 1949), 42.

A rather more conventional reading of an earlier episode in the biblical history may be found in book VII of *The Fruits of the Earth*: 'Saul, in the desert, looking for his asses – You did not find your asses, but instead of them, the kingdom you were not looking for'.[89] Apart from the fact that it follows hard on the heels of a passage devoted to the wonder of the desert, there is little to prepare the reader of *The Fruits* for Gide's fleeting reference to Saul. But this reference to a story which is both recounted (Act 1) and then re-enacted in *Saül* surely reflects what Gide's correspondence confirms: even while he was finishing *The Fruits*, Gide had already identified in the story of Israel's first king both a desert and a desire ripe for his dramatic re-reading.[90] In parsing the relationship between the two works years later, Gide insisted that it was the dangers of unfettered openness (*accueil*) so celebrated by *The Fruits of the Earth* which was the moral of *Saül*.[91] Indeed, even as he was writing the play, Gide had already pondered *Saül*'s relationship to the earlier work, as may be seen in a letter to Paul Valéry on 22 October 1898:

> It would be better to understand that what I am writing, *Saul*, is to be read as a negation of *The Fruits* – as is clear from these sentences that I felt I needed to add to [Saul's] monologue at the beginning, to make it a bit more clear: 'The slightest noise, the faintest scent distracts me, my senses are open to the outside world and I miss nothing lovely which passes me. Later, the witch will say and he [Saul] will repeat: "Everything which delights me is my enemy".'[92]

With five acts at his disposal, instead of Feuchtwanger's one, Gide is able to situate his version of Saul's encounter with the witch of Endor (1 Sam. 28) within the wider narrative of David's rise but especially Saul's demise (1 Sam. 16–31). Indeed, mindful of the way in which 1 Samuel describes both Saul's delight in David and his eventual usurpation by him, Gide's theme as he himself articulates it above may seem unremarkable. What is rather more novel, however, is Gide's construal of the source of Saul's demise as his indulging of his homoerotic desire for David.

89. Ibid., 146.
90. Indeed, while Gide's *Saül* was published by Mercure only in 1903 and staged for the first time as late as 1922 (by Jacques Copeau at the Vieux Colombier), Gide was writing it as *The Fruits of the Earth* went to press in 1897.
91. See the letters from Gide to Poucel (27 November 1927) and to a Reverend Ferrari (15 March 1928) excerpted by Patrick Pollard, *André Gide: Homosexual Moralist* (New Haven: Yale University Press, 1991), 335.
92. André Gide and Paul Valéry, *André Gide, Paul Valéry: Correspondance, 1890–1942*, ed. Robert Mallet (Paris: Gallimard, 1955), 339.

That the love of Gide's Saul in the play is not for his wife, the Queen, is made clear both by his perception of their animosity ('If she proposes anything, it must be something that will do me harm', 'The woman detests me', 'I hate her'[93]) and especially the Queen's own account of Saul's renunciation of her, which she offers to the high priest, Nabal:

> Saul never loved me. After he married me he made a pretence of turning some show of flame towards me; but it was a very short-lived pretence. You can't imagine, Nabal, the coldness of his embraces! As soon as I was with child, they ceased altogether... I know, I know he took concubines; but now he has repudiated them all.[94]

In their loveless and eventually asexual marriage, it is the Queen who manages the kingdom, and in Gide's play it is she who recruits David, eventually to fight Goliath, but initially to help her learn the 'secret' revealed to Saul and the reader by the stars: that Saul will be succeeded by someone other than Jonathan (i.e. an unknown enemy). The first inkling of the delight which will destroy Saul is offered to the audience when David is ushered in to see him and Saul says, 'It's true that he's young, Ah but he's terribly good-looking!'[95]

It is, however, only when Saul observes from behind a curtain the intimacies between David and his son, Jonathan, that the audience begins to more fully appreciate that the secret driving the narrative does not merely relate to Saul's succession but also his sexual feelings for David.[96] Indeed, it is worth noting that Jonathan's own attraction to David and his confession of it in Gide's scene goes well beyond the biblical Jonathan's gifting of his robe and weapons to David as tokens of his loyalty and love (1 Sam. 18.3-4), which evidently inspired it in part:

> Oh if only I were a goatherd like you, naked under my sheepskin, in the open air! How beautiful you are, David! How I wish I could walk with you on the hills. You would clear every stone from my path; at noon we would bathe our weary feet in the cool waters. Then we would lie down among the vines. You would sing. In what lofty words I would tell you of my love!ized[97]

93. Gide, *Saul*, 179–80; see also 204.
94. André Gide, *The Return of the Prodigal: Preceded by Five Other Treatises, with Saul, a Drama in Five Acts*, trans. Dorothy Bussy (London: Secker & Warburg, 1953), 168–9.
95. Gide, *Saul*, 192.
96. In Act II, Saul's men snigger that David would not have been allowed to fight Goliath were it not for the king's 'secret', but the secret is not disclosed at this point.
97. Gide, *Saul*, 219–20.

Moreover, that Jonathan's affections are reciprocated by David to some degree seems clear, when he says: 'You are more lovely now in your white tunic than in all your regal finery...it was for your sake I came down from the mountains... Comfort your weakness here, in my arms.' It is at this point of physical intimacy that the observing Saul is overcome by his mounting jealousy, murmuring 'Oh! Not that! Oh! Not that!' before rushing out from his hiding place shouting, 'And Saul, then? And Saul?', which in turn puts David to flight.

Having earlier expressed his pleasure that David would see him without his crown, Gide's Saul now has his beard shaved in order to look 'younger', so that David will 'like him'.[98] Despite already suspecting that the object of his desire is the enemy who will usurp him and displace his son, Gide's Saul seeks confirmation from the ghost of Samuel summoned up by the witch of Endor (1 Sam. 28) whom Saul suspects has been told that he loves David. Unlike Feuchtwanger's Saul who is, as we have seen, dismissed by the witch with contempt, Gide's Saul seeks to protect his secret by killing the witch, whose dying words offer the final warning alluded to by Gide in his letter above to Valéry:

Witch (*in the throes of death*)

Shut your door!! Close your eyes! Stop your ears and let not love's perfume...

Saul (*with a start of fear*)

What?

Witch (*with an effort*)

...find a way into your heart. All that is delightful to you is your enemy. Free yourself! Saul...Saul...[99]

It is at this point that Gide offers, as the last scene of the third act, his own version of 'David before Saul', the biblical scene which so captivated other playwrights and artists of the period, including, as we have seen, both Zarek and Brecht.

Gide's version of this scene opens with David singing and playing the end of one song and then beginning another, which he has composed especially for the king. While both David's songs appear to be calculated

---

98. Ibid., 226–7.
99. Ibid., 247.

to rouse Saul himself to fight the Philistines, the second of them bores Saul and prompts him to ask whether David knows anything more cheerful.[100] Wishing then to talk, Saul seeks and manages to extract from Gide's David a rather laconic and unenthusiastic affirmation that the king looks better without a beard, which in turn prompts Saul to admit that 'It was for you I had it cut…David', because Saul thought the beard made him look older in David's eyes.[101] The stage directions note David's embarrassment and resumption of his playing, which enrages Saul to the point of nearly striking David, and which then in turn prompts David to move to leave. David's departure, a seemingly clear marker of his discomfort with Saul's feelings for him, is pre-empted by Saul's resumption of the conversation. When David replies 'in some confusion' to Saul's question about what he prays to God for, Saul's response, increasingly angry, prompts David 'at the end of his tether' to make 'a move to go away', which in turn leads Saul to bait David, 'Oh there he is now wanting to go off!' When David cannot oblige the king's request for a merry song, Gide's Saul tells David to 'Just play! For that matter, your singing disturbs my thoughts. One can't always be entertained'.[102] It is as David continues to play, that Saul begins to yield to his feelings as his: 'secret, alive within me, cries aloud with all its strength', consuming his soul 'eating it away day and night like an ever wakeful fire', stirred by the music. Despite admonishing himself in terms reminiscent of the opening scene ('Stop your ears against his voice! All that comes near to me is hostile to me! Shut down, gates of my eyes! All deliciousness is hostile!') Saul's secret cannot be contained any longer:

Saul

Delicious! Delicious! Oh! To be with him, a goatherd like him, beside the running brooks! Oh! To see him all day long! To wander with him in the ardour of the desert, as once, alas! Long ago, seeking for my she-asses.

---

100. Ibid., 249. As A. L. Lerner, *Passing the Love of Women: A Study of Gide's Saül and its Biblical Roots* (Lanham: University Press of America, 1980), 63–4 also notes, the songs draw upon words and themes of Pss. 57 and especially 45.

101. Gide, *Saul*, 250. While Pollard, *André Gide*, 331, rightly dismisses as simplistic the suggestion that Saul's shaving of his beard establishes his homosexual identity (so Jean Hytier, *André Gide*, trans. Richard Howard [Garden City: Doubleday, 1962], 160), Pollard himself fails to appreciate the text's own signalling of its significance: Saul has his beard removed in order to make himself appear younger and more attractive to David.

102. Gide, *Saul*, 252.

In the heat of the air, I should burn! And then I should feel my soul less burning – my soul which this music stirs – and which rushes from my lips – towards you, Daoud, delicious.

*(At this **David** flings his harp to the ground so that it breaks. **Saul** seems to be waking out of a dream)*

Saul

Where am I? David! David! Stop! Stop!

David

Farewell Saul! No longer for you alone will your secret be intolerable! *(He goes out)*.[103]

While the play concludes with Saul's psychological disintegration and eventual death, this scene marks the king's final interaction with Gide's David and the disclosure of the secret which has increasingly haunted Saul.

As has been noted by others, the suggestion that homoerotic desire *per se* is the vice against which the play warns is obviously complicated by Gide's portrayal of David and Jonathan, the homoerotic overtones of which would find a clear resonance in Zarek's own portrayal of David and Jonathan in 1920, as we have seen.[104] In Gide's play, however, what makes Saul's (as opposed to Jonathan's) desire for David destructive and therefore dangerous to Saul? Various possibilities suggest themselves. While Jonathan is not presented as differing from David in age, Saul's homoerotic desire for David is clearly that of an older man for a younger one. Yet, while David's deep (possibly erotic) affection for Jonathan may suggest that it is Saul's age which makes him unattractive to David, the latter gives no sign that this is why he requites Jonathan's love but not Saul's. Indeed, while the play makes clear that David is initially embarrassed and confused by Saul's desire for him and eventually repelled by it, to the point of flight, it does not explain why.[105] Perhaps it is simply that David's heart has already been won by the son.

103. Ibid., 253–4.
104. Noted by Pollard, *André Gide*, 334, as well as Lerner, *Passing the Love of Women*, 47.
105. Lerner, *Passing the Love of Women*, 47, appears to be persuaded that this is the (or at least a) crucial distinction, as does Pollard, *André Gide*, 334 (despite his seeming demurral).

While these various interpretive options have their attractions, the wider structure of the play in which Saul's homoerotic desire is situated may point in a slightly different direction. The final yielding of Saul to his demons – the personified temptations/vices which appear at the outset of the play and then reappear regularly before eventually consuming Saul – confirms Gide's own insistence that his play is concerned with the generalised danger of yielding to sensual desires which are ultimately destructive. On this reading, while Saul's homoerotic desire for David is undeniably the chief emblem of this danger within the play, Gide's *Saül* does not intend to warn specifically against homoerotic affection, nor even pederastic desire *per se*, but rather against erotic desire for anyone which will bring about one's own downfall. Given Gide's grappling with his own sexuality, it is hardly surprising, and by no means incidental to the play, that this erotic desire is configured in pederastic terms. But to suggest that this is *not* incidental is *not* the same as suggesting that it is the central point which Gide saw the play as a whole as making.[106] Rather, it simply suggests that while for some writers, Samson and Delilah may have been the Bible's most obvious illustration of the destructive dangers of yielding to erotic desire, for Gide it was instead the older Saul's 'great love' for the younger David found in 1 Samuel.

Even a cursory comparison of Gide's *Saül* with Brecht's scene of 'David before Saul' (B9) suggests some striking similarities. For instance, while the songs which the respective Davids sing are very different, both Brecht's Saul and Gide's Saul take a particular interest in them and express their opinions and preferences. Notably, both Sauls also express their preference for the music and a disinterest in the words of the songs – Brecht's Saul because David's words are irrelevant, Gide's Saul because David's words disturb him. So too, in both scenes, when the conversation becomes uncomfortable and David attempts to leave, both Sauls successfully arrest their departure, and increasingly dominate the conversations. Crucially, in both Brecht's and Gide's scenes, the source of David's discomfort is, as we have seen, Saul's erotic attraction to him.

---

106. While this point has been appreciated by Katherine Brown Downey, *Perverse Midrash: Oscar Wilde, André Gide and the Censorship of Biblical Drama* (London: Continuum, 2004), 138, she further suggests that the play primarily makes use of homoerotic desire as a metaphor for a generalised spiritual desire. Yet, if Saul is clearly frustrated in both his desire for David and God, his homoerotic desire seems less emblematic of spiritual desire than it is representative of the carnal/sensualised desires embodied in the 'demons' who dominate both the play and, increasingly, its protagonist.

Perhaps most tellingly of all, in both scenes, this attraction is explicitly named by Saul as a 'secret' which he then reveals to David as the scene unfolds. Indeed, in both scenes, Saul's attraction is confirmed not only by what he says to David, but also by what he claims to have done to demonstrate his intentions: Gide's Saul draws David's attention to his freshly shaven beard, while Brecht's Saul reminds David that he had unclothed himself before him. While the reference to the shaving of the beard underlines the pederastic quality of Saul's attraction to David in Gide's scene, Brecht creates a similar (and perhaps even heightened) effect by having his Saul refer to David as 'my child' and 'young' throughout the scene. Finally, in both scenes, Saul's eventual disclosure of his secret and his declarations of erotic desire first lead to David's retreat into embarrassing and awkward silence and then to David's physical flight from a love he cannot requite. Indeed, while Brecht's Saul wonders with whom David will share the secret of Saul's love for him, so too Gide's David, as he departs in haste, intimates that Saul's secret will no longer be his alone.

If the above similarities seem to suggest Brecht's acquaintance with Gide's *Saül*, this is hardly surprising. While in later years Brecht would be unimpressed with Gide's disaffection with the Soviet experiment,[107] the young Brecht's review of a German translation of Gide's other play about David, *Bethsabée* (Bathsheba) for Augsburg's *Der Volkswille* (14 December 1920) suggests nothing but admiration for Gide's biblical endeavours:[108]

> André Gidé's unconscionably beautiful *Bathsheba*, a delicate ivory painting with a startlingly deep psychological foundation. Here culture, poetry, conscience achieve a wonderfully pure, harmonious unity.[109]

That Gide's *Saül* was also read by Brecht in German translation around the time he was working on his *David* and made a similarly favourable

---

107. Chetana Nagavajara, *Brecht and France* (Bern: Peter Lang, 1994), 63–4.
108. *BFA* 21, 89.
109. While Claude Foucart, 'L'Ulysse Francais et son Odyssée Intellectuelle: André Gide vu par Bertolt Brecht', *Bulletin des Amis D'André Gide* 10, no. 56 (1982): 481–503 (482), suggests that Brecht read Franz Blei's German translation of *Bethsabée* (Bathsheba) which first appeared in the second issue of the short-lived periodical *Hyperion* (1908, 108–24), it seems very clear (cf. *BFA* 21, 621–2) that Brecht reviewed the re-publication of Blei's translation in the sixth volume of *Der Dramatische Wille*, a nine-volume series published by Kiepenheuer in 1919.

impression would appear to offer the best explanation for the striking resonance of B9 with certain aspects of Gide's version of 'David before Saul', as we have seen above.[110]

Yet to observe the similarities between the two scenes also highlights the differences. Brecht's scene is much the fuller and longer of the two, and preserves certain aspects of the biblical tradition (e.g. Saul's attempt to kill David) which are passed over in Gide's version. The young Brecht's language is characteristically raw and rough in comparison with the smoothness of Gide's dialogue, though the latter is different again from the exalted tone of the exchanges between Saul and David in Zarek's scene. Indeed, despite Gide's and Brecht's shared focus on Saul's disclosure of his erotic attraction to David – and the latter's flight from it – Saul's articulation of his desire in the two versions strikes a quite different tone. Gide's Saul eventually dissolves into a fit of sensual ecstasy, overcome by the erotic temptation of David's physical presence, but never explicitly names his love for David. By contrast, Brecht's Saul repeatedly declares his love for David from the moment he reveals his 'secret', as he attempts to persuade David to acquiesce to his love. These differences are also mirrored in the response of the Brechtian and Gidean Davids as the scenes reach their equally violent conclusions. In Gide's scene, Saul's final ecstatic uttering of 'Daoud, delicious' – the name which Gide's David allows Jonathan alone to use for him – prompts David to hurl his harp to the ground, shattering the instrument and Saul's erotic reverie, but also signalling David's contempt for Saul's emotional incontinence. In Brecht's scene, by contrast, it is David's sardonic if not sarcastic rejection of Saul's confession of love ('I'm glad my song revived you') which so outrages Saul that it is he who hurls his spear at the retreating David.

* * *

Given the enormous popularity of David and Saul and their stories as subjects for theatrical adaptation in the late nineteenth and early twentieth centuries, much more might be done to situate Brecht's *David* amidst other such adaptations of his age. Nevertheless, our selected comparison of Brecht's fragments with the efforts of Feuchtwanger, Gide and

---

110. It is unclear whether Brecht read the German translation of *Saül* in the pages of the periodical *Schaubühne* where it first appeared in 1907 (André Gide, 'Saul', trans. Félix-Paul Grève, *Schaubühne* 3, no. 32 [1907]: 105–10) or when the translation was published in its own right two years later: André Gide, *Saul: ein Schauspiel in fünf Aufzügen*, trans. Félix Paul Grève (Berlin-Westend: Erich Reiss Verlag, 1909).

Zarek – and in some cases their reflections on those efforts – points to the value of such an approach in attempting to assess the *David* fragments and how they were produced.

Our comparison of Brecht's scenes with Otto Zarek's play and especially his scene of 'David before Saul' serves to parse Brecht's own recollections of the latter's role in his own process. To an extent, Brecht's own predictable emphasis in his diaries on the difference between his approach and Zarek's appears to be reflected not merely in the contrasts of language, tone and style in their respective scenes of 'David before Saul', but also in Zarek's primary focus on Saul's relationship with God and Brecht's focus on Saul's relationship with David. Indeed, whatever the challenges of mapping Brecht's diaries onto his *David* fragments and Zarek's play as we have them, such differences likely corroborate Brecht's understanding of his own effort as a direct reaction to what he perceived as the inadequacies of Zarek's own. That even Brecht's B10 may in some sense be seen as reactive to Zarek's *David* is suggested by the absence of anything remotely comparable to B10 in Zarek's play, as well as the fact that Brecht's insolent, indolent and opinionated David is so very different from the one found in the pages of Zarek's *David*.

If Brecht's 'use' of Zarek's *David* in his own adapting of the biblical tradition thus constitutes a certain, reactive kind of 're-writing' typical of the young Brecht and willingly owned by him, Brecht's use of Gide's *Saül* would seem to represent a 're-writing' of a rather different sort. We've already noted that shortly after this time Brecht would collaborate with Feuchtwanger on *Edward II* (1924), a play whose debt to the sixteenth-century play by Christopher Marlowe was of course entirely clear. Rather less clear, at least when it was performed, was the debt which Brecht's own original play *In the Jungle* (1923) owed to Rimbaud's *Une saison en enfer*, from which it quoted frequently but without attribution. At the time, Brecht responded that such debts were impossible to acknowledge in performance, but when similar accusations resurfaced in 1929 in relation to *Threepenny Opera* and its unattributed use of Ammer's translation of Villon's poetry, Brecht admitted his casual approach to matters of intellectual property.[111]

While the question of Brecht's use of sources in his work (including in his early plays) continues to be explored by commentators,[112] Brecht's use of Gide's *Saül* detected here in the *David* fragments for the first time

---

111. *BFA* 18, 100. See Parker, *Bertolt Brecht*, 217, 247.

112. See, for instance, H. M. Brown, 'Between Plagiarism and Parody: The Function of the Rimbaud Quotations in Brecht's *Im Dickicht der Städte*', *Modern Language Review* 82 (1987): 662–74.

clearly differs from *In the Jungle*'s use of Rimbaud, for there are no direct quotations of Gide's play here. Given Brecht's thematic indebtedness in B9 to Gide's scene in *Saül*, however, might the later Brecht's insistence that 'anyone can be creative, it's rewriting other people that's a challenge' be invoked as a means of accounting for Brecht's creation of his 'David before Saul'?[113] The *David* fragments' self-evident debt to the Bible would appear to fall into the same category as Brecht's use of Marlowe's play (the re-writing of a classic text), but it is now clear that Brecht was by no means simply re-writing the biblical David, but also earlier re-writings of the biblical David, reacting against Zarek's on one hand and emulating Gide's on the other. Of course, it may be doubted whether Brecht would have publicly acknowledged his debt to Gide's work as readily as his private distaste for Zarek's, but the fact that Brecht's *David* was never finished, let alone published, means that we shall never know.

As we have seen, Zarek's play seems to reflect an interest in the idea of the triumph of youth over the old guard and the chief idea of Feuchtwanger's *Saul*, according to the author at least, is the impact of a 'will to (royal) power' on the lives of David, Saul and the witch of Endor. But the question of 'ideas' and their place in Brecht's *David* fragments and in his thinking about them is sharpened by the influence of Gide's *Saül*. As we have seen, in Gide's play, Saul's erotic desire for David, which reaches its climax in 'David before Saul', appears to be emblematic of the dangers of yielding to destructive desires. Indeed, that this qualifies as the 'idea' (or at least the chief idea) of Gide's *Saül* is suggested not only by an analysis of the play itself, but also by Gide's own reflections, both as he was writing the play and years later. What is altogether less certain is of what, if anything, Saul's erotic desire for David might have been emblematic in Brecht's plan for his play. After all, Brecht's B10 hardly prepares the reader for Saul's outpouring of erotic desire for David, or indeed the more general 'idea' that yielding to desires is dangerous. Moreover, while we saw that Brecht's young David is full of ideas in the B10 and even has a few in B9 when he is 'before Saul', the scenes offer no inkling that the play of which Brecht imagined them to be a part would possess an 'idea' of the sort that Zarek, Gide and Feuchtwanger admired and believed their dramas to offer. Indeed, as we have seen in the previous chapter, B10 is radically different from B9 in various ways, including its setting, tone and cast of characters, with the sole exception being the young David himself, who appears in both. Insofar as this is the case, it might be argued that

---

113. Eric Bentley, *Bentley on Brecht*, 3rd ed. (Evanston: Northwestern University Press, 2008), 390.

the two scenes taken together do achieve the ambition for *David* which Brecht voiced in his diaries, namely that it would be a 'piece of David's life' (*ein Stück aus seinem Leben*) equal to but not more than 'simply the young David' (*einfach den Jungen David*). While it might be objected that in seeking to present 'simply the young David' Brecht ends up offering up the very sort of 'idea' or 'point' which he criticised in others and sought to avoid in his play, he would undoubtedly insist that this is an 'idea' of a quite different order.

If, in this and other ways, Brecht's *David* may be distinguished from the efforts of Gide, Feuchtwanger and Zarek, the fact that all four playwrights found in 1 Samuel material worthy of adaptation surely reflects the fact that the stories of Saul and David were, as Nebel has established, *de rigeur* in the first decades of the twentieth century, not least amongst German playwrights. The dramatic decline in interest in such plays after 1920 suggests that both Brecht and Zarek were rather late to the party and may explain in part why Zarek's play was never performed at the time and Brecht's never finished.[114] But the fact that all four playwrights were entranced by the dramatic prospects of Saul and David at a relatively early stage of their respective careers – Feuchtwanger and Gide at the turn of the century and Brecht and Zarek two decades later – may also suggest something more than curious coincidence. Did the prospect of re-writing the sacred stories of their youth appeal to the young playwrights' desire to assert their artistic maturation and existential autonomy over and against the religion of their childhood? If so, the stories of Saul and David must have naturally appealed, and their adaptation might be understood as something akin to a rite of passage.

---

114. Further support for this may be gleaned from the observation that while David's song was more often used as a serious means of illuminating the David–Saul relationship in German-language adaptations written before 1905, in those written between 1905 and 1920, interest in David's singing appears to wane and becomes increasingly superficial. For the raw data which supports this conclusion, see Nebel, *Harfe, Speer und Krone*, 250–3.

Chapter 5

THE *DAVID* FRAGMENTS IN PRACTICE AND PERFORMANCE

Clearing the Stage: David *in Germany (1995)*

The official premiere of the *David* fragments took place three quarters of a century after the composition of the texts, in a 1995 production in the Hebbel-Theater, Berlin, adapted and directed by Brigitte Grothum. It is clear from the available record, and even from the extensive programme for *David* in 1995, that the premiere explicitly set itself against the artistic impulses of its time in the German theatre, aligning itself instead to a lost past. Choices of casting, especially the decision to include Berliner Ensemble member Ekkehard Schall (1930–2005), signal the attempt to invoke a sense of 'authorial' fidelity to the Brechtian tradition, rather than the 'audience' fidelity of contemporary *Regietheater* (directors' theatre) of 1990s' Berlin.[1] The reviews from the *Berliner Zeitung* reveal a conservative, even reactionary, impulse, quoting the director and adaptor Brigitte Grothum as follows: 'Grothum would like to still show "true theatre", meaning "no obscenities", as one can see on the Berlin stages. Brecht's daughter Barbara adds to this, stating that she would be fine with the production provided no one would be naked, and that on stage there would be no toilet.'[2]

---

1. This continuum that maps faith (on the part of a director) toward an 'author' vs. 'audience' connects to a discourse theorised in the sub-field of Samuel Beckett studies, one of the key tributaries of this project in practice. See Nicholas Johnson, 'A Spectrum of Fidelity, an Ethic of Impossibility: Directing Beckett', in *The Plays of Samuel Beckett*, ed. Katherine Weiss (London: Methuen, 2013), 152–64.

2. 'Brigitte Grothum wolle noch "richtiges Theater" zeigen, also "keinerlei Obszönitäten", wie man sie an Berliner Bühnen sehen könne. Brechts Tochter Barbara

5. The David Fragments in Practice and Performance

The structure of scenes in the *Arbeitsfassung* or 'working script' of the 1995 production shows that the fragments (clearly sourced from the *BFA*, based on the errors and silent corrections) were intercut with biblical material, attempting a 'chronological' sequence based on the life of David as related in the Old Testament.[3] The framing dramaturgically suggests that the entire project is a rehearsal; the director/adaptor featured as a framing device on stage, with a 'B' listed in the early pages standing for 'Brigitte', hinting at a 'metatheatrical' frame and, at least in theory, distancing the audience from an empathic relation to the action. A choral ensemble was used to include songs from a variety of sources, not only expanding the number of voices in Brecht's own song 'Strong is the Bull' in B9 with newly composed music, but also incorporating biblical Psalms sung in Hebrew. In the Berlin production Brecht's diary entries and some of the A sections were presented as projections. The participation of women (a contemporising impulse in both productions, given that the included *David* scenes contain almost no voices identified as female) was achieved through the creation of a female chorus supporting the Bathsheba section (appearing through Old Testament citations, rather than fleshing out the minimal mentions of Bathsheba in the A sections of the Brecht texts).[4] One element in the production that was noted by critics as particularly out of kilter was the presence of late twentieth-century war footage from Israel, a choice that is explicitly justified in Grothum's programme note:

> To be sure, the fundamental tendency of the whole work is rather pacifist, but the reference to the military defence of the Jewish-Israeli nation up to the present day is unavoidable. This adaptation of *David* by Bertolt Brecht should, in my view, present a positive contribution to the renewed friendship between the German and the Jewish people, especially in the 3000th year since the founding of Jerusalem, the city of David, as the capital of the Jewish state.[5]

---

ergänzte, sie sei sehr einverstanden mit der Aufführung, keiner sei nackt, und auf der Bühne stünde kein Klo.' Friedrich Detlef, 'Zum jungen Brecht das Alte Testament', *Berliner Zeitung*, 7 September 1995.

3. The title page of the *Arbeitsfassung* (BBA Z 46/159) reads: *DAVID* / Fragment von Bertolt Brecht / Bearbeitung für die Bühne: Brigitte Grothum / Arbeitsfassung von 21.7.95. It is the most current draft of the script available before the premiere, so it is the basis for the analysis of intended textual structure that follows.

4. *David, Arbeitsfassung*, BBA Z 46/210–212.

5. Programme for *David*, Premiere 4 November 1995, Hebbel-Theater Berlin (dir. Brigitte Grothum).

Critics agreed that the blend of texts was not effective dramaturgically; the *Brecht-Handbuch* refers on multiple occasions to the reviews as 'annihilating';[6] one was entitled 'Unintentional comedy'.[7]

However, one of the most noteworthy aspects of the 1995 Grothum production was its treatment of the fragmentary quality of Brecht's *David*. As Tom Kuhn points out:

> in some cases the 'fragment' may perhaps be a thing in itself, not just a piece broken off some imagined ideal 'whole'… This is an idea that has a long and elevated tradition, especially in German letters, where we think of the Romantics as the archetypal thinkers and theorists of an experience of life and art too tentative, or too fragile, or too tortured to find expression in complete and rounded works.[8]

The 1995 *David* sought to complete something that is constituted partly by its incompleteness, raising an interesting question of responsibility to Brecht as an author. Is one to read a lengthy 'finished' scene such as B10 – a scene with many dramaturgical inconsistencies, not to mention incoherencies – and perform it as is, because it reads as 'finished' in comparison with other sections? Is a half-finished or abandoned synopsis like A1 to be used as a schema on which to build a plot, or does it have a more interesting life arising from its gaps and voids? The attempt to 'fill' and 'resolve' such gaps by means of a biblical chronology is visible from the dramaturgical structure of the Grothum production (see Table 1):

Scene Title	Source Material / Key Events
'Bei Beginn der Vorstellung'	Newly composed framing, plus the song from B9 / Director 'B' appears and begins a run-through of a notional rehearsal of *David*; actors, warming up from pre-set, sing the David song 'Stark ist der Stier' together
Prolog	1 Sam. 8.10-20 (Lutherbibel) / choral performance of edited selections from biblical verse
Szene 1	1 Sam. 16.1-12 (Lutherbibel lightly revised) / duologue performance of edited selections from biblical verse

---

6. Jan Knopf, ed., *Brecht-Handbuch in fünf Bänden. Band 1* (Stuttgart & Weimar: Metzler, 2001), 66.

7. 'Unfreiwillige Komik', *Neues deutschland*, 6 November 1995, https://www.neues-deutschland.de/artikel/578741.unfreiwillige-komik.html.

8. Tom Kuhn, 'General Introduction', in *Brecht and the Writer's Workshop: Fatzer and Other Dramatic Projects* (London and New York: Bloomsbury, 2019), 5.

Szene 2	Brecht's *David*, B10 / continuous group performance of *BFA* B10
Szene 3	1 Sam. 17.1-49 (edited Lutherbibel) / Goliath episode; choral performance of biblical verse, setting Israelites against Philistines; video of Yom Kippur War (1973)
Szene 4	1 Sam. 17.57, 18.1, and 18.4 (Lutherbibel); David–Jonathan dialogue from 1937–1944 project *Goliath* (*BFA* 10.2, 780–2) / Friendship of Jonathan and David explored (interpolating text from much later in Brecht's career, and from a different project with a different David character)
Szene 5	1 Sam. 18.6-11 (edited Lutherbibel); 'transparency' projection of *David* A7 (2); choral song of women comparing Saul killing 1,000, but David 10,000
Szene 6	Brecht's *David*, B9 / continuous duo performance of *BFA* B9
Szene 7	Brecht's *David*, A7 (3–8); 2 Sam. 1.1-26 (Lutherbibel) / transparency projection of A7 (3–8); dialogue relating the death of Saul and Jonathan and David's grief
Szene 8	2 Sam. 2.1-2 (Lutherbibel) / short dialogue about David becoming king; includes one speaker named 'third beggar' as cross-reference to B10 earlier
Szene 9	2 Sam. 5.4-6 (edited Lutherbibel); Hebrew song Yism'chu hashamayim (based on Ps. 96) / 'euphoric' singing is overlaid with 5-6 images of contemporary Jerusalem viewed from the air
Szene 10	2 Sam. 11.2-27 (edited Lutherbibel) / female chorus peforms Bathsheba story, with final section of story delivered via puppetry
Szene 11	2 Sam. 12.9-10 (edited Lutherbibel) and Brecht's *Journale* / sung Hebrew/German prayer begging forgiveness; projection on transparency of diary entry from 20 October 1916.
Szene 12	Brecht's *David*, A2 and B3; Brecht's poem 'Absalom reitet durch den Wald' / Grothum reads A2 from book, after which actors perform the poem
Szene 13	Brecht's *Journale* (10 March 1921); Brecht's *David*, B3, B2, B1, and B4; 2 Sam. 19.5 (Lutherbibel); Brecht's *David*, B5 (edited); Brecht's *Journale* (13 September 1920); newly composed framing to conclude / Narrative of David as king, Absalom's rebellion and death, ending with Grothum saying 'Danke, Probenende' (Thank you, end of rehearsal).

Table 1. Structure of the *Arbeitsfassung* text of *David* (1995) with sources.

Several important features emerge from this dramaturgical approach. First, whatever their assertion of an official 'premiere' might imply, it is clear that there is no authoritative script for *David* emerging from this project, given the substantial quantity of interpolation. Analyzing the word-count of the play shows that Brecht's *BFA* 'David' fragments constitute only about half of the play's overall text (5337 words of the total 9244). The arrangement draws freely on other David-related material from elsewhere in Brecht's writing career, including poetry, journal and operatic compositions. Second, there is a clear attempt to retain temporal direction via the Old Testament sequencing as the *sole* guide: the chapters used from 1 and 2 Samuel only count upward as the play progresses, but Brecht's own chronology of composition, in spite of the authorial emphasis of the whole project, is not respected.

The 1995 staging used the Bible in order to fill in the narrative gaps between the fragments not only in a textual, but also in a social and dramaturgical sense. But might there be an alternative (Brechtian and modernist) approach to such openings in the textual fabric, other than patching or filling them? In our own process leading up to the performance of *The David Fragments*, the 2017 performance that will be the main focus of this chapter, we conducted only limited research into this sole previous production, a strategy that is common among directors who hope to offer innovation to an audience (rather than repetition or tradition). We purchased a copy of the 1995 programme as part of our dramaturgical research, read a number of reviews to identify some of the pitfalls for ourselves, and found images of one costume design from the production, but we did not consult the archival records of the production and its script until after our project was complete, when both projects would exist independently as a basis for our comparison. The starting point for our production was, in that sense, completely different. We asked why, at this point in theatre history and with these materials, a 'completed' or 'finished' *David* should be the goal at all. If Tom Kuhn is correct that 'the idea of the "unfinished" is central to Brecht's whole aesthetic',[9] then what might it mean to perform fragments in the theatre?

Setting the Stage: David *and Practice-as-Research in Ireland*

Translating a text like *David* that is filled with gaps, converting it into a series of events that are temporally and stylistically disjointed and marketing a production as 'fragments' may seem at first – especially to a

---

9. Kuhn, 'General Introduction', 6.

reader less informed about, or perhaps less inclined toward, contemporary theatre – like a kind of folly. But our own quest to ferment *David* within a willing group of reflective early-career practitioners and students, and then to share the distillate with both academic and popular audiences, has both precedents within the Brechtian tradition and, we suggest, a range of philosophical, pedagogical and political implications of interest to the field. A strand of Brecht scholarship that is attuned to Eastern resonances, especially the work of Fredric Jameson in *Brecht and Method* and the vibrant new edition of the *Me-Ti* by Antony Tatlow, has exposed dynamics of activity that might be called 'states of flow', a mode of working with Brecht in praxis that animated our project. Jameson notes how 'Brecht is modern first and foremost by way of his discontinuities and his deeper fragmentation: from that dispersal, we can proceed on into a certain unity, but only after having passed through it'.[10] Tatlow writes that Brecht's non-systematic system of aphorisms, parables and stories in the *Me-Ti* 'steps back towards the events behind the events' but also 'allow[s] the contradictions they explore to speak for themselves'.[11] Seeking to keep faith with Brecht's critical stance as an ongoing (and necessary) form of activity, both scholars show how an absolutist reading fails Brecht, whose opposition to absolutes in ideology is (almost) Brecht's only ideology. That this critical stance would inform our work – both with Brecht's biblical readings and with untranslated and unperformed fragments in general – is both biographically appropriate and geographically resonant in Ireland, where public associations with religion are contentious, and where Brecht's performance legacy is minimal. The result is a kind of productive layering of voids: the gaps inherent in this text, when translated into embodiments or images, become more available to an audience that is also more receptive, due to their own lack of concrete expectation. This obviously differentiates the conditions on the ground in Ireland, where Brecht is taught fairly schematically and historically in reference to *Verfremdungseffekt* and epic theatre, and Germany, where the living legacy of Brecht continues to be a contested and sometimes personal one, negotiated between his undoubted significance as a figure of twentieth-century theatre, his complicated politics in both the Weimar Republic and the DDR, enforced loyalty (and legal obligation) to heirs and the vibrant contemporary politics of German theatre, which invites a more critical look at Brecht's practice in the tradition of, for example, Heiner Müller

---

10. Fredric Jameson, *Brecht and Method* (London and New York: Verso, 1998), 6.

11. Tatlow, 'Introduction', in *Bertolt Brecht's Me-Ti: Book of Interventions in the Flow of Things*, ed. and trans. Antony Tatlow (London: Bloomsbury, 2016), 39.

('to use Brecht without criticizing him is betrayal').[12] There is almost certainly greater freedom in Ireland to experiment with Brecht without baggage or association, and this approach undoubtedly is a first distinction between the methods applied to *David* (1995) as opposed to *The David Fragments* (2017).

At the practical and pedagogical level, Heiner Müller also points the way toward a critical engagement with Brecht within the rehearsal room. In his 2002 article on the adaptation of two lesser-known Brecht fragments by Müller, David Barnett describes a working method that resonates with our own:

> The requirement to divide text among the actors encourages active negotiation in the rehearsal process. Here the pre-performance work takes the Brechtian elimination of actor and spectator to its logical conclusion. The actors are exposed to the experience of the text as a whole and are able to play, observe, re-structure and re-play without authorial restriction... However, [Müller] does offer the actors and directors an opportunity to approach the text in a fashion which leaves fundamental questions open and invites actors to experiment and criticize in a manner conceptualized but never fully realized by Brecht.[13]

Deploying such methods in relation to texts that are not necessarily complete, author-approved, or intended for performance is already a recognised mode of theatre teaching and of laboratory practice. Our experience suggests that these interventions also can produce research that challenges the borders between disciplines, methodologies and institutions. In preparation, we depend on the *David von* (by) Brecht, but in performance, we cast our lot with a *David nach* (after) Brecht (of which more below). His *David* fragments, polished in our circle with the *Ermattungstaktik* (tactics of attrition) of praxis, flow onward into a new work, *The David Fragments*, that we hoped would reflect the dialectics of our time, our place and our ensemble: incomplete but decisive, singular but multiple, biblical but Brechtian.

From the beginning of this collaborative investigation into Brecht's early *David* texts, we imagined that practice-as-research (PaR) would be a key methodology for understanding the world of the fragments, both in terms of their origin (i.e. as written by Brecht) and their contemporary

---

12. 'Brecht gebrauchen, ohne ihn zu kritisieren, ist Verrat'. Heiner Müller, *Rotwelsch* (Berlin: Merve Verlag, 1982), 149.

13. David Barnett, 'Heiner Müller as the End of Brechtian Dramaturgy: Müller on Brecht in Two Lesser-Known Fragments', *Theatre Research International* 27, no. 1 (2002): 52.

resonance (i.e. their function in performance). Though its definition and parameters are a persistent site of controversy, both within theatre studies and within the institutional context of the contemporary university, the aspiration of PaR is straightforward: to use theatre/performance techniques as a means of research. As this chapter will demonstrate, this is not the same as 'doing a play' in a professional sense, even though the act of staging theatre also involves research or may yield useful insights into the text as such, and even though projects that originate as PaR may end up in front of audiences, framed as professional performance. Rather, as we understand it in the context of recent work at Trinity College Dublin (TCD),[14] a PaR project is constructed specifically in the academic space (i.e. at a university or in partnership with a university theatre); it begins with research questions, designing a series of 'experiments' in the 'theatre laboratory' to be investigated; it constitutes an ensemble of theatre artists to explore those questions using time, space and the body; it sets up ways to capture, document and reflect on the outcomes of these experiments, in a light mimicry of the scientific method; finally, it works to disseminate the insights achieved through both event-based (conferences, workshops, presentations, performances) and object-based (articles, chapters, books) modes of research communication. Conceptually, it is important to position PaR as opening a 'third space' between empirical/quantitative and theoretical/qualitative approaches, rather than aligned strictly with one or the other. In fact, PaR can reflect usefully on these traditional 'epistemic encampments'[15] that often translate into divisions in universities between theory vs. practice, arts and humanities vs. STEM, or 'hard' sciences vs. 'soft' sciences, and intervene in these discourses to call attention to the ways in which all research is, in fact, embodied. Even a biblical scholar embedded in archival work conducts research by engaging in a series of performative physical events – travelling, observing, sitting, writing, perhaps bending over to see a papyrus fragment more clearly – and exists in a social context (the 'ensemble') of networks, conferences and collaborations. In terms of 'absolute value' these are neither substantially more

---

14. Major TCD PaR projects with interdisciplinary elements that preceded and informed the *David Fragments* project include the Samuel Beckett Laboratory (founded in 2013 but conducting ongoing research, with publications to date in *Journal of Beckett Studies* and *Research in Drama Education*), *Enemy of the Stars* after Wyndham Lewis (2014–2015, publication in BLAST *at 100*), and *Love à la Mode* after Charles Macklin (2017–2018, publication forthcoming).

15. Jonathan Heron and Nicholas Johnson, 'Critical Pedagogies and the Theatre Laboratory', *Research in Drama Education: The Journal of Applied Theatre and Performance* 22, no. 2 (2017): 282.

or less *embodied* actions than when actors are stretching, memorising, singing, dancing, or playing warm-up games within a community of performers. Thus, PaR entails a radical redefinition of research: 'Research is the strategic deployment of an event to understand or evaluate an object'.[16] This definition is designed to apply to all researchers, rather than to create a special category for those working in performance: when a physicist enters a laboratory to observe what happens when two particles collide, she draws on embodied expertise to order a complex sequence of 'events' with the aim of gathering data on the 'object' under analysis. A theatre laboratory works in precisely the same way, although the means of validating and documenting results may not have the same precise systems of measurement, instead defining its own modes of establishing rigour and communicating outcomes. That Brecht was essential in the development of such an experimental ethos in the theater makes this method especially appropriate for the development of *The David Fragments*.

The *David* project had four distinct phases running over a four-year period: translation in 2015, ensemble workshops in 2016, full-scale theatre production in 2017 and academic dissemination in 2018. The aspiration of any writing about practice (such as this chapter) is to expose the concrete approaches taken when undertaking simultaneous biblical and Brechtian research in a rehearsal studio, especially for readers who may be unfamiliar with PaR as a methodology. The structure pivots off the 'scientific mimicry' discussed above by offering something of a lab report, including a description of the experiments conducted, a discussion of results and some possible conclusions. Though we will continue to say 'we' for the team of Shepherd and Johnson, the names of ensemble members will be used when identifying moments or aspects of the process that require personal attribution.

As one of the most globalised nations in the world, Ireland today contains complex intersections of multiple theatre traditions, so it is worthwhile seeking to identify which strands come together in university-based PaR like *The David Fragments*. There are obvious debts to a Continental approach, given the source material, so the German theatre might be thought of as the strongest lodestar in our process. The German tradition of a socially engaged theatre, active since the Middle Ages in the mystery plays in the public square through to the dramaturgy of Enlightenment figures like Gotthold Ephraim Lessing and Friedrich Schiller, who confirmed the stage as a 'moral institution', supported

---

16. This definition is part of a white paper on practice-as-research in the arts formulated by Nicholas Johnson for Trinity College Dublin; it has been presented to peers internally and externally, but not yet published.

Brecht's own ambition to critique the world (if not actually change it). In cultural shorthand, Germany's theatrical tradition is commonly thought of today as a director's theatre, with a multi-century cycle of revising classic texts in consciously engaged and political ways, as well as representing an ensemble model, in which actors are supported by contractual long-term commitments to state-funded theatre companies that develop a 'house style' and often operate under a strong (frequently male) leader. These features of Germany's landscape appear in Brecht's biography quite clearly around the time of *David*'s composition: the way for him to achieve success as a young playwright was to have one of his plays selected for production by Otto Falckenberg, artistic director of the Münchner Kammerspiele, while the way for him to achieve success as a young director was to rework and restage a classic (Marlowe's *Edward II*, in the 1924 production co-adapted with Lion Feuchtwanger; see Chapter 4, p. 129). During that same historical period, Ireland's concerns were quite different: it was not yet an independent nation at the time that Brecht wrote *David*, and its theatre was resolutely focused on the national struggle and the role of the writer, not the director. In the titling of *The David Fragments* as being 'after' rather than 'by' Bertolt Brecht, we followed the German tradition of using *nach* rather than *von* before the name of the author, a choice which not only acknowledges the fragmentary nature of the source material (in other words, necessitating strong dramaturgical intervention and perhaps invention), but also confirms the substantial agency of the living director/ensemble over that of the dead writer. Other than in research projects, however, such usage is rare in Ireland (even when classics are being revisited).[17]

After the German strand that is intrinsic to the source material, the strongest theoretical influence on this project's design was the North American discourse of performance studies. From 1999 to 2003, the director studied under Paul Edwards, Cindy Gold and Dwight Conquergood (among others) at Northwestern University – one of the two institutions, alongside New York University, where 'performance studies' as a named discipline emerged in the 1980s in contrast (and sometimes opposition) to 'drama studies' or 'theatre studies'. These mentors, in different ways, showed that *everything is performable*, an axiom that now informs TCD's

---

17. Highlighting this approach was the 2018 Berlin Theatertreffen production of Brecht's *Trommeln in der Nacht* by the Münchner Kammerspiele, which sold tickets for one version '*von*' Brecht and a different version '*nach*' Brecht on consecutive nights. The performances offered completely different endings: the first by Brecht, and the second revised by the company. Ticket-holders for one night or the other were contacted by email and offered a link for online viewing of the alternate ending.

creative arts research culture. Edwards is known for adapting novels and short stories for the stage, stitching minute textual and cultural analysis into the fabric of these works in order to bring them to life in classrooms and theatres; his work crosses fluidly between university studio practice and award-winning professional theatre in Chicago. Gold trains actors, has a background in comedy and improvisation and was the first instructor with whom Johnson worked on Brecht in performance. Conquergood was informed by a tradition of embodied ethnography but fused it to a solo performance tradition, using testimony, documentary material and other non-fiction sources to intervene in social constructs in critical ways.[18] Conquergood was especially alert to the ways in which the educational environment of the university itself was susceptible to what he movingly called an 'apartheid of knowledges', or 'the difference between thinking and doing, interpreting and making, conceptualising and creating', an entrenched divide that he called on performance studies to 'refuse and supersede'.[19] He wrote in 2002:

> The division of labour between theory and practice, abstraction and embodiment, is an arbitrary and rigged choice, and, like all binarisms, it is booby-trapped. It's a Faustian bargain. If we go the one-way street of abstraction, then we cut ourselves off from the nourishing ground of participatory experience. If we go the one-way street of practice, then we drive ourselves into an isolated cul-de-sac, a practitioner's workshop or artist's colony. Our radical move is to turn, and return, insistently, to the crossroads.[20]

Though Conquergood's metaphor of the crossroads has been highly influential, later discussions of interdisciplinarity have noted that such a model preserves the binarism under critique. Practice and theory are not, in fact, like two roads meeting, any more than mind and body can be thought of as a strict dualism in a human being: if anything, they are structured as a nebula or entanglement, infinitely complex in their mutuality,

---

18. Key publications arising directly from these disciplinary contexts include Victor Turner and Edward Bruner, eds., *The Anthropology of Experience* (Urbana and Chicago, IL: University of Illinois Press, 1986), Richard Schechner, *Performance Studies: An Introduction*, 3rd ed. (New York and Oxford: Routledge, 2013) and Dwight Conquergood, 'Performance Studies: Interventions and Radical Research', *The Drama Review* 46, no. 2, T174 (2002): 145–54; for a summary of the contours of the development of performance studies in the US, see Shannon Jackson, *Professing Performance: Theatre in the Academy from Philology to Performativity* (Cambridge: Cambridge University Press, 2004), 8–15.
19. Conquergood, 'Performance Studies', 153.
20. Ibid., 153–4.

provoking and complicating one another in a series of feedback loops. It is this more complicated landscape of 'praxis', in which all theory is effectuated and tested in practice and all practice is theorised, that has informed the pedagogy of undergraduate theatre education at TCD, and increasingly to the community of postgraduates and researchers as well. The specific practices and techniques grounding the rehearsal room for *David* are clearly indebted, albeit in the byzantine way that education usually mutates over decades, to ideas that originated in the studios of Northwestern.

Finally, exerting undeniable influence on the Irish scene through its cultural gravity, colonial history and geographic proximity is the United Kingdom, to which the language of PaR itself can be traced. The categories of 'practice-as-research', 'practice-led' or 'practice-based' research, 'performance-as-research', or simply 'PaR' are not particularly relevant in the US, but have been hotly debated in the UK higher education sector since the 1990s.[21] Across the Anglophone Commonwealth, where theatre education was more traditionally related to conservatoires, the roots of theatre-based research extend back to the 1960s, but pioneering projects early in the twenty-first century brought PaR into established methods of enquiry, with several universities even launching degree programmes under this name.[22] Writing in 2013 about the 'principles, protocols, pedagogies, resistances' of PaR, Robin Nelson seeks to answer the question of 'what it is' as follows:

> a research project in which practice is a key method of inquiry and where, in respect of the arts, a practice (creative writing, dance, musical score/ performance, theatre/performance, visual exhibition, film or other cultural practice) is submitted as substantial evidence of a research enquiry.[23]

---

21. Regrettably, the focus of much debate around and between these terms seems relegated to highly technical discussions about protocols for awarding promotions or doctoral degrees for creative outputs, rather than the deeper philosophical or ontological questions about performance that this terminology might seem to raise.

22. Baz Kershaw, one of the key figures of the discipline in the UK, identifies the turn to this mode of knowledge creation as 'a paradigm shift, through which established ontologies and epistemologies of research in arts-related disciplines, potentially, could be radically undone'. See Baz Kershaw, 'Practice as Research through Performance', in *Practice-led Research, Research-led Practice in the Creative Arts*, ed. H. Smith and R. T. Dean (Edinburgh: Edinburgh University Press, 2010), 105.

23. Robin Nelson, *Practice as Research in the Arts: Principles, Protocols, Pedagogies, Resistances* (London: Palgrave Macmillan, 2013), 8–9.

This language, particularly the verb choice of 'submitted', already implies an exclusively academic context for such work. This highlights the distinction usually observed between PaR or arts research in the university context and professional arts practice, which is both more public and usually entails different economic relations than those of research, such as ticket sales, fees, salaries or royalties. Initially, the tendency to see a bifurcation between 'doing a play' and 'doing PaR' was reflected at all levels, from training (acting conservatoires versus departments of drama at research universities) to programming (mass entertainment marketed as such, versus avant-garde or experimental festivals/touring contexts). Increasingly, however, the arenas are blending, and advanced theatre practitioners involve themselves in research and collaboration across media or discipline.

Keeping its options open, TCD trains students in both traditions on different ends of the campus, and rewards both types of outputs as representing 'peer review' when it comes to assessing the work of its researchers. In a manner that is both commonplace and strategic for a small island nation at the edge of Europe, Irish theatre practice and Irish higher education seek to learn from, and triangulate between, the three centres of gravity of the Continent, the UK and the US. Ireland brings to the table its own substantial and independent cultural legacy, a value placed on the arts in the common culture, as a result of which it traditionally 'punches above its weight' in the cultural sphere. Following Robin Nelson, who repeatedly argues for PaR as a 'praxis', contemporary Irish theatre education agitates against the binary of theory/practice as separate streams, advocating instead for their imbrication, creating an 'entangled' event where the theory comes into being in the moment of practice (and vice versa). Language that identifies PaR as inherently interdisciplinary and intersectional is commonplace, as is the notion of such events taking place in a 'third space'. In the work of Brad Haseman[24] and Barbara Bolt,[25] the 'performative' method is offered as a scientific approach that extends beyond quantitative and qualitative research. Akin to qualitative research in that it is 'expressed in non-numeric data', such outputs are also unique, in that they 'present as symbolic forms other

---

24. Brad Haseman, 'A Manifesto for Performative Research', *Media International Australia, Incorporating Culture and Policy,* Practice-led research Special Issue, 118 (2006): 98–106.

25. Barbara Bolt, 'A Performative Paradigm for the Creative Arts?' *Working Papers in Art and Design* 5 (2008), www.herts.ac.uk/_data/assets/pdf_file/0015/.../WPIAAD_vol5_bolt.pdf (accessed 15 October 2015).

than in the words of discursive text'.²⁶ The methodology is consciously multi-modal. While some outputs from within the same project might be 'traditional' for the humanities (i.e. the object of the article or monograph, or the event of the conference or academic consultation), the workshop or laboratory – perhaps the key unit of practice in PaR, even more so than official 'performance' – can also stand independently as an output, or, stated less institutionally, a concrete moment at which new knowledge comes into being. Documentation is thus one of the key sites of debate in PaR, since the immediate participants in the process will likely benefit the most; the question of how to make this moment of new knowledge less ephemeral and more meaningful for those beyond that primary circle is one of the enduring challenges (addressed, in part, by a book project like this one).

The victory of PaR could perhaps be declared when the term is dissolved, when the books about the methodological debate are no longer being published, or when the spirited defences within the academy no longer have to be mounted. At such a time, performance will have become simply another *techne*, which Malcolm Heath (following Aristotle) aligns with the human's 'productive capacity informed by an understanding of its intrinsic rationale'.²⁷ At such a time, going into the studio to work on a text 'on its feet' would simply be integrated as part of the activities that qualified researchers might use to achieve their own understanding (like entering a laboratory or reading a book) or to disseminate knowledge (like speaking at a conference or publishing an article) – indeed, the beauty of PaR is partly that it can do both of these in the same instant.²⁸

Preparing the Stage:
The David Fragments *Workshops (2015–2018)*

One of the characteristics of PaR in the academy, where the strictures of commercial production timetables and budgets are somewhat diminished in force, is an iterative practice of multiple workshops, often over an uncommonly long period of project gestation. *David* was no exception.

---

26. Haseman, 'A Manifesto for Performative Research', 6.

27. Malcom Heath, 'Introduction', in Aristotle, *Poetics* (London: Penguin, 1996), ix. Heath refers to Aristotle's *Nicomachean Ethics* 1140a, to support his understanding of *techne*.

28. These final paragraphs about PaR draw substantially on Nicholas Johnson and Colm Summers, '*Enemy of the Stars* in Performance', in *BLAST at 100: A Modernist Magazine Reconsidered*, ed. Philip Coleman, Kathryn Milligan and Nathan O'Donnell (Leiden and Boston: Brill, 2017), 152–4.

The following section will seek to illustrate the structures, intentions, and outcomes of the process itself, drawing on fine-grained detail of the research questions, experimental methodologies and essential results from the theatre laboratory established to develop *The David Fragments*. In tabular form (see Table 2), the *David* process included the following stages:

Year & Quarter	Activity
2015, Q2	First meeting between Shepherd and Johnson; initial discussion re. the fragments
2015, Q3	Translation work by Johnson, shared and discussed with Shepherd
2015, Q4	First reading of work by past collaborators, assessment/revision of translation
2016, Q1	Planning, reading, fundraising for workshops/production of *The David Fragments*
2016, Q2	Announcement of auditions and interviews, formation of ensemble
2016, Q3	First general workshops with ensemble, Output 1: Research Night translation event
2016, Q4	Second round of workshops with ensemble, development of adaptation
2017, Q1	Third round of workshops with ensemble, further adaptation and planning work Output 2: Shepherd lecture on the project at Oxford University
2017, Q2	Output 3: *(Un)translatable and (Un)performable* conference event; rehearsals
2017, Q3	Outputs 4 & 5: public performances of *David Fragments* in Dublin and London
2017, Q4	Assessment and reflection, initial work on dissemination plans
2018, Q1	Output 6: Johnson lecture at Brecht-Tage in Berlin; research and reflection

Table 2. *Stages of* The David Fragments *practice-as-research project, 2015–2018*

The first reading that involved actors was held on 21 December 2015, and it can be considered in retrospect as part of the translation process, more geared toward creating the preconditions for thinking about staging as opposed to a real rehearsal. If there was a research question for this first experiment, it was: 'Can the *David* fragments (in this draft translation) be poetically or dramatically engaging?' The ensemble of readers assembled for this purpose was intentionally an experienced and trusted group of past collaborators, including an intergenerational blend of current drama students, recent alumni, and two professional collaborators with whom the director had more than a decade of working history. The moment of hearing a new dramatic translation aloud for the first time is a completely different experience than reading it on the page; it is one of the defining characteristics of translating drama that it must work in the voice of the actor, and a threshold question must be whether it can be received by the ears of an audience without requiring either (1) access to the printed text or (2) extra time for reflection in order to understand it. Branching off from the fundamental focus on how a text *sounds* in translation is the delicate question of what the desired effect of the text is, noting that certain passages could be intended to baffle, upset or confuse an audience, as often as a text might 'seek to please'. This issue arises frequently in Brecht's fragments, which contain contradictory, oblique and difficult material as a matter of course, in which any effort to 'make clear' might end up distorting an authorial intent to obfuscate or prevaricate. Additionally, the implications of culture and context undoubtedly change based on the time and place of performance, meaning that translation is not a question of language alone. Though it is a truism that all translations occasionally require renewal and revision, for translated drama there is an inherent fidelity to the present audience that can shift the balance away from authorial control over the text.[29]

As readers of the translation (see Chapter 1) will have noted, the *David* texts are highly heterogeneous, making casting of any reading a delicate operation. Since the organising principle of the draft translation was the designation of scenes 'A1–A8' and 'B1–B11' following the *BFA*, the separation of these nineteen fragments – the shortest being A5 and B6 (13 words each, in German) and the longest being B10 (3098 words in German) – was often easier to do by designating actors to read whole fragments, rather than selecting actors to read for particular characters throughout. Additionally, to read B10 without doubling up any voices would require eighteen actors (made up of seventeen men, if Brecht's gender designations were followed), a company of such a scale that it is rarely assembled in the contemporary theatre (on financial grounds certainly, not to mention the issue of gender imbalance). This logistical fact conceals a deep truth about the *David* project as a whole, and

---

29. For an elaboration of this argument in terms of dramatic translation, see Nicholas Johnson, 'On Translating Ernst Toller's *Die Maschinenstürmer*', *Trinity Journal of Literary Translation* 2 (2014): 76–91.

actually conditioned much of our future work in a subtle way: the only way to grapple with this series of texts, it seemed early on, would be to use an ensemble (of any size) as raw material, with the understanding that the actors might have to shift roles, gender-bend or work together in a non-character-driven manner. Nonetheless, in a long phone call on 15 December 2015 ahead of the reading, we attempted to make sense of the character list by attaching the list of volunteers to particular roles, ultimately abandoning this in many sections where, instead, a solo reader would present the entire section's text. As a principle of casting this reading, it seemed that we were looking more for 'difference' and unusual vocal 'resonances' that would make the text stand out, rather than casting for verisimilitude of either gender or type.

The outcomes of this first reading were partly logistical – the project notebook records a reading time of 46 minutes with some interruptions, suggesting that there was 'enough' of the *David* material to work with in making a show – but as will be obvious already, the first research question was answered in the affirmative. The texts had some life in them, according to these experienced but open readers; during the read there had been flashes of poetic engagement and occasional verbalised responses to Brecht's strong images, as well as laughter at moments of awkwardness in the language (generally faithfully reflecting Brecht, like B1's line that manages to both lumber and rhyme: 'You have the brain of a crane'). Though the notes from this first reading focus mainly on translation issues, identifying errors or moments where the rhythm felt wrong or where actors stumbled, there are a few telling comments that (again) seem to set in motion trajectories in praxis that never disappeared from the process. Actors noted that Brecht had made his David an 'anti-hero', more 'stoner David' than 'King David'. This aligned with David Shepherd's initial approach that pointed out major divergences in the texts from the biblical tradition. Whether the 'spine' of a future stage adaptation could be the final outline provided by Brecht in A10, a kind of sequential history play, or would need to rest more on the centrality of the most extensive (though not necessarily most complete) section, B10, was discussed; we ultimately took the latter path. Three words jump out under a section labeled 'Brechtian treatment' in the notes, attributed to Honi Cooke, who ultimately joined the performance ensemble: 'irreverence', 'music' and 'diary material'. Most interestingly, a highlighted note says that the dramaturgy is 'the reverse of *Enemy*: not play as frame, but a containment within'.[30] This comment, by an ensemble member

30. *David* production notebooks, 21 December 2015.

who had most recently worked on Wyndham Lewis's *Enemy of the Stars* in 2014–2015 – the previous work in the drama department's series of experiments with 'unperformable' texts – indicates that rather than the shape of a massive, difficult object (like Lewis's play) being interrupted by commentary or intentionally fragmented by our performance strategies, *David* was already broken up: it would therefore need a 'frame' to be produced that could contain its variety within it. This deep insight never left the process, and adequately describes the ultimate dramaturgical approach to adaptation. We wanted, however, to go deeper than the Grothum gesture of merely 'framing' the action contained as a draft or a rehearsal, and to find moments with their own theatrical integrity and philosophical resonance with the source material.

In early 2016, sailing on the strength of the reading, we came to the decision that the texts should be developed for production as a play, and began to explore options for funding and opportunities for workshop presentation. Once sufficient detail about the next stages of development were known – namely the funding to proceed with a reading at European Research Night in September 2016, in partnership with the Trinity Centre for Literary and Cultural Translation – we felt comfortable holding open auditions and interviews for positions, so that a group of collaborators on performance, dramaturgy, design and production could begin to feed into the development of the process. It is difficult to overstate the extent to which the modes of working on texts like *David* rest on an ensemble, rather than a singular creative intelligence. The concept of a collective development of the adaptation was not only organically connected to Brecht's praxis – which was, at times, perhaps 'collaborative' to a fault – but also empirically tested in the prior work with difficult, unwieldy projects like *Enemy of the Stars*. Bringing an open and democratic spirit to the studio and allowing an ensemble to generate and own the images that they wish to derive from text and put on stage, with the director more in the role of prompting and 'disturbing' systems of performance, rather than 'directing' specific actions, was found to be significantly more productive in generating interesting theatre.

Casting of actors and hiring of staff is usually a terrifying moment for any theatre project, because so much depends on the makeup of the collaborative team, and so much is basically unpredictable. However, the advantage of casting for an ensemble, rather than for specific characters, is that the auditions can be structured to sort actors for flexibility, freedom, generosity and creativity, rather than simply alignment with a pre-arranged set of characteristics like height, age, sound of voice or skin colour. The sole purpose of the auditions in 2016 was to find a team willing to work on a long-term research project with occasional week-long investigative sessions, without any definite promise of ultimate performance or payment, and without allocating specific roles to specific actors. The sole criteria, essentially, were a willingness to work, together with a capacity to explore creatively. If *David* were being turned into a film instead, a primary question would be about the look and feel of the world, especially the specific time and place of the setting. When casting a film set in the known world, the issue of alignment between actor and character becomes difficult to avoid in terms of age, race, gender and other identity signifiers. In the theatre, by contrast, identity can be a significantly more malleable category, and multiple layers of more indeterminate time and space are easier to suspend in the art form. Thus, we cast a diverse ensemble in terms of gender, in spite of the source texts' limitations in this regard – five men, five women – and in terms of 'generation' (in the university context, this just means that not everyone was from the same year group). One subtle agenda guiding this selection was the pedagogical desire to 'pass on' positive ensemble skills between peers, so we included both experienced alumni from the *Enemy* process and students two years younger, who had not had prior exposure to this form of work, believing that each group would be able to teach the other something valuable: one from the position of knowing, and one from the stance of unknowing, building a more dialectic room.

This ensemble, constituted as a research group with signed 'informed consent' forms under which they agreed to certain protocols of participation in both documentation and qualitative survey, went into the studio for the first time for the week of 12–18 September 2016. The stated goals of this workshop appear in list form in a notebook entry of 16 August [explanations added here in square brackets]:

1. Build ensemble [form bonds of companionship and comfort between members]
2. Prep the 30th [Research night presentation, a public reading focusing on translation]
3. A draft → B draft of translation [development of 'rehearsal' from 'faithful' script]
4. Inspire David [reveal working methods of ensemble performance to the dramaturg, who would be coming from a biblical studies background and would have little rehearsal room experience, possibly affecting his trust in the process]

The ensemble was sent the updated 'faithful' translation and asked to respond to these texts, which some collaborators did electronically in writing, others artistically and visually, and others in the first rehearsal verbally. On 12 September 2016, we asked the ensemble what questions they thought of when they read the texts. Selected responses include:

1. Why does this story need to be told?
2. What is relevant, pertinent or contemporary about these texts?
3. Will audiences pay attention to this merely because it is written by Brecht?
4. Why are these texts so dense and difficult?
5. Where would these events depicted in the texts take place?
6. There were women in David's story and in Brecht's life; why none in Brecht's *David*?

These comments again highlight the training of this particular ensemble and the academic context: the ensemble was concerned with the political meaning of the theatre event, not merely its capacity to entertain, and they felt burdened to make the work count for something that would speak to the present moment. There were also the indicative practical questions, coming especially from the design and production team members, about what type of temporal/spatial frame or scenography could make sense of the diversity of the source material, and how we might navigate the baggage associated with being 'Brechtian'.

A long-standing challenge to staging the work of Brecht, especially in the Anglophone world, is that Brecht himself has now attained the status of a classic author, with a widely taught – if not wholly accepted or universally agreed-upon – set of theoretical practices and staging conventions. Writing at the end of his life about his own irreverent approach to staging classics, Brecht recognised a trap set by the 'routine-bound way [of looking] common to the theater of a depraved bourgeoisie', while also seeking to avoid 'purely formal and superficial "innovations" that are foreign to the work'.[31] He writes in his note 'Classical Status as an Intimidating Factor':

> There is a traditional style of performance that is automatically counted as part of our cultural heritage, although it only harms the true heritage, the work itself; it is really a tradition of damaging the classics. The old

---

31. Bertolt Brecht, 'Classical Status as an Intimidating Factor', in *Brecht on Theatre*, ed. Marc Silberman, Steve Giles and Tom Kuhn (London and New York: Bloomsbury, 2019), 322.

masterpieces become, as it were, dustier and dustier with neglect, and the copyists more or less conscientiously include the dust in their replica. What gets lost above all is the classics' original freshness, the element of surprise (in terms of their period), of newness, of productive stimulus that is the hallmark of such works.[32]

The fact that Brecht's *David* itself has no substantial performance tradition (and that we were not even especially informed about the sole previous attempt) somewhat liberated the ensemble from falling into standard tropes, but there were still two considerable forces exerted on such a process: first, the Bible itself and the impressions or habits that a mainly Irish ensemble might bring to the table when performing characters from Israelite antiquity; second, the theatrical theories of Brecht, which were articulated long after the creation of the *David* texts, but which nonetheless continue to powerfully influence contemporary directing and dramaturgy in Europe. There is always a risk that a 'paint-by-numbers' approach to directing Brecht – in brief, putting up a half-height curtain with projected titles and scene introductions, exposing lighting instruments and costume changes, and interpolating a *Gestus* or a V-effect at every possible moment – might worm its way into a process merely by association with the author, rather than as a considered aesthetic response to a text's inner need. There is also the further danger when staging Brecht's published and/or translated plays professionally that the restrictions imposed by the contract with the copyright holders and their agents will limit the degree of artistic freedom that can be applied. In other words, one classic author who will not generally withstand the Brechtian treatment of the classics is Brecht himself.

Given this background and the constant danger of creating a 'routine' Brechtian work, the *David* project was unusually liberated by both text and context. Since the unfinished fragments are mutually incompatible in terms of structure and inconsistent in narrative and style, they are hardly able to generate prescriptive stage directions. Furthermore, their sequence is the product of editorial, rather than authorial, intelligence; this meant that the order in which we might set them could be our own, as was the decision about which pieces would be included or excluded. The context of a university theatre, fitting the *David* work into ongoing interdisciplinary creative arts practice at Trinity College Dublin, also ensured a supported framework for whatever innovations might have emerged, including a bulwark against the inevitable permissions question. Both European and Irish law are clear on the point that practical research

---

32. Ibid., 321–2.

undertaken on the grounds of universities enjoys substantial protection, even if it includes material that is protected by copyright; though publication and public dissemination are more complex, one certainly has the right to work freely with these texts in a studio as part of pedagogy and practice-as-research.

Though its script was intentionally not consulted in the development of our own *David*, the 'authorised' 1995 Berlin production also provides some precedent for not performing the *David* fragments alone. From the reviews and programme notes of that production, it was clear that the Brechtian scenes were interpolated into an Old Testament chronology; as discussed above, our dramaturgical research and directorial compass suggested that this was the wrong approach for us. Though early ensemble workshops explored the atmosphere of the biblical street as a method to enter the world of a text like fragment B10, especially as it related to a community in which violence was a relatively common experience, we discovered early on that the temporal frame of our production was not to be an exclusively biblical one. Reading the Brecht diaries and considering the churn of artistic production among his friends, fierce intellectual debates in Artur Kutscher's Munich theatre seminars, Brecht's wild parties, the Kammerspiele and the welter of post-WWI and post-Spartacist Bavaria, we found the context of the texts' composition to be the most engaging touchstone. Finally, a third temporal frame was introduced, never to be forgotten throughout the process: that of 2017, when an audience would be in the room with us to seek to understand why this performance should matter to them and how the issues at stake for Brecht in the Weimar era might resonate with our own time and place.

This tripartite temporal frame led naturally to a more diverse set of textual sources. The first of these to be introduced in workshops were the diaries of Brecht from 1919 to 1921, which not only illuminate the origins of the text and speak to his aspirations for the *David* project but also place our work on the play in its social, familial and political context. For example, writing on 6 September 1920, Brecht notes:

> In *David* the real motions of the play need to be linked directly to the political events; all the psychology should be dissolved in action [*Handlung*]—because politics is too interesting to serve as mere props. The audience's palate must be treated so that it relishes whatever is put before it; and this must be done by catering to its pleasures down to the last one. The plot [*Handlung*] has become far too clear and rational.[33]

---

33. Brecht, *Diaries 1920–1922*, 39. Cf. 'Tagebuch 1920', *BFA* 26, 157.

As shown above, the diaries reveal one of the origin moments for the *David* fragments to be Brecht's disdain for his fellow playwright Otto Zarek's reading of his own Saul–David scene, unperformed but published by Müller Verlag in 1921. On 27 July 1920, Brecht wrote: '*Sie sei ihm blutsauer geworden, er habe sie durch eine Intrige möglich gemacht*'[34] (which Willett translates as 'Apparently it had turned sticky and he had made it work by means of plotting'[35]). Brecht wrote his own Saul–David scene the following day.[36] There is also, as discussed in Chapter 4, textual evidence from Hedda Kuhn's recollections that this was not the first time the authors had composed 'duelling' scenes as a form of sport.[37]

The idea of direct competition between writers, and of the curious energy of artistic rivalry within the same friend group, was not at all distant for the young ensemble of *The David Fragments*. As many biographical accounts from the period confirm, Brecht felt himself destined for greatness and was certain of his genius, yet Zarek at the time had the trappings of success: a role as dramaturg at the Kammerspiele and a published play (and as of the autumn of 1920, also one that had been performed). Our ensemble became interested in the drama inherent in this competition for recognition as well as in the fact that the biblical story was a vehicle for seeking status among two young playwrights of the period. Deploying our ensemble of early-career artists (roughly the same age as Brecht and Zarek at the time), we explored the process of mind whereby a creative (but perhaps egotistical) young artist might enter the identical terrain of another, convinced that they can exploit it to greater effect. Johnson translated Zarek's scene from the published version – also rendering it for the first time into English – and the actors performed its leaden, poetic tone to contrast sharply with Brecht's charismatic singing of his Psalms. In an extended improvisation, imagining

34. *BFA* 26, 130.
35. Brecht, *Diaries 1920–1922*, 12. 'Plotting' for 'Intrige' is not a precise translation in our view.
36. See BBA 459/14r for dated title page, confirmed in the entry for 28 July 1920, 'Die Szene Saul–David geschrieben'. *BFA* 26, 130.
37. Hedda Kuhn is quoted: 'In München, in meinem Zimmer in der Adalbertstraße, haben wir, Zarek, Brecht und ich, eine Art Sängerwettstreit veranstaltet. Jeder hat eine Szene über Karl V. zu schreiben. Zarek tat sich leicht, weil er nur etwas aus seinem gleichnamigen Stück zu nehmen brauchte. Auch Brecht hatte etwas geschrieben, darin hatte er an dem Kaiser kein gutes Haar gelassen. Ich wollte deshalb Brecht den Lorbeer zusprechen, aber wir erzielten keine Einigung. Wo die damals geschriebene Szene von Brecht geblieben ist, weiß ich nicht.' Frisch and Obermaier, *Brecht in Augsburg*, 127–8.

themselves at the end of a long night of partying in a bohemian apartment setting and with our 'Zarek' figure earnestly reading to them with our 'Brecht' figure trying not to laugh, the ensemble came to a good understanding of what was at stake in such an encounter for these two aspiring authors. Other improvisations focused on the wider historical frame containing them both, imagining the late-night conversations and consultations about the future of Munich theatre in the post-Spartacist chaos of that city. We held classroom-based workshops that used educational material about key artistic figures of the time – Max Halbe, Max Reinhardt, Erich Mühsam, Oskar Panizza, Frank Wedekind, Georg Fuchs, Wassily Kandinsky and Hugo Ball – and asked our collaborators to take up different positions and characters across the spectrum of opinion, arguing for the superiority of their own aesthetic for setting the future cultural and theatrical direction of interwar Munich.[38] We played with improvised scenarios and documented the outcomes, ranging from informal conversations between friends after a particular show (a familiar setting to our ensemble), to public debates and private dinners riven by factions (hosted and moderated by ourselves, naturally, playing the role of Otto Falckenberg, artistic director of the Kammerspiele at the time).

In short, through such embodied workshop activities that both veered into a pedagogical space and drew on our own research, additional sources arose and were propagated among the ensemble, forming part of the textual and conceptual basis for *The David Fragments* during the later rehearsal and development process. Textually speaking, the dramaturg subsequently created three new dramatic scenes centered on the Kammerspiele: the first, a conflict between Brecht and Zarek (related in the diaries); the second, a conflict between Brecht and Hedda Kuhn (biographically related to this period); the third, an address from Otto Falckenberg, before an invented 'work-in-progress' showing of fragment B10. New material also entered the process, however, through the ensemble practice itself: ideas discussed at meetings with designers, physical explorations from studio work with the cast and improvisations with physical prompts from the more poetic and oblique A-fragments. It is difficult in such cases to identify a specific genesis, and yet the integration of such 'transitional' material is the lifeblood of the final work's structure. Often the translated source text or a

---

38. A key source for this material was Peter Jelavich, *Munich and Theatrical Modernism: Politics, Playwriting, and Performance 1890–1914* (Cambridge: Harvard University Press, 1985).

fragment of historical research brought in by the dramaturg would be a prompt for action, and in a form of what Roman Jakobson called 'intersemiotic translation', this action would enter the performance text.[39]

On Stage: The David Fragments *(2017)*

The assembly of a performance text from such material is akin to a first experimental result in a laboratory: it is not the only way it could have gone, and whether there might be a better solution remains to be seen from further testing. The long gestation process led ultimately to two lists: one of named 'sources' in one column, and 'systems' in the other. 'Sources' included the material devised by the ensemble (often in response to the A fragments), material written by Brecht (often from the B fragments, but certain diary entries as well), material newly composed by the dramaturg and Zarek's *David* writing (to be fit ultimately within one of the composed scenes). The 'systems' list encompassed certain games played during the process, modes of physical or vocal engagement, or textual performance systems that we had created: examples were the 'mind of Brecht' games (one ensemble performs a kinaesthetic response to the interior life of the author writing the scene, while two actors perform the scene elsewhere on stage) or the 'Brechts Anonymous' system (the ensemble confesses the content of intimate personal diary entries to one another as though they are each Brecht, and all in group therapy for their Brechtian behaviour). The adaptation ultimately performed as *The David Fragments* included the following scenes and sources in sequence (see Table 3):

Scene Title	Source Material / Key Performance Systems
Prologue	Brecht's *David*, A1 / physical improvisation based on textual prompts and rehearsal games
Party	Brecht's *David*, A2–A6 / physical improvisation progressing, Young Brecht writing
Clowns	Brecht's diaries / direct audience address from two clowns (entry of 1 September 1920)
Zarek	Composed from research; elements of Zarek's *David* and Brecht's poetry (in song form)

39. Intersemiotic translation is a key concept in our PaR, enabling the generation of performance material out of almost any type of source. Jakobson also calls this process 'transmutation', for example when a verbal sign is turned into something non-verbal. See Roman Jakobson, *Language in Literature*, ed. Krystyna Pomorska and Stephen Rudy (Cambridge: Harvard University Press, 1987), 428–35.

Brechts Anonymous	Brecht's diaries / improvisationally performed by ensemble as though in group therapy
Saul and David	Brecht's *David*, B9 / staging the composition process, with Brecht writing during scene
Footnote	Composed from research; integration of biblical, 1920 and 2017 frames by ensemble
Hedda	Composed from research; elements of Brecht's diaries
The Street Scene	Brecht's *David*, B10 / staged as Kammerspiele private work-in-progress showing, 1920
David–End	Performative gesture composed by ensemble; previously titled 'Collapse'

Table 3. Structure of the final performance text of
The David Fragments (2017) with sources.

As this sequence reveals, the final structure remained somewhat fragmentary and variable, in keeping with the source material. As a matter of principle, we did not pursue the dramatic arc of a single chronological narrative, seeking instead a productive tension – or, as it appears in contemporaneous notes, 'poetic friction' – between the content of the *David* texts, Brecht's own creative milieu ca. 1920 and the live ensemble and audience present at the event in 2017. This interplay between temporal frames was a constant in the performance, generating concomitant variation across styles.

Another distinctive feature of the final production was the use of the cast and its multiplication of characters across different temporal frames. From the first reading onward, there was a malleability of persona in each figure, and with only ten bodies to cover a great many speaking roles, resolving this was a dramaturgical requirement. Ideally, such resolutions add to the integrity of the work overall, by finding alignment that allows an actor – even if playing multiple figures – to gradually elaborate a position and a relation to others. Much of this is connected to the 'theatre of arising' process of improvisation and living systems, through which actors make discoveries that they retain for the production. Since each of the scenes had its own temporality – set in the biblical environment like 'Street Scene' (B10), set in the Kammerspiele of 1920 like 'Zarek' or 'Hedda' and set in a distorted present like 'Clowns' or 'Footnote' – each character needed to know their identity, or perhaps better 'positionality', in each of these spaces. A draft grid of these 'castings' from approximately four weeks before the production is transcribed verbatim here (see Table 4):

ACTOR	Biblical	Weimar	2017
Colm Gleeson	Beggar	Clown	Clown
Aoife Meagher	Beggar	Clown	Clown
James Ireland	David	Brecht	Brecht
Martha Grant	The people	The Spirit of German Theatre & Coffee Woman	[choose attitude to Brecht]
Grace Morgan	Uriah/Citizen Two	Zarek	[choose attitude to Brecht]
Richard Durning	Saul	Neuhofer	[choose attitude to Brecht]
Lenny Buckley	David	[direct analogue to Brecht]	being both, being beyond
Honi Cooke	Bathsheba/ Officer (Isaac)	Hedda	[reactionary]
Laoise Murray	Absalom/ Citizen One	aligned with fascists	[fascist?]
Benedict Esdale	Jesse	Falckenberg	[painfully centrist?]

Table 4. 'Casting' grid from *The David Fragments*
production notebooks, June 2017.

As the square brackets indicate, there were some gaps left open for actors to decide; if their own orientation toward Brecht, based on their own reading and research, ended up a certain way through the process, we encouraged them to avail of that feeling within the '2017' moments of the text, rooting their own politics to the actions on stage. This giving of agency and ownership to actors is part of an educative and contemporary ethos in ensemble theatre.

Upon entering the Samuel Beckett Theatre in Dublin, where the first week-long run of *The David Fragments* took place in June 2017, the audience might identify 1920s German jazz music, but they would quickly notice that a contemporary beat and turntable scratch had been added. Eight ensemble bodies, already on stage performing the improvised 'Prologue' as the audience entered, were dressed in 1920s-inspired costumes but were generating a Brechtian/biblically inspired atmosphere, responding communally to physical prompts based on the actions of Absalom, Bathsheba, and David, with the specific source material (Brecht's A-fragments and our own past workshops with them) undetectable by the audience. At the end of the prologue, only the actor playing the young Brecht remained standing (see Fig. 1), an image that set up a motif of Brecht's persistent survival and adaptation, echoed in the final moments of the piece.

5. The David *Fragments in Practice and Performance*

Figure 1. Young Brecht (James Ireland) with ensemble and title at the end of the Prologue (Photo © Kasia Kaminska)

This aggressively avant-garde and somewhat self-serious beginning of the play was immediately punctured by the rapturous applause and heckling of two clowns (visually inspired by Anita Berber and Sebastian Droste, Berlin cabaret performers of the period, but costumed in fragments of WWI uniforms) who had slipped into the theatre with the audience and were now seated among them. Enacting an idea suggested by Brecht in his diary entry of 1 September 1920 – 'Once I get my hooks on a theatre I shall hire two clowns'[40] – the clowns served dramaturgically as comic relief but were also licensed to improvise, helping to bridge between temporal frames and supporting scene transitions. The adaptation script described the aesthetic of the scenography as follows: 'The elements should be as simple and as specific as possible – ten wooden chairs, one table, paper, fabric. A large-scale surface for back-projection is desirable, i.e. a cyclorama on which skies, colours, and some titles/messages can be projected.'[41] A central circle defined the playing-area, with the full ensemble always activated and present outside, even when not performing within the scene.

40. Brecht, *Diaries 1920–1922*, 32.
41. David Shepherd and Nicholas Johnson, *The David Fragments* after Bertolt Brecht, rehearsal script (adaptation 6.6.17).

The first two performance aesthetics on offer – hermetic, experimental modernism and comedic audience address – were then complemented by a third: naturalism, required by this point to clarify the dramatic content setting up the fragments themselves. In the 'Zarek' scene, set in the Kammerspiele, Brecht arrived to interrupt a flirtatious meeting between Otto Zarek and Siegfried Neuhofer (director of the Munich publisher Georg Müller). After hearing (and insulting) a piece from Zarek's *David*, Young Brecht displayed his noted charisma by wildly playing a composition on his guitar entitled 'Mounted on the Fairground's Magic Horses', whose refrain — 'Oh he's so different' — exposed the audience to one aspect of Brecht's persona in this period. What appeared to be a conventionally naturalistic encounter was later somewhat estranged by the recurrence of the same actors in other roles within Brecht's own fragments: the smarmy paternalism of Neuhofer becomes Saul, then later Jonathan; the Kammerspiele 'coffee girl' dismissed by Zarek is resurrected later as 'The Spirit of German Theatre', revealing her coffee tray to be a Wagnerian shield. This interplay of multiplicity and malleability of identity within the ensemble is the heart of scene five, entitled 'Brechts Anonymous' (see Fig. 2), when Brecht himself becomes plural.

Figure 2. The ensemble during 'Brechts Anonymous'
(Photo © Kasia Kaminska)

The 'Brechts Anonymous' performance system is based on the confessional and personal tone adopted in an 'Alcoholics Anonymous' session, except that the state-of-being-Brecht is the addiction, and all the people in the room (except a facilitator and the clowns) are playing Brecht. Each actor had memorised the same text from Brecht's diaries – an alarming description of a party in which a woman at the party is abused – but the sequence and manner of line delivery was improvised each night, generating a freshness and sense of risk. Having constituted the ensemble as the *mind* of Brecht alongside the figure the audience had seen as Young Brecht, the next scene staged the writing process of B9 (David–Saul). His writing gestures amplified by a microphone under his desk, Brecht composed outside the playing area, while the ensemble within the area responded. Audible modifications (words scratched out or changed, based on the original manuscripts of B9) and pauses for contemplation were inserted and performed by the actors playing David and Saul, to firmly establish the dramaturgical relation between creator and creation (see Fig. 3).

Figure 3. The ensemble during 'Saul and David', with Young Brecht in the foreground (Photo © Kasia Kaminska)

Symbolically, the performers eventually gained the upper hand over the writer, with the whole ensemble overwhelming the writing sound with the chorus to David's song ('Strong is the Bull'). Then the spear thrown by Saul at the end of the scene shattered the frame, accidentally hitting one of the clowns offstage, leading to a scene we named 'Footnote', in which the actors reacted (adversely) to Brecht's writing of the David/Saul scene and his general misbehaviour, until the arrival of 'The Spirit of German Theatre' who blesses him. After another scene in the Kammerspiele with Hedda Kuhn, doubling as a Bathsheba figure, and the 'public' work-in-progress showing of B10, the longest of Brecht's fragments, it is the same spear that falls on the stage at the end of the show, just missing Brecht and penetrating the chair in which he was sitting moments before.

It might seem that such a wide aesthetic range explored over a 75-minute production would only produce confusion or ennui. But the shadow of a chronology remained in the journey taken by the central figure of the Young Brecht, seen first writing amid a wild party in the first scene (Fig. 1), then singing his poetry and listening to a poorly written Saul/David scene by Zarek in the fourth scene, then composing his own Saul/David scene in scene six (Fig. 3) and finally submitting a fragment of *David* for semi-public, work-in-progress consumption in the ninth and penultimate scene. All of these episodes have an approximate historical justification in Brecht's *Diaries*, which were also the source for texts performed within 'Brechts Anonymous' and 'Footnote', though these two scenes operated as interstitial material in the contemporary frame and with a more postdramatic mode of performance, in which verisimilitude is abandoned in favor of dialectic opposition between the source material and the situation on stage, and which relies on the creative intelligence of the ensemble to remain live, responding to the the event as it unfolds.

The reception of the production suggested that critics were aware of the strange border on which such PaR generally exists, somewhere between the educational and the professional.[42] As one review put it in *Draff*:

> There is a rare and deliberate intellectual rigour at play in this piece… Any number of potential virtuoso performances are channelled for the greater good. There's a comprehensive accountability in the action. This is evident in the deft details from the careful tenor of the speech, to the organisation of the stage, to the continual element of the right surprise, as well as allowing for some exquisite moments.[43]

---

42. The Samuel Beckett Theatre, as a Dublin city-centre venue that is also on a campus, alternately produces student work (during term) and indigenous/international professional theatre (out of term), so audiences are often unsure what type/level of practice they might encounter there. Our ensemble blended established professionals with current students and recent alumni; the total production budget of €17,000 and the presence of compensation strongly hints at a professional production, though the university funding and research-oriented context differentiates it from most state-sector or independent-sector projects.

43. Martin Sharry, 'Review of *The David Fragments*', *Draff*, 29 June 2017, https://www.draff.net/the-david-fragments.html (accessed 5 January 2019).

Beyond the Stage: Impacts and Absences

We argued above that while translations always require renewal and revision, for translated *drama* there is an inherent fidelity to the present audience that can shift the balance away from authorial control over the text. Practice-as-research with an experimental ensemble is an expression of this de-centering of power in terms of process: instead of a director dominating a room and instructing actors based on a personal vision of the final product, the collaborators are first identified by a shared curiosity and desire to know, bonded as co-investigators through a conceptual process based on the development of mutual trust, and then introduced to atmospheric or improvisational games or open-ended exercises based on the source material. By documenting this process rigorously, a performance text based on organic 'discoveries' rather than 'decisions' can be developed, in line with our understanding of what contemporary theater aesthetics and our obligation to our audience entail. It is through this ethos that we return to fundamental questions of Brecht's philosophy in the theatre and to how the implications of such a working method might be thought in terms of recent readings of Brecht's living legacy.

The expressive action that closed this production, of the spear first launched by Saul toward David, narrowly missing Brecht, traces an arc that was central to this production and perhaps is meaningful in reflecting on both modernism and PaR: the power retained by the incomplete, unfinished or infelicitious gesture. To play out this metaphor, Brecht was first 'grazed' at a young age by a spear launched from the Bible, replete with images of terrible power and, in Luther's rendering, a literary act that extends further, and embeds deeper, in Brecht's life than the religious faith to which it is attached. Though the biblical Saul misses David, his spear hits Brecht. A host of other writers in the German tradition, modernist and otherwise, then bombard Brecht with further projectiles, suggesting that he might 'write back' to this David story that is so persistently 'on the brain'. But when his time comes to launch, he too misses; that spear travels through time and hits us.

The idea of the spear as a literary act makes clear the temporal frames and historical burdens of the 2017 production, which are also, finally, Brechtian burdens: to be 'of a time' while being 'not of that time', to find a form to accommodate the dialectic spaces between methods/ fashions of theatre and to endure and survive through forms of 'adaptation'. What we imagined initially, even from the first physical workshop, might become an exploration of biblical space and its dusty, desert 'street scenes' within a community of violence, gradually became an excavation of the time and circumstances of Brecht's own composition (with some continuity regarding violence and the street, in Weimar Germany). The first reflection on *The David Fragments* project appearing in Johnson's directorial notebooks, in an entry dated 26 November 2015, is remarkable to return to with an awareness of where the project ended up, showing again the curious way in which the end is always present in the beginning. Instead of trying to resolve either a biblical question about David's reception, or a theatre-studies question about Brecht's fragments, it is written: 'we see the avenue where the performance can be engaged to answer both our questions'.[44] These initial notes acknowledge a difference in the two approaches of the lead collaborators, but they also outline the path through these challenges that was ultimately discovered. Entries under three headings – 'Model', 'World' and 'Problem' – are quoted at length below:

> Model: For me, this is the key – we do not impose order on the disordered. We work instead to get the world on stage, whether mad or no, and let anything be performable, as it is. For him this may be different – [Shepherd] sees 'play' as the word for a real world, really created, the narrative. So his intervention is less to 'fix' the fragments than to 'frame' them – in time, context, Kammerspiele. I think these ideas are not so far apart. We can make them both: use the one as supply for the other.
>
> World: This is the hard part. The space of this project is that there is not any excuse for either Brecht/Weimar or for biblical – instead, something needs creation that is within the realm of the theatrical. I suspect something nearly transparent, suggestive, lucid with both possibilities, but unanchored in time. Perhaps.
>
> Problem: In reading the text I increasingly see the space of pure 'poetics of indigence' – his sarcasm. The very particular form of void there, tactics of attrition, the need to get a movement out of the stuckness, the stillness, and to keep alert to the text's particular wakefulness. And I suspect we will find more, in the oddity. The Isaiah – 'over your cities grass will grow'.[45]

The final line, separate and below this last entry, is 'Trümmer sind an sich Zukunft'. This reference, linked to the Isaiah citation, is part of a quote from the German artist Anselm Kiefer, whose paintings, sculptures and assemblages work through the flow of history itself, with a special focus on German history and myth (as well as several biblical themes). The sentiment, expressed here in shorthand, is that the texts and our work with

---

44. Johnson, Production Notebooks, *The David Fragments*.
45. Ibid.

them are an expression of human endurance through difficulty: David's, Brecht's and our own. The animating impulse of this annotation, at the foundation of the whole project, was to reflect on the fascination of how many spears, finally, did not hit Brecht: escaping the Nazis, escaping the Americans, always writing nonetheless. Without aligning morally or spiritually with all of Brecht's actions, there is something remarkable in his tenacity and persistence, and this becomes all the more poetic when, like *David*, it fails to connect with its target. The humanity in the gesture of the spear-throw, mysteriously fascinating to Brecht from the beginning of his *David* sketches, threaded through our production across all its frames and times, and we believe that this spear is flying still.

Concluding Reflections: After *David*

In 1 Samuel 28, after the prophet Samuel has been returned to the land of the living, it may be recalled that the first thing he asks Saul is 'why have you disturbed me by bringing me up?' (v. 15). Indeed, given how peacefully Brecht's *David* had been left to rest by scholarship up until now, we might well imagine these fragments posing a similar question to us, had their views been sought. Like Saul did of Samuel, we have asked questions of Brecht's afterlife of David in the hope that we might learn something new of value. In concluding this study, it seems only right therefore to reflect briefly not only on what we have learned about Brecht's life of *David* and how such afterlives may be explored, but also about the afterlife of *David* in Brecht's later work – all of which, in their own ways, reflect precisely the sort of fruitful 'entanglements' we have sought to embrace in this interdisciplinary project.

Entangled Lives: The David *Fragments, the Biblical David and the Young Brecht*

Our exploration of character development in Brecht's *David* offers ample illustration of the ways in which the fragments follow the biblical traditions relating to David on one hand, but also subvert and even seemingly react to them on the other. While not developed in any meaningful way, the fragments offer tantalising glimpses of Brecht's interest in elaborating the role of Uriah beyond the biblical tradition – an interest which appears to be borne out by the fascination which the figure of Uriah continued to exert on Brecht in later years. By contrast, Absalom may not have commanded Brecht's attention later on in his career in quite the same way, but others' testimony regarding the importance of Absalom at the beginning of his creative engagement with the David stories is borne out by the fragments' interest in the climax of Absalom's rebellion and his death, and Brecht's exploration of David's sympathy for (and perplexity with) his wayward son.

While David's relationship with his son Absalom is thus a major preoccupation of the biblical tradition (2 Sam. 13–18) which the fragments only barely begin to explore, David's relationship with his father, Jesse, which receives little attention in the biblical tradition, attracts Brecht's interest to a much greater extent. Given that Jesse is so thinly drawn as a character in 1 Samuel, comparison with Brecht's Jesse is not entirely straightforward. For example, it is not impossible that Jesse's eagerness to see his son enlisted in the war effort at the end of B10 might find an originating impulse in the biblical Jesse's insistence on sending David to the battlefront. Nor is it inconceivable that the Brechtian Jesse's disgruntlement with David's neglect of the home front is a reflex of the fact that the biblical David spends virtually none of the narrative at home in Bethlehem. Yet, in the case of the former at least, and possibly in the caustic interaction between Jesse and David at the end of B10, we found it difficult to rule out entirely an autobiographical impulse.

While the biblical Jonathan does remain in the shadow of David after the latter's emergence and plays a much more minor part in the narrative than his father Saul, the role of Brecht's Jonathan in B10 is, as we saw, more minor still. Moreover, while Brecht's Jonathan does issue commands, we saw the distinct possibility that Brecht seeks to deprecate both Jonathan's accomplishments and his authority/status. While the biblical Jonathan is presented as generally quite accomplished, his authority/status yields as David's grows, which may well account for what appeared to be the most striking aspect of Brecht's treatment of Jonathan. Instead of being full of rhetorical questions as is his biblical incarnation, Brecht's Jonathan is incessantly asking David questions intended to elicit information about who he is and why he does what he does. This casting of Jonathan in the role of investigative officer encountering a rather curious witness in David highlights the extent to which, in comparison with the biblical tradition, Brecht's Jonathan serves as 'agent' in service not so much of the plot, but of Brecht's characterisation of David in B10 of which more will be said by way of summary below. Given the enormous popular and scholarly interest in the nature of the biblical Jonathan's relationship with David (homoerotic or otherwise), what is perhaps most striking is that his Brechtian counterpart displays no great passion for David in the fragments. As we will see below, it is not until the *Goliath* opera project of 1937–1944 that Brecht shows renewed interest in this relationship, and makes more of it.

We saw that the perplexity of Jonathan with David in B10 finds a resonance in Brecht's Saul in B9, the only full scene of the fragments in which he appears. But what makes Jonathan's lack of passion all the more noteworthy is the contrast this presents to Brecht's Saul in B9, where Brecht chooses to work out the implications of 1 Sam. 16.21 in making narrative sense of David's serenading of Saul and the latter's attempt to spear him. Perhaps adumbrated in A7, B9 is Brecht's dramatisation of *how* and *why* David's music yields to Saul's violence: namely, because of David's rejection of Saul's great (erotic) love for him (1 Sam. 16.21). Given how much attention has been devoted to passages that may illustrate the erotic possibilities of Jonathan's feelings for David (and vice versa), Brecht's treatment of Saul perhaps invites students of Samuel to reflect more deeply on the dynamics of Saul's 'great love' for David.

Unsurprisingly, it is the character of David which offers the most grist for Brecht's mill, appearing as he does in both of Brecht's most developed scenes, and eventually taking centre stage in the longest of them (B10). In the latter we saw David's indolence (cf. also Saul's allusion to David's loafing in B9) explored by Brecht at considerable length, despite their being little hint of this in David's biblical incarnation, unless Eliab's accusation when David arrives at the battlefront with the Philistines points in this direction. Is there a suggestion of the biblical David's impudence too in Eliab's upbraiding of his brother? If not, it is certainly supplied quite explicitly by Nabal in rebuffing the biblical David's request for victuals (1 Sam. 25). Yet the absence of any interest in this episode on Brecht's part may suggest that his David's impertinence/impudence has been supplied from a different source. The same may also be said for how opinionated Brecht's David is, given that the narrative style of 1 Samuel offers no meaningful opportunity for David or anyone else to extemporise on particular subjects. That war is the chief subject on which Brecht's David offers his opinions is not on its own a clear marker of discontinuity from the biblical traditions of 1 Samuel, which are consumed with armed conflict of one sort or another. However, in comparison with the David of 1 Samuel – who is only too happy to take up arms against anyone and everyone apart from King Saul – what marks out Brecht's David is not only his own reluctance to contribute personally to the Israelite war effort, but also his efforts to persuade others to follow suit.

As we have seen in Chapter 4, it is in his diary entry for 20 August 1920 that Brecht voices most clearly his ambition in writing his life of David:

> [I can] write a kind of history, with no relevance, no point [*ohne Pointe*] to the story, no 'idea' [ohne 'Idee'], just the young David [*einfach den Jungen David*] and a slice of his life [*ein Stück aus seinem Leben*].[1]

1. English from John Willett's translation of the *Diaries*, 18. German from the *BFA* 26, 136. *Stück* in this usage might have been more poetically translated as

That Brecht's diaries themselves might answer to something very like this description suggests that *David's* life was not the only one Brecht was writing at the time. Indeed, no less than in the *David* fragments, we found in the pages of his diaries a kind of history without obvious relevance, point or idea: simply a slice of the young Brecht's life. While the latter is very nearly as 'fragmentary' in its own way as the *David* fragments, it is not entirely surprising that Brecht's and others' accounts of his life at this stage might illuminate his life of David.

We have seen that the fragments' fascination with (especially David's) indolence was seen to resonate perceptibly with Brecht's musings on his own diligence or lack thereof. So too, Brecht's exploration of the young protagonist's impertinence and reactions to it seem unlikely to be a coincidence, given how widespread the perception of the young Brecht as impudent and opinionated was amongst both peers and those within the educational and cultural establishment. Moreover, we saw the resistance to war expressed by Brecht's David (but not by his biblical counterpart) become much more comprehensible in light of the evolution of Brecht's own reaction to the war seen not only in his writings, but also in his efforts to avoid military service. Even the acerbic and sarcastic encounter between the Brechtian Jesse and David, for which there is no biblical precedent, becomes more intelligible when considering Brecht's presentation in his diaries of the complexities of his own relationship with his father. But perhaps the clearest indicators of Brecht's own blurring of the lines between his own persona and David's are his practice at the time of writing his own 'Psalms' – a genre inextricably and uniquely associated with David – and the resonance of these Psalms with the song he writes for 'his' David to sing to Saul in the fragments. Indeed, the value of attending to Brecht's other writings from around the same time was confirmed by the resonances of this scene with *Baal*, not only in terms of its interest in indolence, but especially toward the end in its representation of jealousy, violence and homoeroticism – the latter of which Brecht was also exploring at the time in 'Bargan Gives Up' and 'The Ballad of Friendship'.

If a reading of Brecht's life of David alongside accounts of his own life suggest an entanglement that was crucial to his creative process, our study also suggests the value of situating his *David* within the wider 'later-life/afterlife' of David – not least because of how popular the stories associated with him were amongst European dramatists of the late

'piece', which would have retained the *double entendre* of 'slice' and 'play' (*Stück* is also the name for a theatrical 'piece'.)

nineteenth and early twentieth centuries. As became clear in our exploration of the dramatic efforts and ideas of Zarek, Feuchtwanger and Gide, Brecht's *David* was shaped significantly by his encounter with others' work – especially Zarek's *David* and Gide's *Saül*. While we have seen that Brecht's use of Zarek offers more early confirmation of his desire to re-write in 'reaction against', Brecht's indebtedness to Gide's play represents new evidence of Brecht's equally well-attested tendency to emulate and re-situate the ideas of others in his own creative endeavours. Indeed, if, as we have seen, Brecht's David (especially in B10) is incomprehensible without reference to the life of the young Brecht, Brecht's Saul in B9 turns out to be equally indebted to Gide's *Saül*, not least in mimicking the latter's construal of Saul's violence as arising because of David's rejection of his erotic advances. What this suggests is that while Brecht's life of David may well reflect in some way the life of a young writer genuinely grappling with their own experience of (homo)sexuality, the fragments are more likely to reflect the life of Gide than the life of Brecht, and thus meaningful attempts to understand the 'later-life/afterlife' of a biblical character such as David would do well to attend carefully to the 'lives' after which it comes. The query it raises for biblical scholarship is why the biblical Saul's great love for the younger David has been so much less explored than Jonathan's love for David.

Entangled Methods: Theatre/Brecht Studies and Biblical Reception Studies

We have found that exploring the *David* fragments through an open-ended, university-based and collaborative interdisciplinary research project advanced our understanding, not only of the texts but also of our own disciplines, in numerous (and often unpredictable) ways. The joining in this project of two subject-experts working in their own topic areas – in this case, a director/translator of German expressionist work and someone interested in both the 'biblical' David and the Bible's reception in the twentieth century – proved enriching and generated insights and outcomes far beyond what either party could have produced on their own. In what follows, we will seek to reflect briefly on some of the methodological fruit of our exploration of Brecht's *David*.

In the sub-field of Brecht studies, it is our hope that projects like *The David Fragments* may help us to begin to grasp the nettle of a number of the thorniest issues around what we are to do today with the legacy of Brecht in performance. On the one hand, there is the risk of feeling constrained by a stale, programmatic reading of his theories; in spite of their resistance to consolidation, their change over time and their internal contradictions, in many cultural contexts they are treated as 'digested' and reified, 'made safe' through the logic of reproduction.[2] There is also the risk, at least when Brecht's work enters the commercial sector, of being constrained by the 'hard power' vested in the authorities over the rights. We have found that practice-as-research can usefully *interrupt* such procedures, creating a space dialectically between the old and new Brecht – between privately owned texts and publicly owned ideas, between the educational and political spheres – in a manner that we can only describe as Brechtian. 'Interruption', as Walter Benjamin illuminated, is itself one of the key gestures of the epic theatre.[3] Brecht's non-dogmatic, effectively non-religious, deployment of biblical material within his *David* permitted a useful irreverence in our own process, enabling us to ask questions that might not have been easily asked in productions of Brecht's finished plays for other purposes. We clearly made revisions and additions to *The David Fragments* in our own production that would be associated more with 'new' works for the contemporary theatre than with the restaging of the work of classic authors. However, because these creative amendments and extensions were rooted both in Brecht's *time* of writing *David* and in Brecht's emancipating *methods* of theatrical creation, as opposed to having recourse to the biblical David in the quixotic pursuit of narrative coherence, these interventions contrast with the 'authorised' premiere in Germany in 1995. Indeed, if *fidelity* is a goal of such adaptation, which is the more faithful approach?

There were also new insights about translation that arose from working with these fragments from such an early stage in Brecht's career, as opposed to his 'finished' prose, poetry or drama. Translating fragments like *David* deprives the translator of their presumed ability to assess their work in relation to the notionally perfect version published and edited by the writer themselves as a 'gold standard', leaving the choice of either

---

2. For a critique of Brecht's journey through capitalist, especially Anglosphere culture, see the chapter 'Alienation Affects' in Owen Hatherley, *Militant Modernism* (London: Zero Books, 2008).

3. The centrality of the 'Interruption' or *Unterbrechung* to Brecht's theatre was first argued in Walter Benjamin, 'What is Epic Theater?' in *Illuminations*, trans. Harry Zohn, ed. Hannah Arendt (New York: Schocken Books, 1968), 147–54. It is explored in greater detail by Freddie Rokem, '"Suddenly a stranger comes into the room": Interruptions in Brecht, Benjamin and Kafka', *Studies in Theatre and Performance* 36 (2016): 21–6. The root word of *Unterbrechung – brechen/Bruch* – also appears in the word *Bruchstück*: 'fragment'.

substituting instead an *imaginary* whole that was never actually produced by the writer, or else living with the 'hotbeds of inconsistency'[4] that arise from holding fast to the notion of incompletion. Working with ostensibly partial texts is extremely liberating on the one hand, but terrifying on the other, and it requires substantially more background work – namely, tracing the archival and notebook sources of the fragments – than might be generally expected. The complexity, long duration and division of this project into phases involving readers, actors, designers, technicians and audiences showed again how dramatic translation differs in fundamental ways from prose or poetry translation, where the written word is (usually) the only mediation between the source and the final recipient. Translations of drama, and even more so of dramatic fragments, continuously change under the conditions of public reading, private workshop, professional rehearsal and performance. Returning after such a process to the published text (or text for publication), as we did here, makes for a much richer text than would have been produced initially.

For theatre studies and its ongoing evolution within higher education (where it is still relatively young as a named discipline, and usually has to fight for its status in most universities where STEM fields command the bulk of available research funding), this project confirmed the tremendous value of embodiment as a tool in research. The kinaesthetic pathways of exploring fragmentary, partial, incomplete texts or texts not intended for performance yield a different type of awareness that is both *about* the body and *retained* in the body. While more phenomenological than 'scientific' in terms of the data it represents, surprising outcomes can nonetheless emerge from the 'living systems' that constitute experimental theatre workshops, and these moments themselves raise new questions that would be of interest to many outside of the discipline. When B5 – Brecht's poetic treatment of the death of Absalom – was introduced as a source text for movement-based improvisation in workshops in September 2016, the ensemble read the prompt text for about 60 seconds, and then began a group improvisation where they played extensively with their hands (we had not previously noticed, until this, how much

---

4. In a notable passage from the *Messingkauf* Dialogues (B141, Fourth Night, ca. 1945) when the debate is about performing *King Lear* with radical interventions, the Philosopher notes: 'it wouldn't do any harm if there were some abnormal episodes of this sort – if people were confronted with a few such hotbeds of inconsistency. The old chronicles are full of such things' (99). It seems possible that when he says 'old chronicles', the Philosopher is referring to the Bible.

of Brecht's text had to do with hands). This improvisation gradually concluded with the hanging of one actor's head by its hair, even though the actors had limited knowledge of either the biblical or Brechtian source material at the time. Such eerie examples of 'workshop synchronicity', hardly uncommon as a feature of such laboratory-based work in drama, create an archive of strong memory in the researcher, and it is often impossible to forget these moments when going back later to write about the same text, or to retranslate it. This suggests that something in the *social* life of practice-as-research enriches the often solitary labour of individual research. While more challenging logistically, it clearly also expands one's perspective and insights, and thus reflects a distinctive contribution to the scholarly record. Similarly, a deeper knowledge of the texts has been achieved through having to answer actors', designers' and assistant dramaturgs' questions under the pressures of rehearsal time. Without the long process phase, performance gestation and audience feedback, a 'traditional' approach of archival investigations and written research alone would have delivered a much different book.

As any close reader of Brecht (or Dwight Conquergood, or Karl Marx, or Aristotle) will know, practice is not negotiable as a separate part of theory. *Praxis* is not an 'add-on' to enhance the entertainment value of conceptual labour; it is that labour itself. It is to the credit of the editors of the new *Brecht on Performance*, the companion to the classic *Brecht on Theatre*, that they conclude the newly collected *Messingkauf* and *Modelbooks* with an essay by the teacher Di Trevis, entitled 'Acting is not Theoretical', documenting and reflecting on a workshop with Brecht's theories *in action* with contemporary actors. Similarly, in *Brecht and the Writer's Workshop*, Tom Kuhn concludes the general introduction with a full paragraph about how practical work in the theatre has 'inspired and informed' the work, and how the fragments have been selected as 'living, breathing works that can still make their way in the theatre'.[5] We hope that this book will encourage others to pursue what might be assumed to be 'textual' forms of research in collaboration with readers, performers, artists and audiences, and perhaps provide a model for doing so for the many remaining dramatic fragments (and not only those by Brecht).

Indeed, while the sorts of traditional literary and historical tools previously applied to other afterlives of Saul and David undoubtedly did deepen our understanding of Brecht's *David* and its entanglement

---

5. Tom Kuhn, 'General Introduction', in *Brecht and the Writer's Workshop: Fatzer and other Dramatic Projects* (London: Bloomsbury, 2019), 10.

with other 'lives',[6] the more novel deployment of theatrical performance within the project proved equally important in demonstrable ways. Given the challenges of language and interpretation posed by the fragments, performance (and the translation it facilitated and required) was crucial in 'summoning up' Brecht's *David*, much as the medium summons up the biblical Samuel in 1 Samuel 28. However, it is important to note that like the medium of Endor, 'performance' served as more than mere 'handmaid' in our process by facilitating insights and identifications which enabled and stimulated deeper investigation. Workshop investigation of the diaries and Brecht's relationships with his father and Otto Zarek, for instance, offered crucial stimuli for the investigations which led to insights in Chapters 3 and 4. Moreover, the fruitfulness of performance for our study may be seen in the ways in which it pointed to aspects of the biblical text which might otherwise have been overlooked.

To offer but one example, the fixation on 'hands' by the acting ensemble in their movement-based improvisation based on B5 drew our attention to the prominence of 'hand/s' in Brecht's fragments relating to Absalom and his death.[7] Indeed, Brecht's particular interest in 'hands' may be seen also in B10, where the beggars resolve to flee Saul's conscription:

> That's it then, we run, before someone presses an iron shield into our hands! (*looks at his hands.*) Mine is white and has a damn fine skin, it's not for dirty work, my child. Let's see yours!
>
> *They show each other their hands. From a distance cries and whistles of many men.*

In addition to raising the idea that certain hands are more suitable to certain tasks (violence/dirty work) than others, Brecht's beggar encourages the characters within the narrative and indeed the audience itself to attend carefully to 'hands' for what they tell us.

---

6. In addition to Nebel's *Harfe, Speer und Krone*, see, for instance, Sarah Nicholson, *Three Faces of Saul: An Intertextual Approach to Biblical Tragedy* (London: Bloomsbury, 2002), which includes an analysis of Lamartine's *Saül*.

7. See B5 (Von Absalom) where we read: 'Never cursing, never helping: he / Folded the hands! They lay in the lap. / Never reaching, never resisting / Instead, repudiate the hands.'; cf. also B3, where David cannot understand the violence which follows his son: 'My son Absalom has such soft hands', and Absalom's sees his own plight in terms of (hand/s): 'I want to throw away what my hand can grasp... I want to throw my hand away!'

Indeed, we saw something similar early in B9. After stage directions inform us 'David has a lyre in his hands' as he enters, Saul reminds him that following David's great victories, the crowd 'stares at your hands, because you're the victor'. When later in the scene Saul queries why David sings, and David replies 'Your face changes and your hands get calmer', Saul retorts: 'What business of yours are my hands?' Here, Brecht's David makes it clear that while the crowd may well be watching his hands, David himself is watching Saul's – a fact which Saul evidently finds disconcerting.

While Peter Miscall has rightly noted the significance of the metaphorical use of *yād* 'hand' in the sense of power in 1 Samuel 23 and 24, where the word appears 7 and 11 times in the respective chapters,[8] Brecht's attention to literal 'hands' within his fragments, to their suitability for certain tasks and to what may be learned from them, encourages us to attend to the frequent appearance of Hebrew *yād* 'hand' in 1 Samuel 16–18, the very chapters which Brecht had in mind as he was writing B9 and B10. More specifically, Brecht's fragments invite the reader of the biblical narrative to observe afresh what is (and what is not) to be found in the hands of David and Saul at given points in these chapters.

Thus, in 1 Samuel, David is introduced to Saul in the previous chapter (16.16) as one who will make him well by playing the harp 'with the hand'.[9] That David's hands confer blessing seems to be confirmed later in the chapter first when Jesse sends gifts of food and wine to Saul 'by the hand of David his son' (16.20) and then when David plays the harp 'with his hand' and it makes Saul well, as predicted (16.23). When David's combat with Goliath is described in the following chapter, the narrator makes clear that David lays the Philistine low with a shepherd's staff 'in his hand' and a sling 'in his (other) hand' (17.40) and loads his sling with 'his hand' (17.49), before finally emphasising that 'there was no sword in David's hand' (1 Sam. 17.50) to underline the remarkable nature of David's improbable triumph over Saul's enemy Goliath, whose head David proceeds to bring 'in his hand' to Saul (1 Sam. 17.57). That David's hands can do no wrong is confirmed by David's persistence in playing the harp 'with his hand' in the following chapters, despite Saul's now holding 'in his hand' a spear (18.10 and again in 19.9) which is of

---

8. See Peter Miscall, *1 Samuel: A Literary Reading* (Bloomington: Indiana University Press, 1986), 139–40.

9. Kyle P. McCarter, *1 Samuel* (New York: Doubleday, 1980), 280, notes that the Greek text doesn't refer to David playing 'with the hand' but rightly suggests the likelihood of an inner-Greek corruption.

course launched at David on these occasions.[10] Finally, the suggestion that David's hands are a good guide to his characterisation is suggested in 1 Samuel 21 by David's insistence that the priest Ahimelek furnish him with the food and a sword which are 'in your hand' because David has come without a sword 'in my hand'. When David's request is overheard by Saul's associates and costs Ahimelek and his confreres their life at Saul's hand, David all but recognises that for the first time in 1 Samuel he has blood on his hands.[11] Most instructively for our purposes, this insight only emerged as a result of the entanglement of biblical scholarship and the acting ensemble's attentiveness to Brecht's own preoccupation with 'hands' in the *David* fragments.

While we hope that such an example illustrates the promise and potential of collaboration between those working within biblical reception studies and those exploring creative arts practice in music, theatre, film and beyond, we conclude with some final reflections on exploring the later-life (*Fortleben*) and survival (*Überleben*) of the *David* material within Brecht's oeuvre, and on how *The David Fragments* project might connect with Brecht's own literary and theoretical afterlife (*Nachleben*).

Entangled Afterlives: Goliath *and the Survival of Brecht's* David

One by-product of our efforts to summon up Brecht's *David* has been the 'discovery' of just how many theatrical afterlives of David and Saul from the late nineteenth and early twentieth centuries have been left for dead by biblical reception studies.[12] Our investigation of just three of them (and Gide's is among the most famous) suggests that there is much work to be done, not only because there are so many plays to be explored, but also because in many cases, the work of contextualising is so laborious and demanding. Yet, it is hoped that our exploration of Brecht's fragments in light of the work of Gide, Zarek and Feuchtwanger has offered a glimpse of the promise of such work and the potential it has to help us understand how the Bible was interpreted in the context of modernist movements within the visual and performing arts of the late nineteenth and early twentieth century. While this vein remains as yet almost entirely unmined, the afterlife of Brecht's *David* in his own work also remains a

---

10. The significance of what is to be found in David's and Saul's hands respecetively in both 18.10 and 19.9 is noted by Bodner, *1 Samuel*, 194.

11. See Miscall, *1 Samuel*, 132, for this recognition and Shepherd, *King David*, for a reading of this episode which attends to the question of David's culpability.

12. See Nebel, *Harfe, Speer und Krone*.

desideratum. If tracing all the ways in which Brecht's *David* anticipates and is echoed in the length and breadth of Brecht's later work is well beyond the scope of this study, it is perhaps another fragment, *Goliath*, which offers the most obvious avenue for future exploration. For this reason and in the interests of encouraging such exploration, we offer some final thoughts on why and how *Goliath* might be worthy of investigation beyond what is possible here.

Goliath (1937–1944) offers another telling example of Brecht's creative engagement with biblical material, as well as highlighting the enduring importance of the David story for Brecht during his darkest times: indeed, the opera fragment, running to 36 pages in the *BFA*, is the central branch of *David's* afterlife within Brecht's own work. The schema and libretto for *Goliath* were begun by 8 March 1937 in Svendborg, Denmark. Brecht was collaborating with the composer Hanns Eisler, who was using a difficult and avant-garde twelve-tone technique; additional evidence of correspondence among Brecht's friends about the work appears during this period between Brecht and Margarete Steffin, Walter Benjamin and Bernhard Reich, indicating that it was a busy period for its development. This initial phase of work concluded in November 1937, with Eisler moving to Prague in October and then to America in January 1938. Brecht continued after 1938 to write independently, working on the second act ('David and Jonathan') during his sea crossing in 1941, and then attempted to complete the opera in the exile enclave of Los Angeles between 1941 and 1944. The third and fourth act remain merely sketches.

The key action of *Goliath* transforms the Old Testament conflict between Saul's Israel and the neighbouring Philistines into a domestic struggle for power, the first clue that an allegory for Germany in the 1930s is being elaborated. The first fragment, A1, opens with the title for Act I *Die Goliathwahl*, or the 'Goliath Election', in which the Philistines are embroiled in a conflict with 'The poor people of Gad'. In addition to the relatively transparent reference to Hitler's rise to power, a Marxist philosophical underpinning is in evidence elsewhere in the text: the Philistines throughout represent capital, trade or war, while the 'poor people' are depicted as labourers being consciously played off against one another to prevent solidarity. While clearly resonating with the class conflicts explored in the interim years in fragments like *Der Brotladen*, the fascination with labour seen here in *Goliath* is not necessarily exclusive to a post-Marx Brecht: interests in trade and the social hierarchy are also reflected in the discussions of leatherwares, farming, begging and soldiering in the *David* fragments.

Goliath's dictatorship arises from a rigged election, a bottomless greed for food and an appetite for violence; he is referred to in the text sometimes as *Diktator* and sometimes as *Führer*. David suffers multiple indignities at the hands of Goliath, including the murder of his father Jesse. No longer David's domestic nemesis as in the 1920s, Jesse is now the author of a forbidden book that contains the secrets of successful class struggle. (In one comedic episode, David is unable to greet Goliath appropriately, because this book is hidden underneath his hat.) David's sister is selected to be Goliath's bride,[13] the event depicted in the poem 'Marriage banns of Goliath, issued by the Philistines', newly translated by Tom Kuhn and included in the new English edition of Brecht's poetry.[14] In the action of the poem, Goliath takes Jesse's daughter (David's sister), whom he names Miriam, as a wife; this could reflect a need to enhance the dramatic conflict between David and Goliath, as it seems to have no biblical justification. All factors align to point toward the ultimate justice of David's violence toward Goliath. There is evidence of an operatic scale in the conception of stage images and a push beyond realism; several passages concern the construction of a giant spoon for his giant fist, while a chorus entitled 'Die Meistersinger von Gad' clearly parodies Wagner.

Joy Calico, in her book *Brecht at the Opera* (2008), offers a sustained analysis of *Goliath* with an emphasis on the music. While she is also attuned to *Goliath*'s political resonances and the traces in it of Brecht's past work, including the *David* fragments, her focus on the new work leads to interesting misreadings of the older one:

> Goliath was to have been a tour de force, resonating with layers of biblical and political allusions and put forth in opera on a grand scale: Drafts reveal plans for four substantial acts (The Election of Goliath; David and Goliath [sic]; Goliath's Rule; and Goliath's Decline); a large orchestra… The libretto had its origins in Brecht's fragment *David* (1920–21). That early text, which

---

13. In the biblical tradition, the most interesting thing about the Miriam reference is that while the fragments show no awareness of it, Saul initially presents his daughter as a gift and favour to David, but also in the hope that securing the bride price (Philistine foreskins, which do appear in the A fragments) will lead to the Philistines eliminating David for him (1 Sam. 18). Like everyone else in Saul's family and entourage, Michal loves David, but when David has to flee, he has to leave her behind. When he comes back and is about to displace Saul, he takes her back. David also in 1 Sam. 25 effectively takes Nabal's wife, after the latter is struck down in divine vengeance for a violation of hospitality toward David.

14. The poem, 'Hochzeitsverkündung des Goliath durch die Philister', appears in *BFA* 14, 363 and dates from 1937.

stayed true to the plot of its biblical model, provided the scaffolding for *Goliath*; the opera plan retained the biblical names, a few plot elements, and the central friendship between David and Jonathan. And just as Brecht had used 'Ga' to stand in for Germany in *The Horatians*, so the biblical city of 'Gad' represents Germany in Goliath. Otherwise, the opera is more closely related to the antifascist parable *Round Heads and Pointed Heads* and to another fragment about the nature of dictatorship, the unfinished novel *The Business Affairs of Mr. Julius Caesar* (October 1937).[15]

While *David* reflects the biblical setting abandoned in *Goliath*, the suggestions that it is 'true to the plot of the biblical model' can hardly be sustained based on what we have seen. It is also more than a stretch to claim that the friendship between Jonathan and David is 'central' in the prior work. Admittedly, Calico is correct about the multivalence of Gad, however: the name appears in the original *David* as well (see Chapter 1, p. 55 n. 126), and the clearer alignment of 'Ga' with Germany is not only visible in *The Horatians*, but also in the *Me-Ti*, which Brecht had been working on extensively between 1934 and 1937.[16]

What becomes apparent when looking at *David* and *Goliath* with binocular vision, as it were, is the extent to which Brecht's personal life and views are, as with *David,* imbricated into the writing, and how the biblical source is perhaps even more clearly deployed now by Brecht mostly as a vehicle for engagement and argument in public about contemporary issues. In the early days of the Weimar Republic during *David*'s composition, Brecht was a partisan of 'vitality' in a conflict unfolding against 'intellect'; Brecht was concerned in the Kutscher seminar about how the intellect was 'victorious all along the line',[17] seeking instead to celebrate transfiguration, dance and lively embodiment from his own work on *Baal*. His critique of Zarek's *David* as being overburdened with 'the Idea' and *Intrige* is part of this struggle. It stands to reason, therefore, that his David character of the 1920s was a street-wise raconteur, spouting nonsense, struggling with family, but ultimately destined for greatness in spite of his evident shiftiness and indolence. But by 1937, though Brecht's mental model for David remains that of the outsider, intellect and friendship seem to have become more important. David, depicted as both a

---

15. Joy Calico, *Brecht at the Opera* (Berkeley and Los Angeles: University of California Press, 2008), 91.

16. See the list of attributable names in *Bertolt Brecht's Me-Ti: Book of Interventions in the Flow of Things*, ed. and trans. Antony Tatlow (London and New York: Bloomsbury, 2016), 41.

17. Völker, *Brecht: A Biography*, 13.

farmer and an intellectual in the *Goliath* material, becomes close friends with Jonathan, described sometimes as a weaver and other times as a miller. Especially given the dryness of David and Jonathan's interaction in B10 of the *David* fragments, the intensity of their physical intimacy in *Goliath* remains notable, though the emphasis seems political in tone. In one extended dialogue (B9), they exchange their wet tunics as a token of friendship:

David	I am only a farmer.
Jonathan	I know.
David	And you must be a miller.
Jonathan	Between farmer and miller is enmity.
	Are we now enemies?
David	No.
Jonathan	Because: we have both frozen.
David	Because our tunics are both thin.
Jonathan	And we are both lost
David	If we are not both saved.[18]

The biographical evidence that this passage was written during the sea crossing to America – immediately after the death of Margarete Steffin, a key figure of Brecht's life as both a lover and a teacher of solidarity – reframes the relation depicted here from the homosocial to the elegiac. Such traces of the *David* narrative in Brecht's later work are conceptually and biographically tantalising. They are the branches of a tree that flourished because of its rich soil, deep roots, many gardeners and decisive pruning. Exposing the 'line of *David*' within the tree reveals Brecht's iterative and deeply personal creative process, illuminating his changing narrative through the turbulent times in which he lived.

Beyond the question 'how long do works endure?' that also greatly interested Brecht, the *David* fragments caused us to reflect on how literature might both survive and aid survival through dark times. In the production notebooks for *The David Fragments*, at the end of the entry for 12 September 2016 (the first full-ensemble rehearsal), it is written: 'Afterlives of David. This one: set within the context of afterlives.' As described in detail in Chapter 5, there were ultimately three time frames

---

18. *BFA* 10.2, 781–2. B9, author translation.

that were operative in our performance of *The David Fragments*, and thus three (after)lives to which this could refer: one biblical, one biographical and one contemporary. We imagined at first that the earlier two of these three time periods were 'dark times', in the senses that the people's daily lives were marred either by war or the constant threat of war, and that the distribution of power was unequal and often unjust. A recurring phrase from the early ensemble workshops conducted on *David* in 2016 was 'community of violence' – this phrase captured the notion that economies of injury and death were organising principles and controlling phenomena, grounding our readings of both the biblical environment and the period of Brecht's writing.[19] If we had thought in September 2016 that the biblical period and Weimar Germany were the only spaces riddled with hyper-partisan conflict and burgeoning risk, things looked different eight weeks later: In the entry for 7 November 2016 – one day before the election of Donald Trump in the United States – we find the following:

> The first task is to articulate 'in general' the role of art in communities of violence. What do we mean when we say we should connect politically? What do we mean by 'implicate' audience? What is the role of (for example) a national theatre under such conditions?

The same page includes the 'quote of the day' attributed to David Shepherd, 7 November 2016: 'Words kill slower'. Reading the dates of our own notes retrospectively in relation to the historical events that were happening around us reframes the work somewhat, and mimics the gesture of how we sought to understand Brecht by identifying what was going on around him. In trying to understand the meaning, implications and future of our performance and research of the *David* fragments, we have found it useful to consider what might be called the 'weather' within his work's ecosystem: the dark times in which Brecht grew, adapted himself and survived.

---

19. The first kinaesthetic workshop we ever conducted with the *David* ensemble (12 September 2016) was a silent improvisation to build potential atmospheres of the 'biblical street', in which actors first selected a status position to inhabit, and then observed one another to try and establish their relation (whether they were above or below one another), engaging in the street environment accordingly. Violence and the threat of violence pervaded. In the next phase of work exploring the historical dimensions of Munich in the period of Brecht's writing (4 November 2016), the ensemble created improvised sequences entitled 'The March to War', 'The Death of Eisner' and 'Variations on the Flight of Ludwig' in response to key historical events, working to Weimar-era music (as well as contemporary contrasting selections) that could colour the atmosphere in extreme or illuminating ways.

The fact that David's story is woven into the fabric of Brecht's own from 1919–1921, and that its characters recur in Brecht's writings long after this early phase of work, suggests that we might start to read Brecht's engagement with David ecologically as well as chronologically. If Brecht's life-work is a single tree (or perhaps more aptly, a large rhizome) with its soil fertilised by a buried Bible, then the *David* fragments occur as stages of outgrowth that are ultimately overtaken, but which never wholly disappear. Thin branches or twigs that don't resolve are nonetheless aggregated into the whole, leaching into the flow that gives the tree life, impossible to disentangle: after 1921, *David* is always there. Reading ecologically in context, then: the seeds of *David* germinated between 1919 and 1921 in Bavaria's post-World War I political and economic unrest. The first week of Brecht's writing coincided with the founding in Munich, on 7 March 1919, of the *Volksstaat Bayern* under a coalition led by Johannes Hoffman; this short-lived parliamentary government of a breakaway state followed from the assassination of Kurt Eisner and preceded the declaration of the Bavarian Soviet Republic under Ernst Toller. Adolf Hitler gave his first political speech in the city on 16 October 1919. By the time Hitler had clinched power and Europe was on the cusp of World War II, in the spring of 1937, Brecht himself was in exile. We are fascinated that when European upheaval once again overtakes and upends Brecht's life, he returns to Goliath, so conspicuously passed over in the *David* fragments, to draft an opera and a poem, again radically rewriting the biblical source material as an allegory on the nature of power.

The challenge in retaining the 'arboreal' model of a writer's oeuvre is that when literature comes to us arranged on bookshelves as a series of physical objects, contained and sorted and made apparently more solid though editorial labour, the trees – turned into pages – are dead. The translator, the dramaturg, the director, the teacher and the researcher are all potential mediums – horticulturalists of a kind, experimenting with old genetic material – tasked with resurrecting, cultivating and conducting a 're-membered' Brecht through our own turbulent world. When bringing *David* back to life in 2017, supported by an ensemble of a younger generation for whom the ethical questions of theatre practice are routinely foregrounded, we had to confront the question: what are the politics of such an act of resurrection? How can such manipulation of a writer's legacy be done in a non-exploitative manner? In the *Messingkauf* Dialogues (Second Night, B52, 1939–1941), Brecht's 'Philosopher' character admonishes the others: 'Bear in mind that we are living in dark times, when people's behaviour towards one another is particularly abhorrent... For many people, the exploitation of human beings seems just as natural as our exploitation of nature: human beings are treated like fields or cattle.'[20] Writing in 2019, Tom Kuhn and David Constantine echo the sentiment:

> Anyone who will look honestly at where we are now, at the state we are in, at our frequent helplessness in the face of mechanisms we have ourselves developed and unleashed, at the evasiveness, mendacity, and abject uselessness of much public discourse, anyone confronting all that, who then reads Brecht, will surely acknowledge his up-to-the-minute relevance.[21]

Such a diagnosis of the present, resonating with Brecht's note from one of the worst years of the last century, implies a certain obligation to rethink Brecht politically in the same moment that one brings the work back to life. Kuhn and Constantine lament that 'those who have not read his work, or not with an open mind' continue to think of Brecht, wrongly, as 'dogmatically bound into a politics which, so the "reasoning" goes, became redundant when the walls fell'.[22] As noted above, the risk of dogma also attaches to Brecht in the realm of theatre studies as well, in which young students of acting or directing are often taught a 'schematic' or 'static' Brecht, based on a set of received notions from the older editions of *Brecht on Theatre* (if they are lucky; from Wikipedia, if they are not). A fresh risk, of course, with its own associated danger of inflexible orthodoxies, is that the politics of authors/authorship, including in arenas of their personal and professional morality, are increasingly being considered as salient to an artwork's right to be presented.[23] It is

---

20. Bertolt Brecht, *Messingkauf*, or *Buying Brass*, ed. Steve Giles, in *Brecht on Performance* (London: Bloomsbury, 2019), 59.

21. Tom Kuhn and David Constantine, 'Introduction', in *The Collected Poems of Bertolt Brecht*, 4.

22. Ibid.

23. In our own process, the presence of violence against women, racism and anti-Semitism in Brecht's early diaries generated challenging conversations around the ethics of representation. Particularly difficult for contemporary artists to stomach are the biographical details relating to plagiarism/exploitation and misogyny, detailed most famously in the critique of Brecht levelled by John Fuegi, *Brecht & Co.: Sex, Politics, and the Making of the Modern Drama*, 2nd ed. (New York: Grove, 2002). For a meditation on what '*l'affaire* Fuegi' might mean to contemporary Brechtian praxis and pedagogy, see Nicholas Johnson, '"That book should be burned": The Contested Afterlife of Bertolt Brecht', *Trinity Journal of Postgraduate Research* 5 (2006): 8–19.

no wonder that production of many works of Brecht – namely, the more political and with less of a musical repertoire – has faded from the stage in many countries; in some places Brecht's theatre seems to have hit the 'historical limit' that Theodor Adorno foretold.[24]

At its best, interdisciplinary practice-as-research can scaffold an alternative to dogma and a resistance to comfortable repetitions of the same, offering instead an opening toward community, solidarity and the pedagogy of survival. The *David* ensemble constructed a temporary laboratory in which we traced the entangled branches of Brecht's tree, sought to excavate an area of its roots, and deployed both arts and sciences to reinvigorate these forgotten texts. It is a feature of the ecosystem of a 'living' literature that the remnants of our cultural past can be turned into the seeds of new insights, and as we hope this project has shown, Brecht's *David* offers many such kernels for biblical studies, Brecht studies, translation studies, and theatre studies. Before Saul launches his spear – the same spear that misses David, but that also, in our production, later fails to hit Young Brecht – he cries out: 'But it continues, your song, it's not done yet, your song'. This line might be said of the biblical David, whose life has inspired not only Brecht, but many others before and since. It might be said of Brecht's *David* fragments, which remained buried – indeed, left for dead – but went on to feed his *Goliath*. It could surely be said of Brecht himself, whose life-work continues to 'make trouble', ensuring (at least according to the logic of his poetry) that it 'will never decay'.

---

24. Theodor Adorno, *Aesthetic Theory*, ed. and trans. Robert Hullot-Kentor (Minneapolis: University of Minnesota Press, 1997), 27.

Bibliography

Bertolt Brecht's works

The standard German edition of Brecht's writings (*Werke*) is:

Große kommentierte Berliner und Frankfurter Ausgabe (Berlin and Frankfurt: Aufbau/Suhrkamp, 1988–2000), abbreviated as *BFA*.

References to archival materials in the text are marked 'BBA' for Bertolt-Brecht-Archiv in the Akademie der Künste, Berlin; a number following 'BBA' refers to the archive catalogue number where the reference is to be found.

Brecht, Bertolt. *Bertolt Brecht's Me-Ti: Book of Interventions in the Flow of Things*. Edited and translated by Antony Tatlow. London: Bloomsbury, 2016.
Brecht, Bertolt. *Brecht and the Writer's Workshop: Fatzer and Other Dramatic Projects*. Edited by Tom Kuhn and Charlotte Ryland. London: Bloomsbury, 2019.
Brecht, Bertolt. *Brecht on Performance: Messingkauf and Modelbooks*. Edited by Tom Kuhn, Steve Giles and Marc Silberman. London: Bloomsbury, 2019.
Brecht, Bertolt. *Brecht on Theatre*. Edited by Marc Silberman, Steve Giles and Tom Kuhn. London: Bloomsbury, 2019.
Brecht, Bertolt. *Collected Plays: 1*. Edited by John Willett and Ralph Manheim. Translated by Peter Tegel. London: Bloomsbury, 1994.
Brecht, Bertolt. *The Collected Poems of Bertolt Brecht*. Edited and translated by Tom Kuhn and David Constantine. New York: Norton Liveright, 2019.
Brecht, Bertolt. *Diaries 1920–1922*. Edited by Hertha Ramthun. Translated by John Willett. London: Eyre Methuen, 1979.
Brecht, Bertolt. *Notizbücher* 1 bis 3 (1918–1920). Edited by Martin Kölbel and Peter Villwock. Berlin: Suhrkamp, 2012.
Brecht, Bertolt. *Notizbücher* 4 bis 8 (1920). Edited by Martin Kölbel and Peter Villwock. Berlin: Suhrkamp, 2014.
Brecht, Bertolt. *Notizbücher* 9 bis 12 (1921). Edited by Martin Kölbel and Peter Villwock. Berlin: Suhrkamp, 2017.
Brecht, Bertolt. *Poems, 1913–56*. Edited by John Willett and Ralph Manheim. London: Eyre Methuen, 1976.

Other Works Cited

Abbott, H. Porter. *Beckett Writing Beckett: The Author in the Autograph.* Ithaca: Cornell University Press, 1996.

Ackerman, Susan. *When Heroes Love: The Ambiguity of Eros in the Stories of Gilgamesh and David.* New York: Columbia University Press, 2005.

Adorno, Theodor. *Aesthetic Theory.* Edited and translated by Robert Hullot-Kentor. Minneapolis: University of Minnesota Press, 1997.

Anderson, Lisa Marie. *German Expressionism and the Messianism of a Generation.* Leiden: Brill/Rodopi, 2011.

Angert-Quilter, Theresa, and Lynne Wall. 'The "Spirit Wife" at Endor'. *JSOT* 25 (2001): 55–72.

Apostolos-Cappadona, Diane. 'Introduction'. Pages 1–2 in *Biblical Women in the Arts: Biblical Reception* 5. London: T & T Clark, 2018.

Auld, A. Graeme. *I & II Samuel: A Commentary.* Louisville, KY: Westminster John Knox Press, 2011.

Bach, Inka, and Helmut Galle. *Deutsche Psalmendichtung vom 16. bis zum 20. Jahrundert: Untersuchungen zur Geschichte einer lyrischen Gattung.* Berlin: de Gruyter, 1989.

Baker, K. Scott. 'The "Nature" of Pleasure: Homosexuality as Trope in Early Brecht'. In *Nach der Natur – After Nature*, edited by Franz-Josef Dieters et al., 195–210. Berlin: Rombach, 2010.

Bar-Efrat, Shimon. *Narrative Art in the Bible.* Sheffield: Almond Press, 1989.

Barnett, David. 'Heiner Müller as the End of Brechtian Dramaturgy: Müller on Brecht in Two Lesser-Known Fragments'. *Theatre Research International* 27, no. 1 (2002): 49–57.

Benjamin, Walter. 'Die Aufgabe des Übersetzers'. In *Gesammelte Schriften*, Vol. IV/1, 9–21. Frankfurt am Main: Suhrkamp, 1972.

Benjamin, Walter. 'The Task of the Translator'. In *Selected Writings, Vol. 1: 1913–1926*, edited by Marcus Bullock and Michael W. Jennings. Cambridge, MA: Harvard University Press, 2002.

Benjamin, Walter. 'What Is Epic Theater?' In *Illuminations*, translated by Harry Zohn and edited by Hannah Arendt, 147–54. New York: Schocken, 1968.

Bentley, Eric. *Bentley on Brecht.* 3rd ed. Evanston: Northwestern University Press, 2008.

Berlin, Adele. *Poetics and Interpretation of Biblical Narrative.* Sheffield: Almond Press, 1983.

Bjornstad, Jennifer. '"Damit der liebe Gott weiterschaukeln kann": The Psalms of Bertolt Brecht'. *Der junge Herr Brecht wird Schriftsteller / Young Mr. Brecht Becomes a Writer.* Das Brecht Jahrbuch / The Brecht Yearbook 31 (2006): 170–81.

Blythe, Christopher James. 'The Prophetess of Endor: Reception of 1 Samuel 28 in Nineteenth Century Mormon History'. *JBR* 4, no. 1 (2017): 43–70.

Bodner, Keith. *I Samuel: A Narrative Commentary.* Sheffield: Sheffield Phoenix Press, 2008.

Bolt, Barbara. 'A Performative Paradigm for the Creative Arts?' *Working Papers in Art and Design* 5 (2008), www.herts.ac.uk/_data/assets/pdf_file/0015/.../WPIAAD_vol5_bolt.pdf.
Borchers, Wolf. 'Männliche Homosexualität in der Dramatik der Weimarer Republik'. PhD diss., Universität zu Köln, 2001.
Brandt, Thomas O. 'Brecht und die Bibel'. In *Die Vieldeutigkeit Bertolt Brechts*. Heidelberg: Stiehm, 1968.
Breed, Brennan. *Nomadic Text: A Theory of Biblical Reception History*. Bloomington: Indiana University Press, 2014.
Brown, H. M. 'Between Plagiarism and Parody: The Function of the Rimbaud Quotations in Brecht's *Im Dickicht der Städte*'. *Modern Language Review* 82 (1987): 662–74.
Buracker, William. 'Abner Son of Ner: Characterization and Contribution of Saul's Chief General'. PhD diss., Catholic University of America, Washington, D.C., 2017.
Calico, Joy. *Brecht at the Opera*. Berkeley and Los Angeles: University of California Press, 2008.
Callard, Felicity, and Des Fitzgerald. *Rethinking Interdisciplinarity across the Social Sciences and Neurosciences*. Houndmills: Palgrave Macmillan, 2015.
Clifford, Richard J. *Psalms 1–72*. Nashville: Abingdon Press, 2002.
Clines, David J. A. 'X, X BEN Y, BEN Y: Personal Names in Hebrew Narrative Style'. *VT* 22 (1972): 266–87.
Conquergood, Dwight. 'Performance Studies: Interventions and Radical Research'. *The Drama Review* 46, no. 2, T174 (2002): 145–54.
Demčišák, Ján. *Queer Reading von Brechts Frühwerk*. Marburg: Tectum Verlag, 2012.
Derrida, Jacques. 'Des Tours de Babel' and 'Appendix'. In *Difference in Translation*, edited and translated by Joseph F. Graham, 165–248. Ithaca: Cornell University Press, 1985.
Detlef, Friedrich. 'Zum jungen Brecht das Alte Testament'. *Berliner Zeitung*, 7 September 1995.
Disler, Caroline. 'Benjamin's "Afterlife": A Productive(?) Mistranslation in Memoriam Daniel Simeoni'. *TTR: traduction, terminologie, redaction* 24, no. 1 (2011): 183–221.
Downey, Katherine Brown. *Perverse Midrash: Oscar Wilde, André Gide and the Censorship of Biblical Drama*. London: Continuum, 2004.
Engel, Fritz. 'Verein Junges Deutschland Otto Zareks "Kaiser Karl V"'. *Berliner Tageblatt*, 30 August 1920.
Feuchtwanger, Lion. 'Einige Worte über meine Dramen "König Saul" und "Prinzessin Hilde"'. *Münchener Schauspielpremièren* 1, no. 1 (1905): 37–40.
Firth, David. *1 & 2 Samuel*. Nottingham: Apollos, 2009.
Fokkelman, J. P. *Narrative Art and Poetry in the Books of Samuel: Interpretation Based on Stylistic and Structural Analysis*, Vol. 2: *The Crossing Fates (I Sam. 13–31 and II Sam. 1*. Assen: Van Gorcum, 1986.

Foucart, Claude. 'L'Ulysse Francais et son Odyssée Intellectuelle: André Gide vu par Bertolt Brecht'. *Bulletin des Amis D'André Gide* 10, no. 56 (1982): 481–503.
Fradkin, Ilja. 'Brecht, die Bibel, die Aufklärung und Shakespeare'. *Kunst und Literatur, Sowjetwissenschaft* 13 (1965): 156–75.
Frisch, Werner, and K. W. Obermeier. *Brecht in Augsburg: Erinnerungen, Dokumente, Fotos*. Berlin and Weimar: Aufbau, 1998.
Frontain, Raymond-Jean, and Jan Wojcik. *The David Myth in Western Literature*. West Lafayette: Purdue University Press, 1980.
Fuegi, John. *Brecht & Co.: Sex, Politics, and the Making of the Modern Drama*, 2nd ed. New York: Grove, 2002.
Gide, André, and Paul Valéry. *André Gide, Paul Valéry: Correspondance, 1890–1942*. Edited by Robert Mallet. Paris: Gallimard, 1955.
Gide, André. 'Saul'. Translated by Félix-Paul Grève. *Schaubühne* 3, no. 32 (1907): 105–10.
Gide, André. *Bethsabée*. Translated by Franz Blei. *Hyperion* 2 (1908): 108–24.
Gide, André. *Fruits of the Earth*. Translated by Dorothy Bussy. London: Secker & Warburg, 1949.
Gide, André. *If It Die*. Translated by Dorothy Busy. New York: Penguin, 1950.
Gide, André. *Les Nourritures Terrestres*. Paris: Mercure, 1897.
Gide, André. *Saul: ein Schauspiel in fünf Aufzügen*. Translated by Félix Paul Grève. Berlin-Westend: Erich Reiss Verlag, 1909.
Gide, André. *The Return of the Prodigal: Preceded by Five Other Treatises, with Saul, a Drama in Five Acts*. Translated by Dorothy Bussy. London: Secker & Warburg, 1953.
Gordon, Robert. *I & II Samuel*. Exeter: Paternoster Press, 1986.
Grimm, Reinhold. *Brecht und Nietzsche oder Geständnisse eines Dichters: Fünf Essays und ein Bruchstück*. Frankfurt a.M.: Suhrkamp, 1979.
Grothum, Brigitte, dir. *Programmheft für David*. Premiere 4 November 1995, Hebbel-Theater Berlin.
Gumppenberg, Hanns. 'Rezension, "König Saul - Dramatische Studie in einem Akt von Lion Feuchtwanger" und "Prinzessen Hilde – Romantisches Drama in einem Akt von Lion Feuchtwanger"'. *Das Literarische Echo* 8, no. 2 (1905): 132–4.
Gunn, David M. *The Fate of King Saul: An Interpretation of a Biblical Story*. Sheffield: Sheffield Academic Press, 1980.
Halpern, Baruch. *David's Secret Demons: Messiah, Murderer, Traitor, King*. Grand Rapids, MI: Eerdmans, 2001.
Harness, Kelley. 'Theatrical Reliquaries: Afterlives of St Mary Magdalene in Early Seventeenth-Century Florence'. *Biblical Women in the Arts: Biblical Reception 5* (2018): 159–84.
Haseman, Brad. 'A Manifesto for Performative Research'. *Media International Australia, Incorporating Culture and Policy*. Practice-led research special issue, 118 (2006): 98–106.
Hatherley, Owen. *Militant Modernism*. London: Zero Books, 2008.

Heath, Malcom. 'Introduction'. In Aristotle, *Poetics*. London: Penguin, 1996.
Hell, Cornelius, and Wolfgang Wiesmüller. 'Die Psalmen: Rezeption biblischer Lyrik in Gedichten'. In *Die Bibel in der deutschsprachigen Literature des 20 Jahrhunderts, Band 1: Formen und Motive*, edited by Heinrich Smidinger, 158–204. Mainz: Mattias-Gruenewald, 1999.
Hens-Piazza, Gina. *Of Methods, Monarchs, and Meanings: A Sociorhetorical Approach to Exegesis*. Macon: Mercer University Press, 1996.
Heron, Jonathan, and Nicholas Johnson. 'Critical Pedagogies and the Theatre Laboratory'. *Research in Drama Education: The Journal of Applied Theatre and Performance* 22, no. 2 (2017): 282–7.
Herr, Mireille. *Les Tragédies bibliques au XVIIIe siècle*. Paris: Champion; Geneva: Slatkine, 1988.
Herzfeld-Sander, Margarget, ed. *Essays on German Theater: Lessing, Brecht, Durrenmatt, and Others*. New York: Continuum, 1985.
Hildebrandt, Samuel. 'The Servants of Saul: "Minor" Characters and Royal Commentary in 1 Samuel 9–31'. *JSOT* 40 (2015): 179–200.
Horner, Tom. *Jonathan Loved David: Homosexuality in Biblical Times*. Philadelphia: Westminster Press, 1978.
Hytier, Jean. *André Gide*. Translated by Richard Howard. Garden City: Doubleday, 1962.
Ishikawa-Beyerstedt, Saeko. *Friedrich Hebbels Einfluss auf die Moderne: Seine Rezeption in dramatischen*. Marburg: Tectum, 2014.
Jackson, Shannon. *Professing Performance: Theatre in the Academy from Philology to Performativity*. Cambridge: Cambridge University Press, 2004.
Jakobson, Roman. *Language in Literature*. Edited by Krystyna Pomorska and Stephen Rudy. Cambridge: Harvard University Press, 1987.
Jameson, Fredric. *Brecht and Method*. London and New York: Verso, 1998.
Jelavich, Peter. *Munich and Theatrical Modernism: Politics, Playwriting, and Performance 1890–1914*. Cambridge: Harvard University Press, 1985.
Jobling, David. '"David on the Brain": Bertolt Brecht's projected play "David"'. In *The Fate of King David: The Past and Present of a Biblical Icon*, edited by Tod Linafelt, Claudia V. Camp and Timothy Beal, 229–40. London: T. & T. Clark, 2010.
Jobling, David. 'Saul's Fall and Jonathan's Rise'. *JBL* 95, no. 3 (1976): 367–76.
Johnson, Nicholas. 'A Spectrum of Fidelity, an Ethic of Impossibility: Directing Beckett'. In *The Plays of Samuel Beckett*, edited by Katherine Weiss, 152–64. London: Bloomsbury/Methuen, 2013.
Johnson, Nicholas. '"That book should be burned": The Contested Afterlife of Bertolt Brecht'. *Trinity Journal of Postgraduate Research* 5 (2006): 8–19.
Johnson, Nicholas. 'On Translating Ernst Toller's *Die Maschinenstürmer*.' *Trinity Journal of Literary Translation* II (2014): 76–91.
Johnson, Nicholas, and Colm Summers. '*Enemy of the Stars* in Performance'. In *BLAST at 100: A Modernist Magazine Reconsidered*, edited by Philip Coleman, Kathryn Milligan and Nathan O'Donnell, 147–67. Leiden and Boston: Brill, 2017.

Johnston, Philip S. *Shades of Sheol: Death and Afterlife in the Old Testament.* Leicester: Apollos, 2002.
Joynes, Christine E. 'Revisioning Women in Mark's Gospel Through Art'. *Biblical Reception* 5 (2018): 83–98.
Joynes, Christine E., and Christopher C. Rowland. *Women of the New Testament and their Afterlives.* Sheffield: Sheffield Phoenix Press, 2009.
Kahn, Lothar. *Insight and Action: The Life and Work of Lion Feuchtwanger.* Rutherford: Fairleigh Dickinson University Press, 1975.
Kennedy, Hubert. *The Ideal Gay Man: The Story of* Der Kreis. Binghamton: Haworth Press, 1999.
Kershaw, Baz. 'Practice as Research through Performance'. In *Practice-led Research, Research-led Practice in the Creative Arts*, edited by H. Smith and R. T. Dean, 104–25. Edinburgh: Edinburgh University Press, 2010.
Kessler, Martin. 'Narrative Technique in 1 Sam 16:1-3', *CBQ* 32 (1970): 543–54.
Knopf, Jan, ed. *Brecht-Handbuch in fünf Bänden: Band 1.* Stuttgart and Weimar: Metzler, 2001.
Kornhaber, David. *The Birth of Theater from the Spirit of Philosophy: Nietzsche and the Modern Drama.* Evanston: Northwestern University Press, 2016.
Krašovec, Jože. *Reward, Punishment, and Forgiveness: The Thinking and Beliefs of Ancient Israel in the Light of Greek and Modern Views.* Leiden: Brill, 1999.
Kuhn, Tom. 'General Introduction'. In *Brecht and the Writer's Workshop: Fatzer and Other Dramatic Projects*, edited by Tom Kuhn and Charlotte Ryland, 1–10. London and New York: Bloomsbury, 2019.
Kurnick, David. *Empty Houses: Theatrical Failure and the Novel.* Princeton: Princeton University Press, 2011.
Kutscher, Artur. *Der Theaterprofessor: Ein Leben für die Wissenschaft vom Theater.* Munich: Ehrenwirth, 1960.
Kutscher, Artur. *Frank Wedekind: sein Leben und seine Werke*, Vol. 3. Munich: Georg Müller, 1922–1931.
Lerner, A. L. *Passing the Love of Women: A Study of Gide's* Saül *and its Biblical Roots.* Lanham: University Press of America, 1980.
Linafelt, Todd. *Surviving Lamentations: Catastrophe, Lament and Protest in the Afterlife of a Biblical Book.* Chicago: University of Chicago Press, 2000.
Long, V. Philips. *The Reign and Rejection of King Saul: A Case for Literary and Theological Coherence.* Atlanta: Scholars' Press, 1989.
Lorain, Alexandre. 'Les protagonistes dans la tragédie biblique de la Renaissance'. *Nouvelle Revue du XVIe Siècle* 12, no. 2 (1994): 197–208.
McCarter, Kyle P. *1 Samuel.* New York: Doubleday, 1980.
McKenzie, Steven. *King David: A Biography.* Oxford: Oxford University Press, 2002.
Melchinger, Siegfried. 'Brecht und die Bibel', in *Sie werden lachen – die Bibel: Überraschungen mit dem Buch*, edited by Hans Jürgen Schultz, 227–38. Stuttgart: Kreuz Verlag, 1975.

Meyerfeld, Max. 'Exit Junges Deutschland', Neuen Zürcher Zeitung, 5 September 1920, http://horst-schroeder.com/krit19-33.htm.
Michael, Matthew. 'The Prophet, the Witch and the Ghost: Understanding the Parody of Saul as a "Prophet" and the Purpose of Endor in the Deuteronomistic History'. *JSOT* 38 (2014): 315–46.
Miscall, Peter. *1 Samuel: A Literary Reading*. Bloomington: Indiana University Press, 1986.
Morse, Holly. 'What's in a Name? Analysing the Appellation "Reception History" in Biblical Studies'. *Biblical Reception* 3 (2014): 243–62.
Muilenburg, James. 'A Study in Hebrew Rhetoric: Repetition and Style'. *VTSup* 1 (1953): 97–111.
Muir, Lynette. *The Biblical Drama of Medieval Europe*. Cambridge: Cambridge University Press, 1995.
Müller, Gustav Adolf. 'Rezension, "König Saul - Dramatische Studie in einem Akt von Lion Feuchtwanger" und "Prinzessen Hilde - Romantisches Drama in einem Akt von Lion Feuchtwanger"'. *Münchener Schauspielpremièren* 1, no. 1 (1905): 33–5.
Müller, Heiner. *Rotwelsch*. Berlin: Merve Verlag, 1982.
Münsterer, Hanns Otto. *The Young Brecht*. Translated by Tom Kuhn and Karen J. Leeder. London: Libris, 1992.
Murphy, Francesca. *1 Samuel*. Grand Rapids: Brazos/Baker, 2010.
Murphy, G. Ronald. *Brecht and the Bible: A Study of Religious Nihilism and Human Weakness in Brecht's Drama of Mortažlity and the City*. Durham: University of North Carolina Press, 1983.
Nagavajara, Chetana. *Brecht and France*. Bern: Peter Lang, 1994.
Nebel, Inger. *Harfe, Speer und Krone: Saul und David in deutschsprachigen Dramen 1880–1920*. Gothenburg: Acta Universitatis Gothoburgensis, 2001.
Nelson, Robin. *Practice as Research in the Arts: Principles, Protocols, Pedagogies, Resistances*. London: Palgrave Macmillan, 2013.
Nicholson, Sarah. *Three Faces of Saul: An Intertextual Approach to Biblical Tragedy*. London: Bloomsbury, 2002.
Norris, Faith G. 'The Collaboration of Lion Feuchtwanger and Bertolt Brecht in Edward II'. In *Lion Feuchtwanger: The Man, his Ideas, his Work: A Collection of Critical Essays*, edited by John M. Spalek, 277–306. Los Angeles: Hennessey & Ingalls, 1972.
Parker, Stephen. *Bertolt Brecht: A Literary Life*. London: Bloomsbury Methuen, 2014.
Petzet, Wolfgang. *Theater: Die Münchner Kammerspiele, 1911–1972*. Munich: K. Desch, 1973.
Pyper, H. S. 'The Selfish Text: The Bible and Memetics'. In *Biblical Studies/Cultural Studies: The Third Sheffield Colloquium*, edited by J. C. Exum and S. D. Moore, 70–90. Sheffield: Sheffield Academic Press, 1998.

Pollard, Patrick. *André Gide: Homosexual Moralist*. New Haven: Yale University Press, 1991.

Polzin, Robert. *Samuel and the Deuteronomist: A Literary Study of the Deuteronomic History; Part Two: 1 Samuel*. Bloomington: Indiana University Press, 1989.

Raulff, Ulrich. '"Nachleben": A Warburgian Concept and its Origins', https://www.youtube.com/watch?v=u6Hgw8ooams.

Reimer, David. 'Stories of Forgiveness: Narrative Ethics and the Old Testament'. In *Reflection and Refraction: Studies in Biblical Historiography in Honour of A. Graeme Auld*, edited by Robert Rezetko, Timothy H. Lim and W. Brian Aucker, 359–78. Leiden: Brill, 2007.

Reiss, Hans. *The Writer's Task from Nietzsche to Brecht*. London: Macmillan, 1978.

Rohse, Eberhard. *Der frühe Brecht und die Bibel: Studien zum Augsburger Religionsunterricht und zu den literarischen Versuchen des Gymnasiasten*. Göttingen: Vandenhoeck & Ruprecht, 1983.

Rokem, Freddie. '"Suddenly a stranger comes into the room": Interruptions in Brecht, Benjamin and Kafka'. *Studies in Theatre and Performance* (2015): 21–6.

Roston, Murray. *Biblical Drama in England: From the Middle Ages to the Present Day*. Evanston: Northwestern University Press, 1968.

Rowe, Jonathan. *Sons or Lovers: An Interpretation of David and Jonathan's Friendship*. London: Bloomsbury, 2012.

Schechner, Richard. *Performance Studies: An Introduction*. 3rd ed. New York and Oxon: Routledge, 2013.

Schmidt, Brian B. *Israel's Beneficent Dead: Ancestor Cult and Necromancy in Ancient Israelite Religion and Tradition*. Winona Lake: Eisenbrauns, 1996.

Schroer, Silvia, and Thomas Staubli. 'Saul, David and Jonathan – the Story of a Triangle?'. In *A Feminist Companion to Samuel and Kings*, edited by Athalya Brenner, 22–36. Sheffield: Sheffield Academic Press, 2000.

Schroer, Silvia, and Thomas Staubli. 'Saul, David und Jonathan – eine Dreiecksgeschichte? Ein Beitrag zum Thema "Homosexualität im ersten Testament"'. *Bibel und Kirche* 51 (1996): 15–22.

Sharry, Martin. 'Review of *The David Fragments*'. *Draff*, 29 June 2017, https://www.draff.net/the-david-fragments.html.

Shepherd, David J. 'Knowing Abner'. In *Characters and Characterization in the Book of Samuel*, edited by Keith Bodner and Benjamin J. M. Johnson, 205–25. London: Bloomsbury, 2020.

Shepherd, David J. *King David and the Problem of Bloodguilt*. Oxford: Oxford University Press, forthcoming.

Sheridan, Alan. *André Gide: A Life in the Present*. London: Penguin, 1998.

Sherwood, Yvonne. *A Biblical Text and its Afterlives: The Survival of Jonah in Western Culture*. Cambridge: Cambridge University Press, 2000.

Smith, Jonathan Z. 'Religion and Bible'. *JBL* 128, no. 1 (2009): 5–27.

Smith, Richard. *The Fate of Justice and Righteousness During David's Reign: Narrative Ethics and Rereading the Court History According to 2 Samuel 8:15–20:26*. New York: T. & T. Clark, 2009.

Stadler, Arnold. *Das Buch der Psalmen und die deutschsprachige Lyrik des 20. Jahrhunderts: Zu den Psalmen im Werk Bertolt Brechts und Paul Celans*. Köln: Boehlau, 1989.

Stark, Gary D. *Banned in Berlin: Literary Censorship in Imperial Germany, 1871–1918*. New York: Berghahn Books, 2009.

Sternberg, Meir. *The Poetics of Biblical Narrative: Ideological Literature and the Drama of Reading*. Bloomington: Indiana University Press, 1985.

Stoebe, H. J. *Das Erste Buch Samuelis*. Gütersloh: Gütersloher Verlagshaus Gerd Mohn, 1973.

Swindell, Anthony. *Reworking the Bible: The Literary Reception-History of Fourteen Biblical Stories*. Sheffield: Sheffield Phoenix Press, 2010.

Swindell, Anthony. *Reforging the Bible: More Biblical Stories and their Literary Reception*. Sheffield: Sheffield Phoenix Press, 2014.

Tatlow, Antony. 'Introduction'. In *Bertolt Brecht's Me-Ti: Book of Interventions in the Flow of Things*, edited and translated by Antony Tatlow, 1–40. London: Bloomsbury, 2016.

Thompson, J. A. 'The Significance of the Verb *Love* in the David–Jonathan Narratives in 1 Samuel'. *VT* 24 (1974): 334–8.

Turner, Victor, and Edward Bruner, eds. *The Anthropology of Experience*. Urbana and Chicago: University of Illinois Press, 1986.

'Unfreiwillige Komik'. *Neues deutschland*. 6 November 1995, https://www.neues-deutschland.de/artikel/578741.unfreiwillige-komik.html.

Van Seters, John. *The Biblical Saga of King David*. Winona Lake: Eisenbrauns, 2009.

Völker, Klaus. *Brecht: A Biography*. Translated by John Nowell. London: Marion Boyars, 1979.

Weales, Gerald. 'Review of *The Collected Short Stories of Bertolt Brecht*'. *The Sewanee Review* 92, no. 3 (1984): lxv–lxviii.

Wedekind, Frank. *Simson oder Scham und Eifersucht, dramatisches Gedicht in drei Akten*. Munich: Georg Müller, 1914.

Weidner, Daniel. 'Life after Life: A Figure of Thought in Walter Benjamin'. Conference paper, *Afterlife: Writing and Image in Walter Benjamin and Aby Warburg*, Universidad Federal de Minais Gerais, Belo Horizonte, Brazil, October 2012, http://www.zfl-berlin.org/tl_files/zfl/downloads/personen/weidner/life_after_life.pdf.

Weisstein, Ulrich. 'The Lonely Baal: Brecht's First Play as a Parody of Hanns Johst's *Der Einsame*'. *Modern Drama* 13, no. 3 (1970): 284–303.

White, Marsha. 'Saul and Jonathan in 1 Samuel 1 and 14'. In *Saul in Story and Tradition*, edited by Carl Ehrlich and Marsha White, 119–38. Tübingen: Mohr Siebeck, 2006.

Willett, John. 'Introduction: Brecht on the Threshold'. In *Bertolt Brecht Diaries 1920–1922*, edited by Herta Ramthun and translated by John Willett, ix–xxii. London: Eyre Methuen, 1987.

Woloch, Alexander. *The One vs. the Many: Minor Characters and the Space of the Protagonist in the Novel*. Princeton: Princeton University Press, 2003.

Zarek, Otto. *David: Ein dramatisches Gedicht in fünf Akten.* Munich: Georg Müller Verlag, 1921.
Zarek, Otto. *German Odyssey*. London: J. Cape, 1941. Revised edition Otto Zarek, *Splendour and Shame: My German Odyssey*. Indianapolis: Bobbs-Merrill, 1941.
Zarek, Otto. *Kaiser Karl V: Ein Drama*. Munich: Georg Müller Verlag, 1918.
Zehnder, Markus. 'Observations on the Relationship between David and Jonathan and the Debate on Homosexuality'. *WTJ* 69 (2007): 127–74.

Index of References

Hebrew Bible/Old Testament

Genesis
2.24	110
18	68

Joshua
9	57
13.8	55
13.24	55

1 Samuel
1	40
1.23	101
2.19	15
8.10-20	166
9.2	87, 104
10.9	39
10.19	106
10.26	106
10.27	106
13	30, 97, 106
13.14	39
13.19	68
14	97, 101
14.1	97, 102
14.3	97
14.6	97, 102
14.8	102
14.10	97
14.12	97, 102
14.24	98
14.29-30	98, 102
14.43	102
14.45	98
15	16
15.18	16
16–31	153
16–18	207
16–17	67
16	30, 49, 87, 104, 109
16.1-12	166
16.7	87
16.11	88
16.12	87, 88, 91
16.14	109
16.15	109
16.16	40, 109, 207
16.18	88, 104
16.19	104
16.20	88, 207
16.21-23	104
16.21	42, 104, 109, 113, 145, 200
16.23	40, 109, 207
17–18	119
17	112, 142
17.1-49	167
17.1	106
17.12	88
17.13	88
17.15	88
17.17	87
17.20	92
17.28	93, 116, 119
17.31-39	29
17.34-35	92
17.39	57
17.40	207
17.49	207
17.50	207
17.55-58	100
17.57	167, 207
18–21	31
18	98, 112, 210
18.1-3	29
18.1	98, 100, 105, 167
18.3-4	154
18.3	98, 100, 105
18.4	98, 167
18.6-11	167
18.7-12	105
18.7-8	31, 40
18.7	104
18.9	105
18.10-11	106, 109
18.10	29, 40, 106, 207
18.11	135
18.16	105
18.20	105
18.21	105
18.25	30
18.27	30
18.28	105
19	98
19.1-7	98
19.1	98
19.2-3	102
19.7	98
19.9	135, 207
19.11	29
19.23	87
20	98, 101–3
20.1	102
20.2	102
20.9	102
20.12	102
20.14-17	98
20.17	98, 105
20.27-28	89
20.33	29, 135
20.34	98
20.37	102

1 Samuel (cont.)		28.14	14	14.6	80
20.41	98, 143	28.15	14, 198	14.11	80
21	29, 30, 207	28.17-18	15	14.21	81
22–24	135	28.17	16	14.24	81
22	89	28.18	16	14.25-26	82
22.7	89	28.19	16	14.25	32, 82
22.14	89	28.20	16	14.32	81
22.27	89	31	30, 68, 104	14.33	32
22.28	89			15–18	36, 37
22.30	89	*2 Samuel*		15–17	81
22.31	89	1.1-26	167	15	26, 81
23	99	1.17-18	106	16	81
23.16-18	99, 101	1.17	101	16.9	93
23.18	29	1.19-27	85	17	81
23.26	99	1.23	48	18	81, 85, 86
24	30, 69, 135	1.26	105	18.5-15	37
24.3	49	1.27	101	18.5	81
24.6	135	2–3	76	18.9	81
24.7	135	2.1-2	167	18.14	81
24.16	39, 89	2.4	30	18.15	81
24.17	39, 89	3.3	68	18.17	81
25	116, 200	4	135	18.19	85
25.1	14	5	142	18.21	85
25.10-11	116	5.4-6	167	18.25	85
25.38	126	6.7	126	18.26	85
26	39, 69, 89, 135	11–12	25, 34, 74, 77	18.27	85
				18.33	32, 81, 85
26.7	135	11.1	48	19.4	32, 81
26.9	135	11.2-27	167	19.5	167
26.11	135	11.2	25	20.42	29
26.17	39, 89	11.14-15	25, 79		
26.21	39, 89	11.16	78	*1 Kings*	
26.23	135	12	26, 77	1–2	74
26.25	39, 89	12.9-10	167	1.1	28
27	30	12.14	73	2	28, 70
28	13, 14, 16, 17, 30, 31, 129, 130, 134, 153, 155, 198	12.15	73	11	70
		12.18	73, 126	11.3	70
		13–18	199	17	152
		13	25, 68, 77, 80	21	34
28.7	134	13.4	82	*2 Kings*	
28.8	14	13.20	80	4.34	152
28.9	135	13.21	82		
28.11	14	13.30	80	*1 Chronicles*	
28.13-14	15	13.39	32	8.29	57
28.13	14	14	80, 82		

2 Chronicles		Isaiah		NEW TESTAMENT	
28.11	16	26	14	Matthew	
29.10	16	40.6-8	121	19.5-6	110
30.8	16				
		Jeremiah		Luke	
Psalms		50.11	121	15.27	93
14	124				
52	124	Ezekiel		CLASSICAL AND ANCIENT	
92.7	121	37	14	CHRISTIAN LITERATURE	
96	167			Aristotle	
104.14	121	Daniel		Nicomachean Ethics	
		12	14	1140a	177

INDEX OF AUTHORS

BBA 25, 27, 28, 30, 32, 33, 35, 38, 42, 45, 48, 49, 59, 60, 67, 71, 79, 148, 165, 186
BFA 1, 2, 4, 7, 34, 38, 72, 77, 84, 95, 107, 110–12, 114, 115, 120–2, 133, 137–40, 147–9, 159, 161, 185, 186, 200, 210, 212
NB 28, 30, 35, 67, 78, 79

Abbott, H. P. 6
Ackerman, S. 99
Adorno, T. 215
Anderson, L. M. 127
Angert-Quilter, T. 130
Apostolos-Cappadona, D. 10
Auld, A. G. 14

Bach, I. 123
Baker, K. S. 111
Bar-Efrat, S. 74
Barnett, D. 170
Benjamin, W. 11, 12, 14, 16, 20, 203
Bentley, E. 162
Berlin, A. 74, 90
Bjornstad, J. 124
Blythe, C. J. 130
Bodner, K. 105, 207
Bolt, B. 176
Borchers, W. 111, 142, 143
Brandt, T. O. 8
Brecht, B. 2, 4, 5, 30, 67, 84, 95, 107, 110–12, 114, 115, 122–4, 134, 137–40, 147–9, 183–6, 191, 200, 211, 214
Breed, B. 12
Brown, H. M. 161
Bruner, E. 174
Buracker, W. 75, 76

Calico, J. 211
Callard, F. 19

Clifford, R. J. 124
Clines, D. J. A. 90, 91
Conquergood, D. 174
Constantine, D. 215

Demčišák, J. 111
Derrida, J. 12
Detlef, F. 165
Disler, C. 12
Downey, K. B. 158

Engel, F. 140

Feuchtwanger, L. 132, 133
Firth, D. 90, 104, 105
Fitzgerald, D. 19
Fokkelman, J. P. 104, 105
Foucart, C. 159
Fradkin, I. 8
Frisch, W. 96, 117, 120, 129, 141, 186
Frontain, R.-J. 126
Fuegi, J. 215

Galle, H. 123
Gide, A. 151–7, 160
Gordon, R. 90, 98, 105
Grimm, R. 137
Gumppenberg, H. 129, 131
Gunn, D. M. 135

Halpern, B. 73
Harness, K. 10
Haseman, B. 176, 177
Hatherley, O. 203
Heath, M. 177
Hell, C. 123
Hens-Piazza, G. 82
Heron, J. 171
Herr, M. 126
Herzfeld-Sander, M. 132

Hildebrandt, S. 76
Horner, T. 99
Hytier, J. 156

Ishikawa-Beyerstedt, S. 2

Jackson, S. 174
Jakobson, R. 188
Jameson, F. 169
Jelavich, P. 187
Jobling, D. 9, 78, 97, 108, 142, 143, 148
Johnson, N. 164, 171, 177, 179, 191, 196, 215
Johnston, P. S. 14
Joynes, C. E. 10, 13

Kahn, L. 128, 133, 134
Kennedy, H. 142
Kershaw, B. 175
Kessler, M. 87, 88
Knopf, J. 166
Kornhaber, D. 132
Krašovec, J. 82
Kuhn, T. 8, 166, 168, 205, 210, 215
Kurnick, D. 76
Kutscher, A. 3, 117

Lerner, A. L. 156, 157
Linafelt, T. 11
Long, V. P. 135
Lorain, A. 125

McCarter, K. P. 207
McKenzie, S. 73
Melchinger, S. 8
Meyerfeld, M. 140
Michael, M. 130
Miscall, P. 207, 208
Morse, H. 10
Muilenburg, J. 87
Muir, L. 125
Müller, G. A. 131
Müller, H. 170
Münsterer, H. O. 6, 7, 83, 115, 121
Murphy, G. R. 7, 8, 14, 15

Nagavajara, C. 159
Nebel, I. 8, 109, 126, 127, 130, 134, 143, 144, 163, 205, 208
Nelson, R. 175
Nicholson, S. 205
Norris, F. G. 129

Obermeier, K. W. 96, 117, 120, 129, 141, 186

Parker, S. 1, 95, 96, 120, 121, 161
Petzet, W. 129
Pollard, P. 153, 156, 157
Polzin, R. 15
Pyper, H. S. 10

Raulff, U. 12
Reimer, D. 82
Reiss, H. 137
Rohse, E. 1–3, 136
Rokem, F. 203
Roston, M. 125, 126
Rowe, J. 99
Rowland, C. C. 10
Ryland, C. 8

Schechner, R. 174
Schmidt, B. B. 14
Schroer, S. 99
Sharry, M. 194
Shepherd, D. J. 76, 80, 81, 100, 135, 191, 208
Sheridan, A. 151
Sherwood, Y. 9
Smith, J. Z. 13
Smith, R. 80
Stadler, A. 123
Stark, G. D. 3
Staubli, T. 99
Sternberg, M. 78
Stoebe, H. J. 89
Summers, C. 177
Swindell, A. 9

Tatlow, A. 169
Thompson, J. A. 105
Turner, V. 174

Valéry, P. 153
Van Seters, J. 77
Völker, K. 6, 211

Wall, L. 130
Weales, G. 111
Wedekind, F. 3
Weidner, D. 12
Weisstein, U. 141

White, M. 97
Wiesmüller, W. 123
Willett, J. 6
Wojcik, J. 126
Woloch, A. 75, 76

Zarek, O. 140–2, 145, 146, 150
Zehnder, M. 99, 101

INDEX OF SUBJECTS

abandonment 130, 146
Abigail (character) 74, 142, 144
Abishag (character) 74
Abner (character) 75, 76, 91, 100, 142
Abinadab (character) 88
Absalom (character) 4, 5, 7, 25–27, 32, 35–39, 68, 69, 71, 77–86, 126, 136, 167, 190, 198, 199, 204, 206
'Absalom rides' (Brecht) 83–5
Absalon oder der Beauftragte Gottes 5
adaptation 21, 23, 31, 95, 100, 125, 127, 129–31, 133, 135, 137, 139, 141–3, 145, 147, 149, 151, 153, 155, 157, 159–61, 163, 165, 170, 178, 180–1, 188, 190–1, 195, 203
adultery 3, 26, 73, 79, 80
afterlife 9–17, 20, 21, 198, 201, 202, 205, 208, 209, 212, 215
Agag (character) 16
Amnon (character) 32, 80, 82
Anfang, Der (Johst) 117, 141
Aristotle 177, 205
armour 57, 67, 81, 91, 94, 98, 101, 103, 115, 118, 119
Athalie (Racine) 126
Augsburg 1, 41, 117, 124–5, 127, 159
autobiography/autobiographical 6, 199
autography 6
avant-garde 128, 176, 191, 209

Baal/*Baal* (Brecht) 95, 96, 111, 112, 114, 137, 141, 201, 211
Ball, Hugo 187
'Ballad of Friendship, The' (Brecht) 110, 201
Banholzer, Paula 133
'Bargan Gives Up' (Brecht) 35, 110, 201

Bathsheba (character) 3, 5, 25, 26, 34, 68, 72–4, 77, 79, 80, 82, 83, 126, 135, 159, 165, 167, 190, 193
Beggar 36, 48, 50–60, 62, 64, 90, 101–3, 113–16, 118, 167, 190, 206
Benjamin, Walter 11–14, 16, 20, 21, 100, 203, 209
Berlin 1, 3, 4, 8, 12, 24, 128, 137, 140, 147, 164, 165, 173, 178, 185, 191
Bertolt-Brecht-Archiv 4
Bethlehem 87, 89, 91, 92, 116, 199
Bethsabée (Gide) 159
Bible 1–3, 7–9, 14, 47, 68, 72–4, 77, 78, 82, 83, 87, 93, 95, 99–100, 123, 127, 134, 151, 158, 162, 168, 184, 195, 202, 204, 208, 214
Bible, The (Brecht) 2
bloodguilt/innocent blood 80, 81, 135
Brecht, Berthold (father) 95, 96
Brecht, Bertolt
  childhood 1–3
  diaries xv, 2, 4, 6, 48, 71, 72, 73, 110, 114, 115, 122, 136–41, 148, 149, 165, 167, 180, 188, 191, 200
  works: *Absalon oder der Beauftragte Gottes* 5; 'Absalom rides' 83–5; *Baal* 95, 96, 111, 112, 114, 137, 141, 201, 211;, 'Ballad of Friendship, The' 110, 201; 'Bargan Gives Up' 35, 110, 201; *Bible, The* 2, *Bread Store, The* 78, 209; *David* (see *David*); Desdemona 79; *Der Sieger und der Befreite* 5; *Drums in the Night* 129, 137; *Edward II* 111, 129, 161, 173; *Goliath* 28, 125, 149, 167, 199, 208–16; *A Man is a Man* 78; *Messingkauf Dialogues* 204, 214; 'Ode to my Father' 95; 'Seventh Psalm, The' 121; 'Springtime' 120; *Threepenny Opera, The* 1, 161; *Uriah Letter, The* 28, 79

Index of Subjects

Brechtian theatre 7, 9, 13, 19, 21, 52, 55, 58, 64, 82, 85, 86, 93, 94, 96, 103, 104, 113, 115, 117–19, 121, 124, 148, 160, 164, 168–70, 172, 180, 183–5, 188, 190, 195, 199, 201, 203, 205, 215
Brecht, Frank (son) 3, 7, 95, 128, 187
Brecht, Sophie (mother) 1, 111
Brecht, Walter (brother) 1, 11, 12, 20, 151, 203, 209

Cahiers de André Walter, Les (Gide) 151
censorship 3, 158
character/characterization 2, 4–5, 9, 14, 17, 19, 25, 35, 52, 54, 68, 72–7, 79, 80, 82, 89–91, 93, 94, 96, 97, 100–104, 108, 113, 123, 125, 126, 129, 130, 132, 136, 137, 142, 143, 149, 162, 167, 179–82, 184, 187, 189, 198–200, 202, 206, 211, 214
clowns 115, 188, 189, 191, 193
comedy/comic 106, 166, 174, 191
Conquergood, Dwight 173, 174, 205

David (Zarek) 28, 110, 134, 139, 141, 142
David (Brecht)
  alternate titles 5, 72, 73
  A1 4, 23, 25, 68, 69, 73, 77–80, 83, 166, 179, 188, 209
  A2 5, 27, 85, 167, 188
  A3 27, 85
  A4, 27
  A5, 4, 28, 80, 179
  A6, 28, 188
  A7, 28, 32, 100, 101, 103, 112, 113, 167, 200
  A8, 4, 23, 25, 30, 100, 101, 103, 106, 112, 179
  B1, 4, 23, 25, 32, 38, 82, 167, 179, 180
  B2, 35, 36, 167
  B3, 36, 69, 84, 85, 167, 206
  B4, 36, 167
  B5, 4, 36, 37, 69, 71, 79, 83, 85, 86, 167, 204, 206
  B6, 37, 179
  B7, 38
  B8, 38, 42
  B9, 4, 29, 31, 39, 42, 44, 46, 49, 54–6, 60, 69, 86, 105, 106, 110–15, 121–2, 124, 134, 138, 139, 144, 145, 147–9, 158, 160, 162, 165, 167, 189, 193, 199, 200, 202, 207, 212
  B10, 4, 32, 36, 42, 44, 48, 51–2, 55, 64, 67, 68, 72, 76, 87, 90, 91, 93, 94, 96, 101–4, 106, 113–16, 118, 119, 121, 122, 134, 136, 138, 139, 141, 149, 150, 161, 162, 166, 167, 179, 180, 185, 187, 189, 194, 199, 200, 202, 206, 207, 212
  B11, 4, 23, 24, 32, 58, 67, 113–15, 179
David (1995 Grothum production) 164–7, 181
David et Jonathas (Charpentier) 130
David Fragments (2017 production) 2, 4–10, 12, 14, 16, 18, 20–76, 78–80, 82, 84–6, 88, 90–2, 94, 96, 98, 100, 102, 104, 106, 108, 110, 112–14, 116, 118, 120, 122, 124–8, 130, 132, 134, 136, 138, 140–2, 144, 146, 148, 150, 152, 154, 156, 158, 160–2, 164–98, 200–204, 206, 208–10, 212–14, 216
DDR 169
death 10, 12, 14–16, 25, 26, 32, 36, 37, 61, 63, 73, 76–9, 81, 83–6, 99, 104, 106, 119, 120, 126, 128, 130, 133, 155, 157, 167, 198, 204, 206, 212, 213
demon(s) 73, 158
Der Sieger und der Befreite (Brecht) 5
Desdemona (Brecht) 79
desire 2, 38, 96, 100, 109, 110, 113, 121, 124, 135, 148, 152, 153, 155, 157–60, 162, 163, 182, 195, 202
Deutsches Theater 140
dialogue 4, 5, 16, 24, 38, 54, 76, 77, 82, 84, 91, 101, 102, 118, 131, 149, 160, 167, 204, 212, 214
Die Dame 1
Die Ernte (*The Harvest*) 2
Die Töchter Sauls (Wolff) 142

Draff 194
dramaturg/dramaturgy 18, 19, 23–4, 129, 147, 170, 172, 180–2, 184, 186–8, 205, 214
Drums in the Night (Brecht) 129, 137

ecology 21
Edward II (Brecht) 111, 129, 161, 173
Edwards, Paul 173, 174
Einsamen, Die (Feuchtwanger) 128
Eisler, Hanns 125, 209
Eisner, Kurt 213, 214
election 143, 209, 210, 213
Eliab 87–9, 91, 93, 116, 119, 200
Elisha 126, 152
ensemble 20, 24, 36, 164, 165, 170–3, 178, 180–95, 204, 206, 208, 212–14, 216
entangling/entanglement 18, 174, 198, 201, 205, 208
environment 18, 174, 189, 213
eschatology/eschatological 10–12
Europe/European 75, 125, 176, 181, 184, 201, 214
evolution/evolutionary (process, metaphor, etc.) 10, 11, 16, 20, 21, 125, 201, 204
experiment/experimental 125, 133, 159, 170–2, 176, 178, 181, 188, 192, 195, 204

Falckenberg, Otto 173, 187, 190
familial dysfunction 3
Feuchtwanger, Lion 126–37, 139, 140, 149, 151, 153, 155, 160–3, 173, 202, 208
  works: *Einsamen, Die* 128; *Joel* 129; *Weib des Urias, Das* 126, 129
fidelity 133, 164, 179, 195, 203
film 28, 79, 95, 175, 182, 208
frame/framing 9, 75, 102, 165–7, 180–1, 183, 185, 187, 189, 191, 193–7, 212
friendship 6, 99, 110, 143, 145–8, 165, 167, 201, 211, 212
Fuchs, Georg 187

Ga (for Germany) 55, 211
Gad/Gath 55, 59, 61, 118, 209–11
gene 21
German Odyssey (Zarek) 140
Germany 3, 55, 56, 92, 118, 120, 140, 164, 169, 173, 196, 203, 209, 211, 213
Gestus 184
Gibeah 97
Gide, André 46, 127, 151–63, 202, 208
  works: *Bethsabée* 159; *Cahiers de André Walter, Les* 151; *Nourritures Terrestres, Les* 152–3; *Saül* 346, 127, 151, 153, 156, 158–62, 202, 206
God 5, 15, 16, 35, 38, 39, 44, 48, 49, 66, 70, 72, 73, 82, 102, 104, 105, 123, 124, 130, 136, 144–8, 156, 158, 161
Gold, Cindy 173, 174, 203
Goliath (character) 4, 29, 55, 61, 67, 88, 92, 94, 98, 100, 105, 106, 112, 118, 119, 121, 135, 141, 149, 154, 167, 207–10, 214, 216
Goliath (Brecht) 28, 125, 149, 167, 199, 208–16
grass 41, 44, 121, 122, 196
Grothum, Brigitte 164–7, 181

Halbe, Max 187
hand(s) 5, 15, 36, 37, 39, 40, 52, 60, 65, 71, 73, 76, 84–6, 92, 95, 103–5, 107, 108, 130, 132, 145, 152, 162, 193, 198, 202, 204–8, 210
harp (see lyre) 144, 157, 160, 207
higher education 19, 175–6, 204
Hitler, Adolf 209, 214
homosexuality/homoeroticism 35, 99, 100, 110, 111, 142, 143, 201

idea (dramatic) 5, 21, 78, 113, 115, 116, 127, 129, 132, 134, 137–40, 144, 148, 162, 163, 166, 168, 175, 186, 187, 191, 195, 196, 200–3, 206, 211
impudence/impertinence 52, 53, 58, 62, 104, 115–18, 200, 201
incomprehension 107, 108, 122

indolence/laziness 48, 53, 55, 58, 67, 68, 103, 113–15, 119, 122, 149, 161, 200, 201, 211
interdisciplinary/interdisciplinarity 17–19, 171, 174, 176, 184, 198, 202, 216
interruption 72, 180, 203
intersemiotic translation 188
Ireland (and Irish) 19, 62, 168–70, 172, 173, 175, 176, 190, 191
irony/ironic 12, 13, 87, 94, 104
Ish-bosheth 75, 76, 135, 142
Israel (and Israeli) 14, 30, 32, 34, 55, 68, 70, 82, 85, 88, 97, 102, 104–106, 130, 131, 153, 165, 209
Israelites 14, 30, 59, 68, 70, 87, 91, 116, 118–20, 124, 167, 184, 200

jealousy 3, 105, 155, 201
Jesse (character) 51, 55, 60, 64–7, 77, 87–98, 103, 104, 116, 118, 119, 121, 149, 190, 199, 201, 207, 210
Jesus 28, 152
Jewishness/Jewish/Judaism 14, 56, 124, 128, 136, 165
Joab (character) 25, 32, 75–7, 79–81, 86, 143, 150
Job (character) 72, 95, 151
Joel (Feuchtwanger) 129
Jonathan (character) 3, 13, 28–30, 40, 48, 51–8, 68, 72, 85, 86, 89, 96–107, 109, 111–19, 121, 123, 136, 138, 141–3, 145, 147, 150, 154, 155, 157, 160, 167, 171, 192, 199, 200, 202, 209, 211, 212
Judges 3
Judith (Hebbel) 2, 118
Judith (character) 2

Kammerspiele, Die Münchner 110, 128, 129, 147, 173, 185–7, 189, 192, 193, 196
Kandinsky, Wassily 187
Karl V (Zarek) 137, 140, 141, 147, 186
Kiefer, Anselm 196
King Lear 204
König Saul 126, 127, 129, 131, 132

König und Zauberin (Grosch) 130
Kuhn, Hedda 6, 8, 84, 117, 124, 140, 141, 166, 168, 183, 186, 187, 193, 205, 210, 215

Lessing, Gotthold Ephraim 132, 172
Lewis, Wyndham 171, 181
love 32–5, 42, 43, 45–7, 53, 58, 82, 83, 85, 98–100, 104, 105, 108–11, 113, 122, 130, 137, 142–6, 148, 151, 154–60, 171, 200, 202, 210
Luther's Bible/Lutherbibel 2, 93, 100, 166, 167
lyre 39–42, 45, 104–6, 108, 207

Man Is a Man, A (Brecht) 78
Marlé, Arnold 129
Marlowe, Christopher 161, 162, 173
Marx, Karl/Marxism 205, 209
media 18, 176
mediation 18, 204
medium 14, 17, 18, 21, 31, 130, 131, 134, 136, 137, 206
meme 10, 21
Messingkauf Dialogues (Brecht) 204, 214
Michal (character) 30, 74, 99, 105, 142, 143, 210
Modelbooks 205
modernism/modernist 168, 177, 187, 192, 195, 203, 208
Mühsam, Erich 187
Müller, Georg 3, 140, 141, 192,
Müller, Heiner 169, 170
Müller Verlag 140, 141, 186
Munich 3, 17, 127–9, 131, 133, 140, 141, 147, 185, 187, 192, 213, 214
music 34, 40, 41, 49, 107, 113, 156–8, 165, 180, 190, 200, 208, 210, 213

Nabal (character) 116, 126, 154, 200, 210
Nazi/Nazis 139, 197
necromancy 14
Neuhofer, Siegfried 110, 190, 192
New York University 173
Nietzsche, Friedrich 132, 137

Northwestern University 125, 132, 162, 173
Nourritures Terrestres, Les (Gide) 152–3

'Ode to my Father' (Brecht) 95
opera 1, 125, 130, 161, 199, 209–11, 214

Panizza, Oskar 187
pedagogy 152, 171, 175, 185, 215, 216
performance 3, 18–24, 29, 35, 41, 43, 49, 50, 53, 55, 57, 59, 62, 161, 165–75, 177–85, 187–9, 191–7, 202–6, 213, 215
performance studies 22, 173, 174
performative 49, 171, 176, 177, 189
Philistines 16, 29, 30, 48, 50, 55–61, 68, 87, 88, 96–8, 103, 106, 116, 118, 119, 129, 130, 134, 136, 142, 149, 150, 156, 167, 200, 209, 210
plot 73, 74, 79, 86, 104, 142, 148, 166, 185, 199, 211
practice-as-research/PaR 19, 22, 159, 168, 170–2, 175–8, 185, 188, 194, 195, 203, 205, 216
praxis 169, 170, 175, 176, 180, 181, 205, 215
Pritzel, Lottie 128
psalms 40, 87, 106, 122–4, 165, 186, 201

questions/interrogatives 1, 18, 52, 69, 74, 76, 77, 101–3, 112, 127, 170, 171, 175, 178, 183, 195, 196, 198, 199, 203–5, 214

Reich, Bernhard 209
Reinhardt, Max 140, 187
robe 15, 30, 32, 49, 98, 154

Saison en enfer, Une (Rimbaud) 161
Samson (the work) 2, 3, 158
Samson; or Shame and Jealousy 3
Samuel (character) 3, 6, 13–18, 21, 29–32, 39, 49, 72–7, 80–3, 85–91, 94–101, 103–7, 109, 112, 116, 123, 125–7, 129, 130, 133–5, 143, 150, 153, 155, 158, 163, 164, 168, 171, 190, 194, 198–200, 206–8
Samuel Beckett Theatre 190, 194
sarcasm 56, 93, 196
Saul (character) 3–5, 8, 13–18, 28–31, 39–49, 54–9, 61, 67–9, 72, 75, 76, 85–90, 92, 96–113, 115, 117–19, 121–7, 129–39, 141–50, 153–63, 167, 186, 189, 190, 192–5, 198–202, 205–10, 216
Saul and David (Nielsen) 130
Saül (Gide) 46, 127, 151, 153, 156, 158–62, 202, 206
scenography 183, 191
Schall, Ekkehard 164
Schaubühne, Die 128, 160
Schiller, Friedrich 172
Schwabing 128, 129
secrecy/secret 46, 71, 73, 79, 108, 122, 145, 147, 154–7, 159, 160, 210
'Seventh Psalm, The' (Brecht) 121
Shammah (character) 88
She'ol 14, 16, 17, 21
silence/silent 46, 49, 83, 91, 103, 106, 108, 109, 124, 159
singing/song 27, 40–2, 47, 67, 85, 86, 99, 106–9, 111, 112, 117, 121–4, 140, 143–9, 152, 155, 156, 158, 160, 163, 165–7, 186, 188, 193, 194, 201, 216
sling(shot) 3, 67, 94, 149, 207
Solomon (character) 69, 70, 80
Splendour and Shame: My German Odyssey (see *German Odyssey*)
Spartakus 129, 133
spear 29, 47, 68, 101, 105, 108–9, 112, 113, 135, 160, 193–5, 197, 200, 207, 216
Spiegel, Der 128
spirit 3, 22, 49, 69, 104–5, 107, 109, 121, 130, 132, 133, 146, 147, 181, 190, 192, 193
'Springtime' (Brecht) 120
style 4, 24, 87, 90–1, 147–9, 161, 173, 183, 184, 189, 200
survival 9–11, 13–15, 18, 20, 21, 102, 190, 208, 212, 216
Svendborg (Denmark) 209

Tamar 32, 80, 82
Tekoa, woman of (character) 80
Threepenny Opera, The (Brecht) 1, 161
translator/translation 4–6, 11–13, 16, 18–29, 31, 33–5, 37, 39–47, 49–55, 57, 59, 61–3, 65, 67, 69–71, 78, 82, 84, 93, 94, 101, 105, 117, 122, 123, 144–7, 150, 159–61, 172, 178–83, 186, 188, 195, 200, 202–4, 206, 212, 216
Trinity College Dublin/TCD 19, 171–3, 175, 176, 184

underworld 17
Uriah (character) 25, 26, 28, 34, 68, 77–80, 83, 136, 190, 198
Uriah Letter, The (Brecht) 28, 79

Valentin, Karl 128
V-Effekt or Verfremdungseffekt 169
violence 60, 103, 113, 119, 185, 195, 196, 200–202, 206, 210, 213, 215
Volkstheater, Das Münchner 129

war 2, 17, 48, 54, 56–8, 60, 63, 66, 69, 78, 90–4, 96, 104, 106, 113, 116, 118–22, 125, 140, 142, 150, 165, 167, 199–201, 209, 213–14
Wedekind, Frank 3, 128, 187
Weib des Urias, Das (Feuchtwanger) 126, 129
Weimar Republic 142, 169, 196, 211, 213
workshop(s) 8, 19, 24, 166, 171, 172, 174, 177, 178, 181, 182, 185, 187, 190, 195, 204–6, 213
World War I 96, 119, 150, 185, 191, 214
World War II 214

Zarek, Otto 4, 9, 28, 110, 126, 127, 129, 134, 137, 139–63, 186–90, 192, 202, 206, 208, 211, 219, 226; works: *German Odyssey* 140; *Karl V* 137, 140, 141, 147, 186; *David* 28, 110, 134, 139, 141, 142